P9-BVM-550

The first years at school

SECOND EDITION

Developing Teachers and Teaching

Series Editor: **Christopher Day**, Professor of Education, University of Nottingham.

Teachers and schools will wish not only to survive but also to flourish in a period which holds increased opportunities for self-management – albeit within centrally designed guidelines – combined with increased public and professional accountability. Each of the authors in this series provides perspectives which will both challenge and support practitioners at all levels who wish to extend their critical skills, qualities and knowledge of schools, pupils and teachers.

Current titles:

Angela Anning: *The First Years at School (second edition)*
Les Bell and Chris Day (eds): *Managing the Professional Development of Teachers*
Colin Biott and Jennifer Nias (eds): *Working and Learning Together for Change*
Sally Brown and Donald McIntyre: *Making Sense of Teaching*
Joan Dean: *Professional Development in School*
C. T. Patrick Diamond: *Teacher Education as Transformation*
John Elliott: *Action Research for Educational Change*
John Olson: *Understanding Teaching*
John Smyth: *Teachers as Collaborative Learners*
Patrick Whitaker: *Managing Change in Schools*

The first years at school

Education 4 to 8

SECOND EDITION

Angela Anning

Open University Press
Buckingham • Philadelphia

Open University Press
Celtic Court
22 Ballmoor
Buckingham
MK18 1XW

and
1900 Frost Road, Suite 101
Bristol, PA 19007, USA

First published 1991
Reprinted 1991, 1993, 1994

First published in this second edition 1997

Copyright © Angela Anning 1997

All rights reserved. Except for the quotation of short passages for the purpose of
criticism and review, no part of this publication may be reproduced, stored in a
retrieval system, or transmitted, in any form or by any means, electronic,
mechanical, photocopying, recording or otherwise, without the prior written
permission of the publisher or a licence from the Copyright Licensing Agency
Limited. Details of such licences (for reprographic reproduction) may be
obtained from the Copyright Licensing Agency Ltd of 90 Tottenham Court Road,
London, W1P 9HE.

A catalogue record of this book is available from the British Library

ISBN   0 335 19690 X (pb)

Library of Congress Cataloging-in-Publication Data
Anning, Angela, 1944–
    The first years at school: education 4 to 8 / Angela Anning. – 2nd ed.
       p.   cm. – (Developing teachers and teaching)
    Includes bibliographical references (p.) and indexes.
    ISBN   0–335–19690–X
    1. Education, Preschool – Great Britain.   2. Education, Elementary – Great
Britain.   I. Title.   II. Series.
LB1140.25.G7A55   1996
372.21'0941 – dc20   96–33768
                                                                              CIP

Typeset by Graphicraft Typesetters Ltd, Hong Kong
Printed in Great Britain by St Edmundsbury Press Ltd,
Bury St Edmunds, Suffolk

For Vicky and Simon who taught me most of all

Contents

Series editor's introduction

The first edition of this book was the first of its kind on the education of 4–8-year-old children, and quickly became 'required reading'. Much has happened since its publication and this revised edition brings the text up to date, thus keeping its place at the centre of thinking and practice for all teachers in training, and all those serving teachers who want to take stock of their current thinking and practices. The book has grown out of Angela Anning's twenty years' experience of working alongside and talking with primary teachers and demonstrates a broad and detailed knowledge of research and other commentaries on the state of schooling for this most important cohort of children. In a very real sense, then, it is both practical and reflective.

In reviewing the historical and ideological traditions of British infant and primary schools and nursery education, she characterizes infant teachers of the 1990s as being caught between child-centred progressivism and the utilitarian demands of the Elementary School tradition. In her discussion of views of children's learning, the author presents a valuable detailed and authoritative critique of accepted thinking about the cognitive, social and emotional development of children. Citing recent classroom-based research she emphasizes the need for teachers to intervene more to extend children's thinking in contexts which are familiar to them; she also makes a vital distinction between the need for teachers to take account of each child's past learning experiences which are different and their need to recognize that not every child learns differently. Allied with this, Anning details, through careful argument and examples of teachers in action in the classroom, the complexities of the teacher's roles, particularly the use of language intervention, role-modelling and expectations. She discusses the curriculum in practice, the effects of different models of organization and structures. She argues the need for teachers to offer moral frameworks to children beneath the visible surface of practice.

The final chapters of the book provide an analytical commentary upon the National Curriculum 'post Dearing'. In her overview of Key Stage 1 reforms, the author places these alongside current research on the quality of teaching and learning, and the latest developments in knowledge generated about the national curriculum subjects. She identifies both positive and negative outcomes of curriculum reforms for early years teachers. Whilst they have resulted in more rigorous planning, this has been accompanied by high levels of stress. She is critical of the special needs policy and code of practice which, she observes, has had the effect of depriving children in their first three formative years of schooling of specialist help and appropriate resources. In moving into the twenty-first century, she proposes an entitlement for a recognized quality of education for the pre-fives, a return to teaching broad curriculum areas (HMI 1985), and a 'process' mode of planning into which subjects can be reconciled. Then, as now, it will be teachers who 'from the heart of any education system', will not be afraid to address 'in an analytical way' the challenges which this book so persuasively presents.

The book is filled with practice-based knowledge about the curriculum, children, and teaching and learning. As such it should commend itself to all who have an interest in promoting quality education through the management, planning, teaching and assessment of the curriculum for 4–8-year-olds in the 1990s and beyond.

Christopher Day

Preface

The 1990s was a period of tumultuous changes in schools in the UK. Under the terms of the Education Reform Act 1988 a National Curriculum was laid down for all children aged 5 to 16 in state schools. A national programme of testing all children at ages 7, 11, 14 and 16 was set up. Local financial management introduced a new element of control to governing bodies in the financing and running of schools. A four-yearly programme of inspection of all maintained schools by Ofsted (Office for Standards in Education) was introduced. All these radical changes were introduced as the 1990s unfolded and the teachers of Key Stage 1 children spearheaded the curriculum and assessment reforms.

Yet the infant schools within which I work with teachers and students carry forward, with any changes imposed by outsiders, a history and culture which underpin any new initiatives. This book was written with the intention of clarifying why things are as they are in children's first years in school. It also aims to explore some of the exciting new areas of research into the processes of educating young children. But my principal concern is that it is important that we understand why we are as we are in order that we may speculate about and gain some control over what might happen next.

I would like to make it clear that my analysis of classroom practices is as much an attempt to understand my own dilemmas as a teacher of young children as it is to offer more distanced observations of Key Stage 1 teachers and pupils at work. I have a deep sense of commitment to the education of young children, and a loyalty to the teachers with whom I have worked. I have never forgotten how much of the personal is expressed in the day-to-day functioning of a professional educator at work and how debilitating self-doubts can be; so my hope is that the questions I raise will not be seen as destructive criticism.

This quotation from Penelope Lively best crystallizes my feelings about the teachers and pupils I have known:

You are public property – the received past. But you are also private; my view of you is my own, your relevance to me is personal.

(Penelope Lively, *Moon Tiger*, Penguin, 1988: 29)

Histories and ideologies

An analysis of the past can help us to understand what is happening now and to anticipate what may happen in the future in schools. Just as every teacher's behaviour in school is influenced by his or her own personal and professional experiences, so every school is influenced by a range of local, political, economic and personnel changes and in turn every LEA is influenced by wider political and social changes. An awareness of these imperatives can make things that are happening in schools that appear incomprehensible suddenly become clear. Anybody who has moved to a new job recently and has struggled through the period of adjustment to an alien working culture will testify to this process of dawning enlightenment as past histories, conveyed through staffroom talk, clarify all manner of idiosyncratic school rules and habits. These flashes of insight are reassuring. Understanding how and why situations have arisen can help the individual to come to terms with uncomfortable current realities. In this chapter changes within the historical and ideological traditions of British primary and infant schooling will be reviewed. A discussion of the past will serve to illuminate some of the habits and assumptions underlying infant school practice today and give some insights into what may happen in the future.

Historical perspectives

In Britain infants from the age of 3 were admitted to schools throughout the nineteenth century. For many this meant attending the notorious dame schools, often bleak childminding provision for working mothers. Others were sent with older brothers and sisters to the monitorial schools. The 'babies' class' for pre-5-year-olds and the infant class for children over 5 might take sixty to eighty children. The children sat in the fixed, tiered galleries that contemporary children in their projects about 'schooling long ago' love to role-play . . . for an hour or so! Sitting still for day after day with older children drilling them in writing (always with the right hand), letter recognition, object recognition lessons and copying objects for drawing lessons must have been a tedious way for such young children to spend their days. In more enlightened times, practical activities recommended by Froebel (1826), one of the great innovators in nineteenth-century education to whom we shall return later in the chapter, were introduced into the curriculum, but these activities were done in unison, with perhaps one child in each row handling by rote the soft spheres, wooden spheres, cylinders and cubes and boxes of shapes which make up the Froebel 'gifts' as the teacher called out instructions. The physical constraints of sitting still were relieved only by drill or marching lessons in the school yards.

A handful of more fortunate children attended the few free kindergartens which were set up by various charitable trusts for slum children in Salford, London and Edinburgh. In these philanthropic institutions the emphasis was on physical and medical care. In 1816 Robert Owen, as manager of a cotton mill in Scotland, pioneered the New Lanark Infant School. Owen had visited Jean Pestalozzi's school in Switzerland. Pestalozzi emphasized the importance of children learning through experience and deplored rote learning (see Curtis and Boultwood 1962). Owen was impressed with the Pestalozzi school and based the curriculum of the New Lanark Infant School on similar principles. The children were divided into two age groups (2–4-year-olds and 4–6-year-olds) before they went into the schoolroom at 7 – the equivalent of Standard 1 in the elementary schools. The emphasis was on outdoor play, nature study, music, dancing and (perhaps in deference to our colonial aspirations) geography.

Infant schools were set up in many of the major cities from 1818 onwards. They were seen as agents of moral and social rescue and training and emphasized rote learning of reading, writing and numeracy, sewing and manual dexterity activities in the classrooms and physical training in the playgrounds. Many of them were under the auspices of various denominations of the church; in general a tone of moral righteousness pervaded both the textbooks and the teacher attitudes. The National Society for the Education of the Poorer Classes in the Principles of the Established Church set up in 1811 was the kind of body that influenced the beginnings of the British elementary school tradition.

From the middle of the nineteenth century state funds were allocated to assist in the establishment of a national system of education. From 1833 small state grants were offered towards the building of some schools. As public funds were released, demands for accountability grew. In 1858 a Commission was appointed under the chairmanship of the Duke of Newcastle 'to enquire into the present state of popular education in England and to consider and report what measures, if any, are required for the extension of sound and cheap elementary instruction to all classes of the people'. The results of the Royal Commission were published in 1861. By the terms of the Revised Code their recommendations were put into effect in 1862. Children were first formally tested within schools in Standard 1 at 7. Teachers were paid according to the results their pupils gained in the standard tests, as well as on minimal attendance – hence the still evident neuroticism in schools about registers. Schools were inspected by HMIs to ensure that they were conforming to the requirements of the code.

In the summer of 1870 both Houses of Parliament debated the compulsory school starting age. One argument claimed that 'five was a tender age for compulsory attendance'; another that 'it was never too early to inculcate habits of decency, cleanliness and order' (quoted in Whitbread 1972). In the end the clinching argument was that 'The difficulty was to obtain education without trenching on the time for gaining a living: beginning early and ending early would present a solution' (NEU 1870: 441–2). On this instrumental note the English education system's unique policy of entry to school at the age of 5 was established.

The curriculum of the elementary schools was based on the notion of social utility – 'what is useful to teach the sons and daughters of the working classes'. Thus an emphasis on basic skill competence dominated the infant classes' timetables. Parents were required to pay fees of from a penny to two pence a week. Children from the age of 3 could be taken into schools and the 'babies' rooms' continued to offer training in alphabet recitation, picture recognition and marching to music. The young children of the middle classes were educated at home by tutors or in private schools. In the late nineteenth century it was estimated that only 41 per cent of working-class children aged 6 to 10 attended grant-aided elementary schools (NEU 1870: 6). In 1870 School Boards were established as was the principle that new schools should be financed by a combination of low fees, local rates and central government funding, while the voluntary schools funded by the church ran alongside this provision. Upon this principle local authority primary schools and church schools still coexist today. An Act of 1876 enforced compulsory school attendance on children over 5. In 1891 it was determined that parents could demand free education for their children. In 1893 the employment age for children was raised to 11 and in 1918 the statutory school leaving age was raised to 14. The rigid government control over the elementary school curriculum was gradually eased by a series of Revised Codes. In 1926 central control over the curriculum was finally lifted. From then on elementary school teachers were 'guided' by a handbook of suggestions rather than constrained by a set of regulations. It is sometimes hard to believe that all this was happening within living memory and ironic to realize that sixty years later, by the terms of the Education Reform Act 1988, we have come full circle back to a centrally controlled National Curriculum.

The 1930s saw an expansion of nursery education in Britain with pioneering work by the McMillan sisters and Susan Isaacs (to which we shall return on pp. 13–15). It was the Hadow Reports of 1931 and 1933 (Board of Education) that marked the beginnings of the concept of 'primary education'. In the first report it was recommended that infants (3–7) and juniors (7–11) should be taught separately but with close liaison between the two sectors and that 'the curriculum is to be thought of in terms of activity and experience rather than of knowledge to be acquired and facts to be stored'. The curriculum was considered under three broad headings: natural activities (including play), expressive training (including handwork), and formal instruction in the 3Rs. It was recommended that the teaching of reading should begin at 6.

The 1933 report recommended that there should be special facilities – premises and staffing ratios – for very young children in primary schools. The purpose of nursery 'training' should be to assist the unfolding of the child's natural powers. Its functions should be educational but the methods recommended were for children to be encouraged to observe, handle objects and make things, working in small groups in order to learn from their own actions. Class instruction was discouraged.

In the Education Act 1944 infant education was subsumed into primary education. The Act marked fundamental changes in attitudes towards an entitlement to education for all. This was partly the result of the feeling that since everybody had contributed to the war effort then everybody was rightful heir to a welfare state which guaranteed a minimum standard of health, education and economic status regardless of social class. The statutory school starting age was to remain at 5, but there was an obligation for local authorities to provide nursery classes. Most children started school in the term after their fifth birthday; thus an accident of birth could determine whether a child spent between six and nine terms in infant schooling. Once inside the school most 5-year-olds would find a diet of look and say reading, phonics, basic computation, copy writing and occasional Friday afternoon play activities.

Progressive schools were pushing ahead with innovations such as integrated days – where a number of curriculum activities would be going on simultaneously with children working through tasks at their own pace – and vertical grouping arrangements – where children were taught in mixed age groups. But as with many of the shifts in policy we have identified so far, the effects of changes in other phases of education filtered down into infant schools. The school leaving age was to be raised to 16, and in order to assist the processes of secondary reorganization, the Education Act 1964 made it possible for LEAs to vary the age of transfer of pupils from one stage of schooling to the next. This legislation paved the way for the recommendations of the Plowden Report 1967 (CACE 1967) that young children would be best served by an educational system which provided nursery education for all whose parents wished for it, first schools for children from 5 to 8, and middle schools for 8–12-year-olds. By 1975 there were 2093 first schools spread amongst forty-eight LEAs. Nevertheless most children aged 5 to 8 in the UK are educated in infant schools for ages 5 to 7, or primary schools for ages 5 to 11. It is also clear that despite the official school starting age of 5, more and more children are entering their first school at 4, an issue which will be addressed later.

The Plowden Report marked a great upsurge of confidence in the child-centred approach to education defined by Hadow in the 1930s. The most famous passage from Plowden is still used as the clarion call of the so-called Progressive movement in primary education:

> at the heart of the education process lies the child. No advances in policy, no acquisitions of new equipment have their desired effect unless they are in harmony with the nature of the child, unless they are fundamentally acceptable to him.
>
> (CACE 1967: para 9)

There was an underlying belief in education as a good thing in itself, part of a liberal view of the entitlement of the British public to a publicly funded education system.

Running alongside the concept of 'entitlement' of all children to a state education was a growing concern about the effects of 'social deprivation': of low income, poor housing, racism. In infant and nursery schools in the 1960s and early 1970s there was a naive belief that compensatory education would serve to combat the known effects of social disadvantage on children's educational achievements. In the inner cities, money was pumped into an expansion of nursery classes attached to infant schools through the Urban Aid programmes. A major concern was to raise the level of language competence of working-class children. Plenty of Peabody Language Kits, a highly structured language teaching programme complete with plastic fruit for 'real' first-hand learning experiences, were shipped across from the USA to provide opportunities for young children to have structured language teaching sessions. However, it soon became apparent that in order for the programmes to have any real and lasting effect on the children, it was essential to involve parents in what was going on at school. These home/school initiatives were followed up by extensive programmes of involving parents in listening to children reading (see e.g. J. Tizard *et al.* 1982; Topping 1984, 1985). The involvement of parents in the governing bodies of schools also became a political issue. In 1977 the Taylor Report (DES 1977a) recommended that parents should make up one-quarter of the governing bodies of schools. The recommendation was finally implemented in Sections 1 to 4 of the Education Act (2) 1986, which now form the basis of the new regulations for the composition of governing bodies.

Everything seemed possible in the 1960s. There was a genuine optimism about the role of education in the development of both the individual and the society within which the individual would flourish. But the student demonstrations in the late 1960s in Paris and in the British universities – Essex, the London School of Economics, and Leeds – rocked the Establishment. The babies reared under the edicts of Benjamin Spock (1946), whose child-rearing manual was on the shelf of countless parents of the 1950s and 1960s, and in the so-called progressive classrooms of the Plowden era, had turned into rebellious, long-haired, young adults refusing to submit to adult authority.

Inevitably a reaction set in against Progressive Education. In 1969 the first right-wing Black Paper appeared (see Cox and Dyson 1971) criticizing the supposed *laissez-faire* attitude of schools towards basic skill teaching and maintaining that standards of education were declining. In 1975 a junior school in Islington, the William Tyndale school, was the subject of a government inquiry which resulted in the publication of the Auld Report (Auld 1976). The headteacher, Terry Ellis, and the deputy headteacher, Brian Haddow, were criticized for their liberal attitudes towards allowing children to choose their own ways of working to the point where children in the school became 'bored and listless'. At the same time a research project by Neville Bennett (Bennett 1976), into the effectiveness of thirty-seven primary teachers designated as formal or informal in their teaching styles, gave the superficial impression that pupils achieved 'better' results in schools with formal teachers. In fact the *most* successful teacher in the study was an informal teacher who set clear goals and was well organized in her style of working in the classroom. The press chose to take a simplistic view of the results and used them to hammer the cause of progressivism.

This kind of public anxiety was reflected in 1976 in a speech by the then Prime Minister, James Callaghan, at Ruskin College, It is worth quoting extracts from this important landmark of a speech, delivered by a Labour politician, which heralded the educational policy changes of Thatcherism in the 1980s. He argued that

> parents, teachers, learned and professional bodies, representatives of higher education and both sides of industry, together with the Government, all have an important part to play in formulating and expressing the purpose of education and the standards that we need.

Callaghan went on to identify the complaints of employers that 'new recruits from the schools sometimes do not have the basic tools to do the job that is required'. He also talked in guarded terms about

> the unease felt by parents and teachers about the new informal methods of teaching which seem to produce excellent results when they are in well-qualified hands but are much more dubious in their effects when they are not.

He concluded

> There is a challenge to us all in these days and the challenge in educa-
> tion is to examine its priorities and to secure as high efficiency as you
> can by the skilful use of £6 billion of existing resources. Let me repeat
> some of the fields that need study because they cause concern. There
> are the methods and aims of informal instruction. The strong case for
> the so-called core curriculum of basic knowledge. What is the proper
> way of monitoring the use of resources in order to maintain a proper
> national standard of performance? What is the role of the inspectorate
> in relation to national standards and their maintenance? And there is
> a need to improve relations between industry and education.
> (Reported in the *Times Educational Supplement* 22 October 1976)

Other research into primary classrooms in the 1970s did not report the kind
of mayhem that the press ascribed to 'progressive' state schooling. The
ORACLE project based at Leicester University found little evidence in the
junior classrooms studied over a three-year period to substantiate 'the claim
that anarchy and confusion prevail in primary school classrooms' (Galton *et
al.* 1980: 156). An HMI survey of primary schools published in 1978 actually
warned teachers against an over-emphasis on basic skill teaching.

> Anxiety is sometimes expressed that maintaining a wide curriculum in
> primary schools may be possible only at the expense of the essential,
> elementary skills of reading, writing and mathematics. The evidence
> from the HMI survey of primary education in England does not bear
> out this anxiety. A broad curriculum can include many opportunities
> for the application and practice of the skills of reading, writing and
> calculating. It should be planned to include them, and every oppor-
> tunity should then be taken to improve children's abilities in these
> essential skills.
> (DES 1978a: 12)

Nevertheless the call for accountability signalled by the Ruskin College speech
escalated into a full-blooded yell. The DES issued Circular 14/77 (DES 1977b)
asking all local authorities to answer questions about the arrangements they
had for curricular delivery in schools. In a report on the responses published in 1979 it was suggested that 'not all authorities have a clear view of
the desirable structure of the school curriculum, especially the core elements'. The belief was expressed that the Secretaries of State 'should seek
to give a lead in the process of reaching a national consensus on a desirable framework for the curriculum and consider the development of such a
framework a priority for the education service' (DES 1979: 6). 'The secret
garden' of the curriculum referred to by the then Conservative Minister of
Education, Sir David Eccles, in a debate in the House of Commons in 1960

(reported in Manzer 1970) where anybody other than teachers 'who attempted to trespass there were very firmly warned off' was about to be invaded. Moreover, it became clear that the separation of infant, junior/ middle and secondary schools curricula was to be discouraged. Documents pouring from the DES during the 1980s focused on curriculum matters from 5 to 16, for example *The School Curriculum* (DES 1981a), *The Curriculum from 5 to 16* (DES 1985b) and *Educational Reform: Government Proposals for Schools* (DES 1987). The curriculum was seen very much as a continuum: 'the 5–16 curriculum needs to be constructed and delivered as a continuous and coherent whole, in which the primary phase prepares for the secondary phase, and the latter builds on the former' (DES 1985b: para 65).

With unemployment running at high levels and public disagreements between the Labour Party and the unions, the stage was set for a landslide electoral defeat. In 1979 Margaret Thatcher began a long reign during the course of which successive Secretaries of State for Education wielded increasing power over every aspect of education. The first tentative moves towards centralized control escalated into the vast changes in the traditions of Welsh and English primary education heralded by the 'Great' Education Reform Bill of 1988. Whether infant teachers liked it or not they were thrust into the maelstrom of educational change legislated for within the terms of the Education Reform Act 1988 (NCC/WO 1989a), and into the mainstream of debate about curriculum content, assessment, changes in governing bodies and local financial management. Indeed infant schools became the focus of particular attention when the National Curriculum was introduced to 5-year-olds first in September 1989, with the first round of assessment of the targets of attainment being practised on those children in the summer term of 1991 when they were aged 7.

Ideologies

In trying to understand infant and first schools as they are now it is also essential to be aware of the history of ideas which have influenced the ideologies of infant teachers. As Nan Whitbread (1972) points out, the ideologies of nursery and infant teachers have been meshed together by historical events. Though there are vociferous opponents in both 'camps' to moves to lump nursery and infant education together as Early Years Education, in fact the increasing emphasis on nursery education being provided in classes or units attached to infant or primary schools, the closure of separate nursery schools and the huge increase in 4-year-olds being admitted into reception classes have all conspired to force nursery and infant teachers to work alongside each other. The closure of nursery schools has been justified on the grounds that it is better for the children and their parents to have an 'all through' notion of the first few years in school and that nursery classes are therefore preferable. This notion is a reflection of the current emphasis on continuity and progression within the National Curriculum 5 to 16. The admission of 4-year-olds into the reception classes of primary schools has been justified on the grounds that they are better off with an early start to school. The more likely reasons are that these policy changes have been *ad hoc* responses to financial constraints and have resulted in nursery education on the cheap for many young children.

There is evidence from the longitudinal Child Health and Education Study at Bristol (Osborn and Milbank 1987) that children who have experienced nursery education in nursery schools achieved higher scores on a range of tests of competence in language, numeracy and verbal reasoning when tested at age 5 and age 10 than those who have attended nursery classes (though in fact the best results were achieved by those children who had attended small home-based playgroups!). One explanation of these results may be that nursery schools are more likely to be staffed by teachers with nursery education training – rarely the case with nursery classes – and that children at nursery schools are therefore given a better start to their schooling. However, the social contexts in which parents will travel some distance to take their children to nursery schools out of a belief in their value, and the data on home-based playgroups, indicate that parental attitudes and circumstances in the study affected the children's long-term gains in educational achievement. Nevertheless there is indisputable evidence of the inadequate staffing, resources and curriculum provision being offered to many of the 4-year-olds in reception classes (NFER/SCDC 1987; Bennett and Kell 1989; Cleave and Brown 1989, 1991a, 1991b; Anning and Billett 1995) in comparison with the legal requirements of staffing and resourcing of the nursery provision to which this age group is entitled.

Whatever the vagaries in the provision and funding of the education of young children, infant classrooms sit uneasily between ideologies shared with their nursery colleagues and those of their primary class teacher colleagues. Lesley Webb wrote, 'One must not overlook or underestimate the existence of the "common law" of English nursery education, nor assume that because it is often unformulated and too rarely subjected to analysis its writs no longer run' (Webb 1974: 4). Robin Alexander has described the origins of primary teachers' ideology of child-centredness (Alexander 1984: 15). Yet many infant school students and indeed practising teachers perpetuate practices derived from these received ideas without ever recognizing the origins of their beliefs or in fact questioning the validity of what they habitually do. Why do we claim to base the curriculum of young children on play activities? Why do we have home corners? Why do we send children out to play for up to two hours a day on to freezing, barren school playgrounds? Why do we have reading schemes, unifix cubes, Lego or jigsaws? Why are we so nervous about 'teaching' creative activities or handwriting? Why do we have those mysteriously misnamed 'choosing times'? In order to grapple with these kinds of questions we need to review some of the major influences on beliefs about nursery and primary education, since the two traditions flow into infant classrooms like currents in a tidal estuary.

Froebel

It is to Froebel (1782–1852) that we owe the legacy of valuing play to the point of what Dearden (1968) describes as eulogizing it. Froebel had an almost mystical belief in the value of spontaneous play, 'the highest level of child development' (Froebel 1826: para 30). He wrote 'Play at this time is not trivial, it is highly serious and of deep significance.' Dearden quotes the whimsical extract from Rousseau's *Emile* (*Book 2*) which encapsulates the notion of school learning as being the antithesis of pleasure:

> The hour strikes, the scene is changed. All of a sudden his eye grows dim, his mirth is fled. Farewell mirth, farewell untrammelled sports in which he delighted. A stern, angry man takes him by the hand, saying gravely, 'Come with me, sir', and he is led away. As they are entering the room, I catch a glimpse of books. . . . The poor child allows himself to be dragged away; he casts a sorrowful look on all about him, and departs in silence, his eyes swollen with tears he dare not shed, and his heart bursting with the sighs he dare not utter.
>
> (Quoted in Dearden 1968: 94)

Play has been defined as a 'non-serious' activity and an activity which is 'spontaneous and self-generated' (Lowenfeld 1935: 37) but this definition sits uneasily alongside Froebel's more austere version of learning through play. Froebel expected that children should play with the Gifts which made up the resources for the key Occupations for learning in a carefully prescribed manner. It is fascinating to note that when the Occupations were done by rote in the tiered galleries of the monitorial schools, the purpose was defined as 'to train hand and eye', an appropriate technical skill for future artisans. More fascinating still is the repetition of history in the choice of technology as the first foundation subject of the National Curriculum to be introduced to 5-year-olds in 1990 in the belief that this will provide a firm basis for the supply of skilled technicians for the work-force of the twenty-first century! The legacy of Froebel's belief that practical craft work – making up geometric designs with coloured wooden squares and triangles, paper-folding and weaving, stick-laying and construction, sewing and embroidery – leading to sensory and language training should be central features of the school curriculum is still in evidence in infant classrooms. Think about the table-top toys that start many infant children's daily dose of education, and the number of student school practice topics based on 'The Senses'.

Montessori

Maria Montessori (1870–1952) was a doctor and psychologist. Her hand-book *The Montessori Method* was first published in English in 1914, in the USA, and the first edition of 5000 copies sold out within four days. Maria Montessori had pioneered her *Casa dei Bambini* (Children's House) in the slums of Rome. It is worth quoting an extract from the handbook to get the full flavour of the revolutionary learning environment Montessori prescribed for young children:

> The 'Children's House' . . . ought to be a real house; that is to say, a set of rooms with a garden of which the children are the masters. A garden which contains shelters is ideal, because the children can play or sleep under them, and can also bring their tables out to work and dine. In this way they may live almost entirely in the open air, and are protected at the same time from rain and sun.
>
> The central and principal room of the building, often also the only room at the disposal of the children, is the room for 'intellectual work'. To this central room can be added other smaller rooms according to the means and opportunities of the place: for example a bathroom, a dining-room, a little parlor or common room, a room for manual work, a gymnasium and rest-room.
>
> The special characteristic of the equipment of these houses is that it is adapted for children and not adults. They contain not only didactic material specially fitted for the intellectual development of the child, but also complete equipment for the management of the miniature family. The furniture is light so that the children can move it about, and it is painted in some light color so that the children can wash it with soap and water. There are low tables of various shapes and sizes – square, rectangular and round, large and small. The rectangular shape is the most common as two or more children can work at it together. The seats are small wooden chairs, but there are also small wicker armchairs and sofas.
>
> In the working-room there are two indispensable pieces of furniture. One of these is a very long cupboard with large doors. It is very low so that a small child can set on the top of it small objects such as mats, flowers etc. Inside this cupboard is kept the didactic material which is the common property of all the children.
>
> The other is a chest of drawers containing two or three columns of little drawers, each of which has a bright handle (or a handle of some colour to contrast with the background) and a small card with a name upon it. Every child has his own drawer, in which to put things belonging to him.
>
> (Montessori 1972: 37–9)

There are so many elements here of an idealized infant classroom environment that it makes one smile inwardly to recognize how firmly Montessori still has a hold over us. Montessori believed that children should learn in an environment which replicated their home lives but to child-size scale: 'this method seeks to give all this to the child in reality – making him an actor in a living scene' (Montessori 1972: 47).

Children were to spend their days cooking, cleaning, and playing outside in the garden. In this sense, our house corners are a pale imitation of Montessori's intentions. It is also interesting that the English tradition of nursery education, with a much greater emphasis on the value of fantasy play, renamed the Children's House the Wendy House of J. M. Barrie's *Peter Pan* (Barrie 1915) and now of course those concerned with gender issues in early years education have insisted that boys should not feel excluded from domesticity by Wendy's ownership and so it has been renamed again with the gender-neutral label 'the home corner'.

In the room designated for 'intellectual work', children would be expected to select from particular shelves, according to their levels of competence, sets of the didactic materials – carefully prescribed sets of wooden rods, sticks, cubes, insets (we still have an obsession with wooden rather than plastic aids for learning in infant classrooms!), card alphabets and numbers, lacing and buttoning exercises, bells, etc. – often bringing small mats to table tops or the floor so that they could frame a space for their work with the apparatus. The role of the teacher was simply to set up the child-centred learning environment and to observe the children's progress through the set procedures defined by the structured apparatus – 'the teacher in our method is more of an observer than a teacher, therefore this is what the teacher must know, how to observe'.

> It is necessary for the teacher to guide the child without letting him feel her presence too much, so that she may be always ready to supply the desired help, but may never be the obstacle between the child and his experience. . . . There is no need for intervention. 'Wait while observing.' That is the motto for the educator.
>
> (Montessori 1972: 131–2)

The legacy of not intervening in the child's personal voyage of discovery, which was to be developed by John Dewey, remains as a strong force within the ideologies of infant teachers, and is a theme which will be explored in some detail later in this book.

Steiner

Rudolf Steiner's (1861–1925) vision of education was to help each person to find his or her right place in life and to fulfil a personal destiny. He believed in the absolute supremacy of the individual over the demands of the institution or state. He believed that 'There are three affective agents in education: compulsion, ambition and love. We do without the first two' (Steiner 1926). He saw teachers as enablers or creators who would stay with one class, at least for a two-hour 'main lesson' which starts each day, throughout their schooling.

The Steiner curriculum is divided into three stages: the kindergarten from age 4 to 6 when children develop through practical experiences and imitation; the second stage from 6 to 14 when the emphasis is on imagination and feeling and the third stage from 14 to 18 when children are considered to be ready for intellectual abstraction and analysis. The teaching methods he pioneered are almost ritualistic – a great deal of oral work woven through with storying, drama, music, poetry, sewing, and a stylized movement to speech and music called Eurithmy. Stages at which children are ready to tackle formal academic work are strictly laid down. Children aged 6 and 7 are introduced to the alphabet by stories and pictures about individual letters, but children are not expected to learn to read, for example, until their eighth year.

The schools are staffed by a non-hierarchical 'republic of teachers', often on very low wages. Steiner schools sprang up in the UK between the 1960s and the 1980s as 'alternative schools' to the state primary system. Steiner has come to be called the 'guru of the Greens', but apart from his appeal to the so-called hippy parents who opt for Steiner schooling for their children, we have all retained from Guru Steiner the intense concern for the individual child in the English tradition of early education, the slightly fey approach of some infant teachers to the 'mystery and wonder' of childhood and the Plowdenesque notion that 'at the heart of education lies the child'. When Pat Ashton and colleagues (1975) asked primary teachers to rank their aims for education, of the seventy-two aims listed in her study, six of the top eight were to do with personal and social development and the sixth was, in fact, 'The child should be an individual developing in his [sic] own way.'

McMillan

The formidable McMillan sisters, Margaret (1860–1931) and Rachel (1859–1917), worked in Bradford and London to establish 'open air' nursery schools. The open verandahs down one side of each classroom were designed to stop the spread of TB, ear, eye and throat infections. Without antibiotics these infections could cause real distress amongst young children. Many headteachers in inner city schools in the 1970s and 1980s have waited in exasperation for these draughty verandahs to be closed in to make extra corridor or storage space. The McMillans worked directly from the philanthropic tradition of the late nineteenth century. Margaret was openly political, campaigning within the traditions of the Independent Labour Party in the 1920s, in her demands for schools to cater for the physical and social needs of slum children. Children were seen to need physical nurturing – well-scrubbed bodies, a wholesome diet, regular medical inspections – before they might be subjected to intellectual work. Given the physical conditions of inner city life in the 1920s, the McMillans had their priorities right; but the obsession with fresh air and exercise *per se* as intrinsically good for children can still dominate much of the infant school day. In fact it is hard to know how else we could justify the percentage of the school day which is written off as 'playing out', often on uncompromisingly bare tarmac school yards with no attention whatsoever paid to the quality of play the children are experiencing.

In *Education Through Imagination* (1923) Margaret McMillan wrote 'To educate the hand and to safeguard the speech impulse: that is perhaps the main work – of a formal kind – of the nursery school.' The sisters were also strongly influenced by William Morris and John Ruskin's writing and believed in the importance of aesthetics in the curriculum. They believed in the need for 'a new order of workman' capable of exercising 'enterprise, initiative – plus what is learned – Imagination'. Teaching was organized into small groups – six in a group for children under 5 and twelve for 5 pluses – with a young girl 'helper' working with the children, but all under the direction of a trained teacher. There was a benign, domestic and essentially maternal atmosphere in the classrooms.

Isaacs

Later Susan Isaacs (1885–1948) was to explore the intellectual growth of young children from her base at the Malting House School in Cambridge. She worked in a different tradition from the socialist reforming zeal of the McMillan sisters. The Malting House School was financed by a wealthy business man, Geoffrey Pike, and the children, aged between $2^1/_2$ and 9 years, were well-heeled and often exceptionally bright. Susan Isaacs devoted much of her research into the minds of young children towards those with psychological problems. She was strongly influenced by Melanie Klein's (Klein 1949) work on Freudian theories of children's emotional and social development. She was concerned that the teacher should develop 'true scientific understanding' of young children's learning. Isaacs wrote in her pamphlet on *The Educational Value of the Nursery School*:

> Children need not only the right play-material, but skilled help in their own efforts to learn and understand, and in their struggles with their anti-social impulses. To know what is the right word to say to the shy or inhibited child, the angry and destructive child, to have the right answer ready to an intellectual problem, to see when to introduce the child to a new piece of number apparatus, to understand when to interfere and when to leave alone, when to check defiance or stop a

quarrel, and when to allow the child to solve his own problem, when to encourage and when to remain silent, is not a wisdom that comes simply by nature. Certainly it rests upon natural qualities. The nursery school teacher no less than the mother must have love and sympathy, natural insight and the patience to learn; but children need more than this in their struggles with the many problems we have glimpsed. They need true scientific understanding as well as mother-wit and mother-love.

(Isaacs 1948: 72)

Susan Isaacs used close and systematic observations of children engaged in problem-solving activities in normal nursery school settings, rather than in laboratory conditions, to develop her understanding of children's intellectual growth. Of all the early pioneers her stance probably will sit most comfortably alongside the ideologies of many infant teachers in the 1990s. She described how she viewed the function of nursery education:

The children are free to explore and experiment with the physical world, the way things are made, the fashion in which they break and burn, the properties of water and gas and electric light, the rain, sunshine, the mud and the frost. They are free to create either by fantasy or imaginative play or by real handling of clay and wood and bricks. The teacher is there to meet this free enquiry and activity by his skill in bringing together the material and the situations which may give children the means of answering their own questions about the world.

(reported in van der Eycken and Turner 1969: 39)

It is significant that Susan Isaacs saw the role of the teacher as not only supportive but also interventionist. The teacher must 'have the right answer ready for an intellectual problem' and is there to 'meet' the children's free enquiry and activity with careful structuring of learning experiences and situations. Though she valued observation of young children as highly as Maria Montessori and appreciated the values of the maternal nurturing role, she saw the role of the teacher as far more specialized, positive and active in promoting the child's learning.

Conflicting imperatives

Two separate strands of theorizing began to dominate educational publications in the twentieth century of interest to infant teachers. The developmental psychological tradition focused on the stages through which children's learning progressed. Sociological studies of classrooms focused on the contextual influences on children's progress in schools. These theories will be set against the third imperative influencing infant classrooms, the instrumental view of early years education inherited from the Elementary Schools.

The developmental psychological tradition

The Froebelian naturalist developmental tradition argued that the teacher's role was to set up a learning environment where children might learn through first-hand experiences. The influence of psychology, particularly of the theories of Jean Piaget (which will be explored in Chapter 2), was powerful. Children were expected to move through defined stages of learning towards maturity of thought.

The kinds of principles which underpinned the developmental psychological model applied to professional practice are exemplified in the following list of 'generalizations' which appears in a book emanating from the Froebel Institute as late as 1969 (Brearley *et al.* 1969). The group of authors was chaired by Molly Brearley:

1 Children are unique persons and their individuality is to be acknowledged and respected.
2 Each person constructs his own mind as a result of interaction with things and people in his environment, and interaction between his own inner experiences.
3 Learning is continuous and knowledge cumulative.
4 The concept of 'stages' in intellectual development is useful in helping to understand some distinguishable phases of development in a child's thought.
5 Children encouraged in co-operative efforts with other children and with teachers will collaborate in the search for and the sharing of knowledge.
6 The mental processes involved in the search for knowledge and understanding contain their own self-expanding and extending propulsion.

(Brearley *et al.* 1969: 159)

Each child was to be seen as an 'individual' in the classroom. The following manifesto of a primary teacher, reported by Coe (1966), typifies this belief:

I know all my children as individuals. Of course there are times when we come together and share activities like music making, drama or perhaps just quietly listening to a story. But in basic work I give twenty different lessons. The children work individually, each at their own pace, and I circulate among them, helping, guiding and correcting. Always I have the particular need of the child in mind. Sometimes the children work in groups helping each other. Class lessons? They just wouldn't work. . . . I never teach a class. I teach children.

(Coe 1966: 77)

The ideology of 'liberal romanticism' (Richards 1982) which starts from the individual child when developing educational principles and sees the teacher as working 'alongside' the child was best demonstrated in the 1960s and

1970s in the village schools of Oxfordshire or in Leicestershire or the former West Riding of Yorkshire. These geographical clusters of 'progressivism' in primary schools were associated with charismatic characters like Robin Tanner, Alec Clegg or Sybil Marshall. Sybil Marshall's book *An Experiment in Education* (published in 1963) still reads as an inspirational document and its breathless enthusiasm for educating children explains the profound influence those great educators had on a generation of teachers and children:

> Education must have an end in view, for it is not an end in itself. The end can only be the knowledge of what it means really to live, and the wisdom to accept and make the most of what life offers each individual person.
>
> (Marshall 1963: 170)

Many infant teachers today would claim to espouse such an ideology.

Classroom 'realities' – the sociologists' views

However, in the 1970s a more rigorously analytical study of infant school practice from a predominantly 'left-wing' political standpoint began to prevail as issues of inequality in education were explored by researchers. Research studies like Sharp and Green's seminal sociological analysis of infant classrooms. *Education and Social Control: A Study in Progressive Primary Education* (1975) and King's *All Things Bright and Beautiful? A Sociological Study of Infants' Classrooms* (1978) challenged the ideology of 'liberal romanticism'. The researchers' frameworks of reference were poles apart from those of infant school teachers and they confidently offered evidence that infant teachers were unable to act in classrooms in the way their rhetoric *claimed* that they were acting. For example in the classrooms studied by Sharp and Green and by King children were not treated as individuals, nor given free choice of activities, nor allowed to develop at their own pace. There was evidence also that the teachers' typifications of pupils affected the way they responded to different groups of children within their classes, and that teacher responses to children and their expectations of them had tangible effects on pupil progress in schooling. These findings will be discussed later in this book in some detail since they represent some of the first attempts to collect evidence of the 'realities' rather than the 'rhetoric' of English infant school practice.

Teaching the basics – the elementary school tradition

The 'realities' were in fact strongly influenced by the alternative major ideology stemming from the elementary school tradition which determines the beliefs of infant school teachers: the utilitarian view that education is about introducing children to the basic skills which will make them into useful and productive citizens and workers. Basic skills are largely interpreted as numeracy and literacy and, above all in infant schools, as learning to read. In these 'basics' the style of instruction in infant classrooms has continued to be largely didactic, though often the didacticism is presented in the 'soft' form of individualized, group or structured scheme-based teaching. The model of instruction implicit in the elementary school ideology implies an interventionist stance, rather than the non-interventionist role of the teacher implicit in a child-centred model of infant education. Evidence from recent research studies of infant classrooms indicates that it is basic skills teaching that continues to occupy most teacher and indeed pupil time (DES 1982a; Bennett *et al.* 1984; Tizard *et al.* 1988; Alexander 1992).

In one sense, infant teachers are simply responding to the demands of society, or more specifically of parents, to get on with 'proper' schooling. On the whole parents favour the old elementary school tradition of instruction in the 3Rs – reading, writing and arithmetic. Froebel, Steiner, Montessori, and Discovery Learning are seen by the majority of parents as the province of a minority of intellectuals and middle-class romantic liberals who mostly have a shrewd knowledge of how to work the education system anyway. 'Normal' parents are suspicious of learning through play. What is more, most local education authorities and in-school tests at infant stages have been in literacy and numeracy, above all in reading, and infant teachers have been answerable to those test results. Ironically, though infant teachers were hostile towards the notion of testing children on a National Curriculum at the age of 7 as recommended by the Task Group on Assessment and Testing in Schools (DES 1988a), when this model was finally put into practice, the pressure on infant teachers to pay real rather than rhetorical attention to practical experiential learning was greater than ever before. The report recommended that testing at 7 should be cross-curricular and based on 'normal' infant classroom practice, which was assumed to include group work, a schematic approach to curriculum planning and practical learning activities. Piloting of Standard Assessment Tasks based on those principles in the summer of 1990, proved how complex this approach to testing is. Nevertheless it is salutary to remind ourselves that testing in the elementary school system, upon which payment by results was based, was also first implemented in Standard 1, the 7-year-olds' class, in 1862. Perhaps infant teachers are wise to be cautious about the long-term use to which centrally imposed test results might be put.

It must be pointed out that teachers working in inner cities have found the quintessentially English village school philosophies, inherited from Sybil Marshall, Alec Clegg and Robin Tanner, difficult to implement in the very different contexts of strife-riven inner city life. The premise that all children *want* to learn does not always seem to hold in the middle of Hulme, Toxteth or Newham! However, since this model has often been held up as 'The Ideal' during their training, teachers have been made to feel guilty that they have fallen short of such lofty aspirations. Hence the gap between the rhetoric

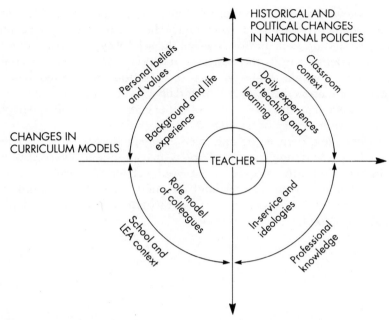

Figure 1 Conflicting influences on the teacher

and the reality exposed by the research of Sharp and Green and King has remained a constant feature of infant school life.

Thus infant teachers in the 1990s find themselves caught between the relentless currents of child-centred progressivism and utilitarian demands to teach the basic skills. Marooned in such an uncomfortable position, it will not be surprising if they feel vulnerable and confused as to how they should set about reaching the shore. Their uncertainty has been further compounded by legislation which prescribed National Curriculum core and foundation subject content and assessment procedures for 5–7-year-olds mainly on the basis of a secondary school curriculum system backed down into infant classrooms.

The complex working context in which teachers find themselves is perhaps best summarized in Figure 1.

On one axis education is inevitably caught up in the processes of changes in the national priorities and policies of whichever political group currently wields the most power. On the other arm of the axis, the ideologies of local and national hierarchies in educational policy-making and administration determine the curriculum models imposed upon schools. At times a set of political interests may be at odds with a conflicting set of educational policies determined by strong vested interests within the education profession. The teacher is buffeted backwards and forwards along the two axes by the power of these external forces.

But I believe that the power of the forces represented within the four enclosing segments of Figure 1 upon the teacher is *much* stronger than the pressure exerted upon them from outside the school system. This power is largely unrecognized by both politicians and policy-makers. In the course of the argument within the book, each of these four interrelated areas of influence acting upon the teacher – their daily classroom context, their professional knowledge, the role model of colleagues, and teachers' personal beliefs and values – will be examined.

In this complex, demanding and ever-changing climate, infant teachers are struggling to find their way. The hope is that subsequent chapters of this book, in trying to clarify issues related to young children's learning, the role of the teacher of young children and the infant school curriculum, will support them in their struggle and give due recognition to their considerable and underrated professional expertise.

2
Children learning

All teachers are exposed to some aspects of psychology during initial training. However, it is clear that infant teachers are no exceptions in finding it
difficult to make the links between what Edgar Stones (1984) has described
as 'galloping through the gurus' and the hectic realities of trying to understand
how the young children in their classrooms learn. In other words the 'knowledge' of psychology courses offered to teachers at initial or in-service level
is not transferred easily by teachers to their day-to-day practices. Why should
this be so?

In the first place, the kind of psychology offered to teachers has not on
the whole been drawn from the realities that they recognize. Traditionally
for most teachers in post now, the dominant models offered in educational
psychology courses were Behaviourism, particularly by B. F. Skinner (1974),
and the radically different model of Developmental Psychology proposed by
Jean Piaget (Piaget 1971). The behaviourist psychologists were presented as
viewing the child as a *tabula rasa* at birth. The child learns by passively
reacting to stimuli and to the reinforcements which the environment or people
within that environment provide. Students in training were offered accounts
of rats and pigeons being put through various uncomfortable experiences as
the basis for demonstrations of behaviourist theory in action. Naturally they
found the insights gained from the study of the hapless creatures' responses
to the levers, mazes, buzzers and food dispensers in these experiments difficult to transfer to their experiences with children in classrooms! At the other
extreme, the Piagetian view has presented the child as actively constructing
his or her own thinking by acting upon the physical and social environment.
All children were seen to develop through a series of clearly defined stages
towards logical thinking. Most research evidence offered in support of the

developmental psychology model was drawn from observations of children in home or laboratory conditions. Again, teachers have found it difficult to make useful links between the model and their daily work with children in classrooms.

It seems that psychological theories have either not been explained with sufficient clarity to engage the interest and commitment of the teaching profession – there is a great deal of jargon to plough through – or the implications for classrooms have not been clearly defined, or the theories offered have been so contradictory that teachers have simply given up in exasperation and rejected the whole package (see Barrow 1984).

Bruner (1980) wrote, 'It is only when research helps one to see with one's own eyes that it gets beneath the skin': this highlights a second significant issue. It is only recently that teachers of young children have begun to engage in research and higher degree work in their own right. Even when it was glaringly obvious that the 'knowledge' offered on conventional educational psychology courses was not transferable to their life in classrooms, teachers were themselves reluctant to challenge the conventional wisdom offered to them by the discipline of psychology. Particularly in the field of early years education, a predominantly female work-force has been socialized by the kinds of social processes of parental aspirations, careers advice at school and patterns of male-dominated promotion in primary education (see De Lyon and Migniuolo 1989) into low expectations of their own academic capabilities and the sense that somebody up there knew better than they did. It is sobering to realize that equal pay for women teachers was fully implemented only in 1961! Hence teachers actually rank knowledge of child development and psychology high on their list of what 'knowledge' is useful to teachers despite their obvious difficulties in making use of this expertise.

What happened then was that teachers, because of misplaced deference towards the 'gurus' of psychology, adopted basic psychological frameworks for talking about their classroom practices, what Walkerdine (1985) calls 'the conceptualizations which form the bedrock of modern practices', without rigorously analysing the underlying theories. They express the conceptualizations in common-sense terms such as 'individualized learning', 'experience', 'readiness' and 'concepts'. In other words, they extract from the mass of 'knowledge' offered only those aspects of psychological theory that seem most relevant to their classroom practice. They simply convert the mysteries of psychological theories into classroom common sense and borrow from the psychologists some of the more accessible terms. In doing so they tend to use the terminology more as slogans than as tools for analysing the learning behaviours and processes of the pupils in their classrooms.

Drawing upon both psychological conceptualizations and the ideologies outlined in Chapter 1, most infant teachers would have claimed to subscribe to the following tenets about young children's learning:

1 Children develop in sequential stages from concrete to abstract levels of thinking.
2 A child must be 'ready' to move on to the next developmental stage and must not be forced to move to a higher level of cognitive functioning (e.g. in beginning to read, in recording numbers, in learning to conserve).
3 Children learn through first-hand experiences, particularly through play activities.
4 Children need to develop competence in language use to function effectively as school learners.
5 In social development children move from egocentrism to the ability to empathize with others.
6 Every child is an individual learning in his or her own unique way.

There is a new generation of researchers working hard to operate within the conceptual frameworks of teachers *and* a new generation of teachers who are determined to engage with and generate new ideas about children's learning. The work of Bruner (1960, 1966) and Vygotsky (1962) has become central to a new paradigm (see Wood 1990 for a full account). The six tenets will be examined in the light of some recent research which has attempted to bridge the gap between the 'disengaged' nature of psychological theorizing and the application of educational psychology to classroom realities. In each of the following six sections of the chapter the 'accepted' psychological thinking embedded within the tenets listed above will be reassessed in the light of new research and classroom evidence.

Children develop in sequential stages from concrete to abstract levels of thinking

This has been one of the most influential beliefs in infant classrooms since the 1950s. It has also caused teachers to underestimate the ability of young children to reason, and encouraged them to focus on what children cannot do 'yet' rather than to build on what they *can* do now. However, in the 1970s and 1980s, there was a radical change in emphasis to a much more open-ended and positive view of children's capabilities.

The Piagetian stages

Piaget labels the first eighteen months of a child's life the Sensori Motor phase; eighteen months to 4–5 years the stage of Intuitive Thought; and 4–5 to 7–8 years the stage of Concrete Operations. (See Brown and Desforges 1979, for a full critique of the Piagetian model of developmental stages.)

One of the most significant contributions towards helping teachers to reassess their understanding of the ways in which young children think and

learn was Margaret Donaldson's book *Children's Minds* (Donaldson 1978).
Using evidence gained from research studies based at the University of Edinburgh, she argued for a reinterpretation of the Piagetian view of children's
cognitive development. Investigations were set up replicating some of the
Piagetian tests but with important differences in the methodology of administering the tests to young children and in the nature of the tasks the children
were set. The tasks were designed so that they made 'human sense' to the
children. So, for example, the classic Piagetian 'Three Mountains Test' (see
Piaget and Inhelder 1956) required children to say what they thought a doll
could see when that doll was placed at various points around a model of
three mountains distinguished from each other by features such as a house
on top of one, snow on another, and a red cross on the third. Children were
asked to choose from a set of ten pictures of the three mountains model
taken from various angles, or to reconstruct a cardboard version of the model,
to demonstrate what they thought the doll could see. Children under the
age of 6 or 7 tended to choose the picture – or construct the model – which
represented their own view of the three mountains from where they were
sitting. This led Piaget to argue that the children were unable to 'decentre'
from their own egocentric view of the world.

In a task devised by Martin Hughes for the Edinburgh studies, children
were asked to explore the idea of whether a policeman, positioned at various points in a model of two intersecting walls, could see a boy who was
hiding from him. After some exploratory talk, when the children were famili-
arized with the hypothetical situation of the boy hiding from the policeman
and the function of the model in helping to explain the propositions, the
children were then asked to hide the boy from two policemen, each of
which were placed at the ends of two of the walls. With children between
the ages of $3^{1}/_{2}$ and 5 ninety per cent gave correct responses to the task.
Hughes introduced a third policeman, complicated the arrangements of the
intersecting walls still further, and still 3-year-olds achieved success rates of
sixty per cent and 4-year-olds of ninety per cent on the tasks.

Donaldson argued that the children were able to demonstrate competence
on the activities set up by Hughes because they were dealing with a situation
to which they could relate. Most young children are familiar with the game
of hide and seek and through television, or in some cases through family
circumstances, they are also familiar with the notion of a baddie hiding from
some figures of authority! Not many of our school population are familiar
with viewing mountains from various strategic positions.

> The point is that the motives and intentions of the characters [in Hughes'
> version of the experiment] are entirely comprehensible, even to a child
> of three. The task requires the child to act in ways which are in line
> with certain very basic human purposes and interactions (escape and
> pursuit) – it makes human sense. Thus it is not at all hard to convey

to the child what he is supposed to do: he apprehends it instantly. It then turns out that neither is it hard for him to do it. In other words, in this context he shows none of the difficulty in 'decentring' which Piaget ascribes to him.

(Donaldson 1978: 24)

Another significant factor in the methodology adopted by the Edinburgh team was that the language that the adult researchers used in giving instructions was carefully structured and related to the purposes of the experimental activities so that the children were in no doubt as to what the tasks were about. With a clear sense of purpose, the children were thus able to demonstrate what they could do.

The team also explored young children's concepts of conservation using a variety of activities. They discovered that children's performance on standard Piagetian tests designed to investigate conservation of number, volume, length, etc. was affected by their assumptions that adults must have a reason for rearranging rows of buttons or sticks or pouring water from one container to another. On standard Piagetian tests, the children's responses were therefore geared to answer adult questions with the replies they imagined the adults wanted to hear. When the agents of change in an experiment were seen by the children as less adult-led and deliberate – almost as accidental events – children seemed to be freed from their sense that the adults questioning them knew what they were doing and therefore *required* certain responses. For example a classic Piagetian test of the child's ability to conserve numbers is to lay out two rows of the same number of buttons, ask children if there are the same number of buttons in each row, then rearrange one of the rows so that the buttons are spread further apart and repeat the question. In 'classic' Piagetian experiments, most young children appear to confuse the length of the row with the number of buttons, and respond that the longer row has more buttons. However, when James McGarrigle introduced the concept of a naughty teddy messing around with the buttons the children responded quite differently:

McGarrigle found that this version of the task – where the transformation was ostensibly accidental – was dealt with much more successfully than the traditional version; many more children between the age of four and six 'conserved' – that is continued to say that the crucial attribute was the same.

(Donaldson 1978: 64)

The concept of sequential stages and schooling

Donaldson argues persuasively that we have been conditioned to underestimate the rational powers of young children. She also argues that many of the activities we set young children in schools and the teaching strategies we adopt demonstrate the qualities of the Piagetian test situations. They deprive children of the opportunities to demonstrate what they are able to do. She argues that the purpose of school tasks is rarely made clear to young children. The Socratic questioning style of interaction of much classroom talk between the teacher and pupils forces children into an uneasy sense of always having to search for answers they believe the teacher wants to hear. Lastly, the kind of tasks offered to young children are often remote from their own experiences of learning in real-life situations. She challenges the belief that teachers should wait until children are 'ready' to move from concrete to abstract levels of thinking. Instead teachers should actively encourage children to move towards the 'disembedded thinking' which characterizes the 'formal' modes of learning in schools. Children should be encouraged to use talk to move from the here and now, freeing language from its embeddedness in present events. Teachers should model uses of language as a symbol system which empowers children with the ability to express their abstract thinking, *but* within learning contexts which are meaningful to the children.

> . . . the normal child comes to school with well-established skills as a thinker. But his thinking is directed outwards on to the real, meaningful, shifting, distracting world. What is going to be required for success in our educational system is that he should learn to turn language and thought in upon themselves. He must be able to direct his own thought processes in a thoughtful manner. He must become able not just to talk but to choose what he will say, not just to interpret but to weigh possible interpretations. His conceptual system must expand in the direction of increasing ability to represent itself. He must become capable of manipulating symbols.
>
> (Donaldson 1978: 88–9)

In other words children should be *taught* how to extend their powers of thinking towards abstraction; we should not simply wait for it to happen.

A child must be 'ready' to move on to the next developmental stage and must not be forced to move to a higher level of cognitive functioning

The cognitive curriculum

In the past teachers of young children have not emphasized cognitive development as high amongst their educational aims. In two studies of the aims of nursery teachers (Taylor *et al.* 1972; Clift *et al.* 1980) teachers overwhelmingly emphasized 'social' aims. This contrasts with traditions of early years education in the USA where cognitive development is emphasized at the levels of curriculum planning, regular testing and economic accountability.

Because of the traditions of the English nursery school discussed in Chapter 1, there is still a strong resistance in our school cultures to what the Americans define as the Cognitive Curriculum (see e.g. Copple *et al.* 1979) and more recently the High/Scope curriculum (Hohmann *et al.* 1979). This in part explains the heated arguments raging over the efficacy of translating the High/Scope system into British schools. The Highscope curriculum emphasizes the need for each child to be directly involved in planning his or her own activities, negotiated with an adult, by a method known as 'Plan–Do–Review'. Children are encouraged to set goals for themselves for the day's activities in the nursery and to reflect on how far they achieved these goals at the end of the session. For teachers imbued with the English nursery school tradition of free play, the High/Scope curriculum is seen as too adult-structured.

However, for many teachers of young children the new emphasis on teaching children how to think is exciting. The work of Vygotsky (1962, 1978) (for many years accessible only to Russian-speaking students but now available in English translation) emphasizes the role of internalized inner speech in structuring children's cognitive activities. This is a very different view of the role of language in learning from the Piagetian view. Piaget believed that language is the externalized evidence of children's active learning experiences rather than a tool for thinking. But Vygotsky also has a quite different view of the role of the adult in children's learning. He sees the process of human mental development as functioning at two levels – the actual, present level and the potential next level. He calls the gap between the two levels 'the zone of proximal development', and he sees the role of the teacher as directed towards encouraging children to move from the actual to the potential level of development. The teacher is to encourage children to do *without* help what they can do only at present *with* help. This process of teacher support for children's learning is what Bruner calls 'scaffolding' learning and will be referred to again in Chapter 3, which will focus on teachers' strategies. So there is a clear contrast between Vygotsky's view of the role of the teacher in actively working to improve children's levels of development and his view of knowledge as acquired by essentially social and external processes, and Piaget's view of the teacher expertly setting up experiences by which the child will learn through his or her own individual actions and exploratory behaviours.

Schemas

There is interest too in the ways in which young children organize their learning experiences. For example Chris Athey (1981), working at the Froebel Institute, has been researching into schemas, which she defines as 'patterns of repeatable and generalisable actions which can be applied to objects or events'. Children in the nursery attached to the Institute were observed by staff and researchers, but parents were also encouraged to observe the children at home. Thus, the children were observed using schemas across a range of nursery and home-based activities.

One such schema is the topological space notion of 'enclosure' (see also Piaget and Inhelder 1956). It is characterized by an absorption with enveloping space – e.g. the building of brick enclosures which are then used to represent a variety of imaginary objects such as a car, a boat, a castle. The schemas will then be explored in a whole variety of subsequent related exploratory activities. Athey gives the following example:

> Over several months Louise systematically explored enveloping space and certain associated schemas. She always carefully wrapped things up. For instance, she wrapped her clay pancake up (it was too hot to hold). She went round covering things up. When she had covered up the windows of her model house she said, 'Now it's dark inside.' She covered a worm with sand saying: 'YOU know they live under the sand . . . at night he'll be asleep.' She made a hole right through her 'home' book. Her mother was embarrassed and carefully mended the book. Louise made 'a sofa with a hole in it'. She wrapped 'sausages' in tin foil to 'cook' them. She wrapped up her mother's shoes at home and 'posted the parcel' in the rubbish bin, 'the post box'. When she arrived in school she painted 'a parcel with mummy's shoes in it'. Using different materials, Louise told a long story (on audio tape) about her cat. The persistent theme was the cat going inside and outside the dustbin and bringing what was inside the dustbin into the house and so on. Her persistent concerns had become sufficiently internalised for her to have an interesting conversation about them.
>
> (Athey 1980: 8)

Beryl McDougall, for many years an influential Early Years Adviser for Cleveland, pursued the study of schemas with nursery staff and parents in Cleveland Schools. In an edition of their newsletter, *Rumpus* (Nicholls 1986), McDougall gave another example of a child experimenting with a schema:

> the action and muscular sensation of going round an object can be represented:
>> by language, i.e. the words 'going round' are symbols of the actual event
>> by another action, e.g. pushing a toy vehicle round the object by graphics, e.g. drawing a circle.
>
> Added complexity is again acquired when these representational schemas are coordinated as, for example, when the circle and the dab (in painting) are coordinated to create a face with eyes and nostrils or a body with buttons down the front.
>
> (Athey in Nicholls 1986: 6)

Once parents and teachers/nursery nurses are alerted to these recurring patterns of behaviour, they are less inclined to dismiss children's play behaviour as 'flitting'. They begin to make connections for the children between one set of play experiences and others. It may be that the child moves physically from running round and round a climbing frame, or later chants a continuous refrain about going 'round and round the garden like a teddy bear' as she plays with making circles with her fingers in the sand pit. Minutes later she might be pushing a toy fire engine round a pile of Lego. Her drawings and paintings over a period of weeks may show endless variations on large and small circle motifs. Her behaviour in play is in fact the projection of different manifestations of a consistent preoccupation. She is trying to come to terms with roundness.

In the same *Rumpus* newsletter Chris Athey was quoted as saying:

> I was watching a child who was spinning his pencil on a table with a twist of his finger. I said, 'You're making it go round, aren't you?' Immediately he looked at me with interest. I mentioned some of the things I had seen going round, such as wheels and a cement mixer, and used the word 'rotate'. Excitedly he added things he knew. Once you show in your conversation with a child that you've cottoned on to his current schema, you're his friend for life.
>
> (Athey, in Nicholls 1986: 21)

The schemas appear to serve the purpose for the young child of categorizing experiences or insights in order to make sense of them and are operating in a much more complex way than simply assigning verbal labels to like or unlike objects or events. As Jerome Bruner pointed out, there are tools of the mind as well as tools of the hand, and Athey's final comment is significant because it demonstrates an adult interest in sharing with a child the tools of thinking which are helping him to understand the world. It is true that what a child brings to a learning experience from his or her own previous learning is always novel, but equally true that the kind of *strategies* which learners are likely to use are identifiable and generalizable to any number of children. In other words, there is a difference between emphasizing the individuality of each child's past learning experiences and insisting that every child learns differently. Coming to an understanding of this may help the teachers of young children to see the task of educating a class of twenty-five 'individuals' as a more manageable prospect. Cathy Nutbrown (1994) has explored the relationship between 'schema' research and the early years curriculum.

Metacognition

There is also new interest in children's understanding of their own thought processes, their awareness of how to cope with particular kinds of problems, their ability to remember – what is called 'metacognition'. Sara Meadows (Meadows and Cashdan 1988) points out that if children are helped to gain insights into how they think, plan, remember and set about different types of problems they are likely to gain confidence in tackling new tasks.

> Children are very commonly novices on tasks where adults have become experts with many well-learned routines. It is part of the process of education to facilitate the child's sharing of this expertise. It is important to recognise that it is both specific expertise – how to paint a straight line on the paper – and generalised expertise – how to hold tools, adjust their use to the particular task, judge where to start and where to stop, and so forth. A general 'feel' for the task as a whole is crucial.
>
> (Meadows and Cashdan 1988: 55–6)

Meadows believes that adults should provide role models for children by demonstrating their own planning, strategies for remembering things, or systematic approaches to solving problems. This is not to suggest that children should be drilled in 'strategies for thinking' in isolation from a real and perceived purpose. It is not appropriate for young children to be given lessons in problem-solving of the de Bono 'How to weigh an elephant' variety. In the home an apprenticeship model of learning is provided for children quite naturally. A parent might use a board in the kitchen where important notes about forthcoming school and family events are pinned up, shopping lists may be made before the weekly trip to the supermarket, or a sketch of where new floor covering is to be laid may be scribbled on the back of an envelope. This sharing of strategies for regulating behaviour and perhaps for saving time and minimizing frustration in achieving a goal is rarely in evidence in infant classrooms. Yet 'Thinking about your thinking seems to be an effective way of getting better at it, and also to be a source of self-confidence' (Meadows and Cashdan 1988: 56). There is no reason why young children should not also benefit from being given actual examples of how to think deliberately through problems as part of a negotiated system for organizing the day's learning activities. The Highscope model offers an example of how this can be achieved with individual children, but young children can also see the point of talking through with their teachers whole-class patterns of planning and the mechanics of functioning as a group in classrooms, and can benefit from working together on real problems such as access to cloakroom storage systems or maximizing the use of hall times. As Wood (1990: 55) argues, 'instruction and schooling play a central role in helping children to discover how to pay attention, concentrate and learn effectively' so that they can learn how to regulate their own intellectual activities.

Children learn through first-hand experiences, particularly through play activities

The value of play

Early years educators have always set a high value on children's ability to learn through play. In part this is a reflection of the importance they ascribe to learning through 'first-hand experiences'. A belief in the value of play has permeated through the kinds of ideologies reviewed in the first chapter. Play is seen to be an essential component of children's 'normal' development. This culturally based conviction is best crystallized in Susan Isaac's often quoted statement:

> Play is indeed the child's work, and the means whereby he grows and develops. Active play can be looked upon as a sign of mental health; and its absence, either of some inborn defect, or of mental illness.
>
> (Isaacs 1929)

In fact, as P. K. Smith and Cowie (1988: Ch. 5) point out in *Understanding Children's Development*, we have little empirical evidence upon which to base our belief in the value of play in young children's learning. After reviewing research studies which have been carried out, the authors conclude:

> Considerable empirical investigation has now been made into the benefits of play, but 'the jury is still out'. Most of the investigations have concentrated on the supposed cognitive benefits of play, and have been made in an explicitly educational framework. Yet, as we have seen, the evidence for strong cognitive benefits, either from theory, observation, correlational or experimental studies is not convincing. If anything, the evidence is better for the benefits of play for social competence. This has been less thoroughly studied, while the postulated benefits of play for emotional release and catharsis have scarcely received any well-controlled experimental study at all.
>
> (P. K. Smith and Cowie 1988: 139)

We have discussed Dearden's (1968) reference to the 'eulogizing of play', and there is a sense in which educators of young children have been accused of sentimentalizing play, reducing it to the level of idealization of those Mabel Lucie Atwell postcards of darling children at play, pretty, spotlessly clean, smiling and unreal. However, there may be another underlying and fundamental reason for the accusation that teachers of young children indulge in 'preciousness'. The fact is that 'play' has been defined as trivial by a male-dominated society which emphasizes the rational, scientific side of learning and the power of rational thought. Work is the serious, rational business of life and play is for leisure and fun. Politicians and policymakers throughout the 1990s derided the vocabulary of infant teachers, and the word 'play' (unless it was associated with rugby or golf) was singled out for particular derision (Anning 1995a).

Moreover, the concept of learning through play involves acknowledging the role of imagination and, dare one say it, the emotions in intellectual development (Egan 1991). There is a profound distrust of any alternative imaginative/affective approach to education amongst the dominant scientific/rational tradition in education and, as was argued in Chapter 1, teachers of young children are inevitably caught up in the determining societal and political beliefs about the purpose and value of education. The elementary school tradition certainly put play in its 'proper' place – the self-contained and special times of Friday afternoons and 'playtime' in the yard, the territory of the children, well away from the boundaries of the serious business in classrooms. There are many infant schools where these patterns of 'play' are still operating; though the rhetoric of the profession would not lead one to expect to see such patterns in the 1990s. It is noticeable that in the United States 'play' seems to have a better press. For example, play is a central focus of papers presented in the Early Childhood Education section of the annual American Research in Education conferences. Fromberg (1990: 237) reported a number of positive findings from research on the contribution of play to young children's development. However, she points out that 'at the same time that the research literature on the value of play appears to expand geometrically the presence of play in early childhood classrooms has been dwindling'.

What is play?

Dearden also points out that we have not clearly defined the characteristics of play. It is another of those words that tends to be used at a slogan-like level by teachers of young children. In infant schools play can be

1 rushing around the school playground
2 manipulating table-top toys
3 impersonating mums and dads in the home corner
4 joining in adult-directed and rule-bound games of lotto or Happy Families
5 simply 'horsing about'.

Attempts *have* been made to define types of play behaviour. For example Piaget distinguished between practice play, which involves repetition of actions until they are progressively mastered, symbolic play, which involves the manipulation of symbols, and games with rules (Piaget 1962). He argued that children will develop the ability to handle increasing levels of abstraction in their play behaviours – children aged 18 months may use a real brush to pretend to brush their hair, 3–4-year-olds might use a substitute body part such as their fingers to represent the brush, and 6–8-year-olds will probably simply use an imaginary brush to carry out the action.

A more sophisticated attempt to categorize play behaviours, but not by isolating them from other behaviours in a classroom, has been made by Meadows and Cashdan (1983) in a study of nursery classrooms. Play was rated, along with other behaviours, on dimensions such as social parti- cipation, degree of child's involvement, number of operations, themes or skills involved, extent to which materials were used and apparent goals of the child.

Purposes of play

It may be helpful to reflect briefly upon theoretical claims about the purposes of play. Theories about the function of play range from Karl Groos's view that play is preparation for life, or Stanley Hall's belief that play behaviours are a reflection of our evolutionary past, to the Freudian view that play provides a safe opportunity for children to come to terms with their wishes and anxieties. (For a full account of theories of play see standard texts by Millar 1968, Garvey 1977 and Smith 1984.)

If infant teachers are asked to address the issue of the function of play in children's development they are likely to suggest that play is important for physical development, for social development and the child's mental health, and for cognitive development; in all these aspects there are clear references back to 'classic' theories of the function of play. Each of these three functions will be discussed.

1 Play promoting physical development

If we take the function of play as promoting the physical development of the child, there is evidently a spontaneous urge amongst young children to try out and practise physical activities for the sake of enjoyment and the sense of achievement they gain from progressive mastery of large motor skills such as running, jumping, climbing, kicking and catching balls, etc. Fine motor skills are practised in activities such as building blocks, posting shapes into containers and mark making. These skills are clearly transferred to the real tasks of, for example, moving around to gain independence, or manipulating clothes in the tricky business of getting dressed without adult help. We tend to forget how rapidly young children are developing a whole range of physical accomplishments in their first years at school and how much their self esteem is bound up with progressive mastery of physical skills. Montessori's curriculum provided carefully structured opportunities for the mastery of physical skills; it is interesting to note that Piaget carried out his early research into children's learning at a modified Montessori school and was for many years president of the Swiss Montessori Society. Piaget saw the functions of play as consolidating existing skills by practising known schemas with minor variations and also as giving children a sense of 'ego continuity' as they gained confidence through the mastery of physical actions in a climate where it was safe to fail. Expressing this concept of mastery in another way, Bruner wrote, 'Play provides an excellent opportunity to try combinations of behaviour that wouldn't be tried under functional pressure' (Bruner 1972).

2   Play promoting social development and the child's mental health

The function of play in promoting social development is often taken for granted but as we have already indicated has not been well researched, and is rarely systematically provided for in schools. Social development will be discussed on pp. 40–43.

The related concept of play as a therapeutic process, an agent of mental hygiene, is a legacy, through Susan Isaacs' work (Isaacs 1948) and Melanie Klein's influence (Klein 1949) of the Freudian tradition. There is new evidence that we have underestimated children's competencies in learning to handle the emotional demands of relationships. For example, Judy Dunn's research (reported in Bruner and Haste 1987: Ch. 1) indicates that far from being so egocentric that they were unable to empathize with another's point of view, 2-year-olds were able to demonstrate their awareness of and understanding of the feelings of other members of the family. They demonstrated this understanding in talk and behaviour towards others. In the following example, talk was stimulated by a 2-year-old, Virginia L., looking at a book with her mother.

Child: Great big bonfire.
Mother: Big bonfire, yes, it is a great big bonfire. What is it burning up the bonfire?
Child: Burning birdies. All hungry.
Mother: They've got to fly away because they've burned the tree that the birdies used to live in, haven't they? And look at all the little bunny rabbits crying.
Child: They sad.
Mother: That's right, they're sad.

(Bruner and Haste 1987: 33)

The children in Dunn's study also demonstrated that they understood how to be agents of pleasure, comfort or pain by their actions which included affectionate physical responses, comforting siblings or parents in obvious distress and deliberate teasing. She describes one very sophisticated teasing strategy used by a 2-year-old. Her older sister had three pretend friends named Lily, Allelluia and Peepee. If the sisters argued, the 2-year-old would announce that *she* was Allelluia and revel in her older sister's obvious sense of outrage! Many examples of playing out feeling states were observed in the children's pretend play. It was also apparent that children whose parents spoke to them about feelings were more likely to articulate their own ideas about emotional states. Significantly the research indicated that mothers talked more often about feelings to girl children, who in turn produced more talk about feelings than boys. These findings are important when set alongside recent evidence about differences between women and men in the way they refer to feelings in talking about moral issues and have important implications for the education of boys and girls at all levels of schooling (Gilligan 1982).

We have already referred to the tendency for the education of the emotions to be regarded with grave suspicion within our male dominated 'stiff upper lip' culture. Infant teachers are aware of the power of children's emotional reactions to events both in school and in their lives outside, but perhaps because of pressures to concentrate on the tried and tested basic skills curriculum, they are not acknowledging the importance of structuring opportunities in their curriculum planning for children to come to terms with both the positive and negative effects of feelings or the skills of developing relationships with others. The arts are an obvious area in which children can be encouraged to explore feelings within a safe framework (this theme will be returned to in Chapter 5 on the curriculum in infant schools) but there is a great deal of scope in many collaborative learning activities for social development and the expression of feelings to be much more overtly 'taught'.

One particularly fascinating line of research has been into what Csiksentmihalyi (1979) calls 'flow' in play events. The Froebelian view of play as being a highly spiritual activity for the child, mediating between the emotions, spirit and intellect, the unfolding of the divine 'essence' of the child, is extended through Csiksentmihalyi's work. 'Flow' is characterized by that blissful sense of involvement that adults can recapture in pursuits such as listening to music, rock-climbing, dancing, sexual activities or indeed in some cases academic work! The involvement is total – a loss of self-consciousness, but at the same time an awareness of being in control of the self's absorption in the activity. In this instance it might be children who can teach adults a thing or two. The ease with which they can become totally absorbed in an activity and sustain that absorption over long periods of time can be impressive. It demonstrates that children, given the appropriate learning conditions, *can* concentrate for long periods.

3   *Play promoting intellectual development*

The third function that teachers claim for play in infant classrooms is that of promoting intellectual development. Evidence is thin on the ground to support this claim, and in fact what evidence we have makes depressing reading. It is in pre-school settings that most research has been done into levels of cognitive challenge in play. Meadows and Cashdan (1983) found that the free play offered to the children in twenty nursery school classes in an Outer London borough did not appear to challenge them intellectually:

Life was pleasant enough for most of the children – fights, quarrels or upsets were rare – but so were discovery, achievement after endeavour and intellectual challenge. Some play bouts were brief and desultory, some went on interminably at the same repetitive activity, as if the child couldn't get out of a rut. Some of the rising fives were clearly bored with the available curriculum and were getting their kicks out of rough and tumble or other social activities. Some children managed a choice of activities that took them out of the teacher's orbit completely, apart from token compliance with story sessions. Others, less boisterous, remained on the margins of activities, drifting unengaged from one space to another without even sustaining either conversation or involvement with task or material. Though the classroom norm was happy, goal-directed use of the resources provided, enough children fell below this level, and so few rose to the heights of creativity, co-operation and challenge, that we could not feel the free play curriculum was fulfilling our hopes.

(Meadows and Cashdan 1983: 35)

In another major study, again of pre-school provision, in this case using playgroups and nursery classes and schools in Oxfordshire to collect evidence, Kathy Sylva and her colleagues (Sylva *et al.* 1980) observed the learning behaviour of children. They made an analysis of the level of cognitive challenge offered by play activities within the nursery curriculum. High yield of cognitive challenge – defined by the challenge of the task and the way in which the child carried it out – was achieved when children were involved in music (when not led by an adult), small-scale construction, art (where children choose their own medium), large-scale construction and structured materials. The qualities which were common to these activities were that they had clear goals and involved materials that provided 'real world feedback'; that is 'They show the child whether a given sequence of behaviours has "worked" or hasn't' (Sylva *et al.* 1980: 63). Moderate yield of cognitive challenge was achieved in pretend, scale version or manipulation activities; and low yield in non-playful interaction, informal games and rule-bound games, and gross motor play. However, in these 'moderate and low yield' activities, there was often a high degree of social interaction between the children. The final group of activities, 'the lowest yield', including social play, horsing around and giggling, 'seemed motivated by the desire for the pleasure of physical exercise or of repetition'. They offered the children little opportunity for planning or elaborating play behaviours.

Sylva's team also investigated the length of time children concentrated on play activities – and at this level of analysis, pretend play scored highly along with the activities already defined as offering a high level of cognitive challenge. Finally, the team observed that children achieved levels of complex play with a high degree of cognitive challenge when they were playing in pairs or in social groups paralleled to others, and in the case of the 4-year-olds (rather than the 3-year-olds) observed, when in the company of an adult.

It is difficult to find hard evidence from infant classrooms about the level of intellectual challenge of play experiences in which children engage. In a study of infant classrooms in the now defunct ILEA (Tizard *et al.* 1988) there was little evidence of *any* kind of play activities in the classes on 7-year-olds studied. In a recent study of 4-year-olds in infant classrooms (Bennett and Kell 1989) fewer than 6 per cent of all activities observed were categorized as 'play' and 'play was used as a filler activity of unclear purposes'. (Both these studies will be discussed in detail in Chapter 4 when we examine the curriculum offered in infant classrooms.)

Children need to develop competence in language use to function effectively as school learners

Many infant teachers working in classrooms in the 1990s were trained within the traditions of the 'deficit model' of language development. Through the work of Basil Bernstein (1971, 1975) and Joan Tough (1976) in particular, we were encouraged to focus on children's levels of language competence which were identified by their use of increasingly complex language struc-tures, and their ability to use language for a greater variety of purposes. The role of the adult was seen to be one of fostering the child's progress towards greater levels of competence by styles of questioning, or by demonstrating different ways of using language. Working-class children were seen to need this kind of adult support far more than middle-class children.

The role of discourse

Recent thinking about the role of language in children's cognitive develop-ment has switched the emphasis to the role of discourse in children's language development. The shift parallels the emphasis on the child learning as a social being rather than as an individual explorer of the world, the Vygotskian rather than Piagetian paradigm. There is also a much greater concentration on what children *can* do with language rather than what they cannot do. Language development is seen as a social process, and in order to study children's linguistic capabilities research studies have adopted methodo-logies which allow the child to be studied in the social context which is most natural to them – that is at home rather than exclusively in school or in a laboratory.

This has had unfortunate consequences in one sense. Teachers are being told that the styles of interaction they adopt in schools disadvantage chil-dren in that they offer a restricted number of daily adult–child interactions in comparison to those offered at home and that the quality of school adult–child interactions is inferior to that offered at home regardless of the class label given to that home. One of the most influential studies of this kind was Tizard and Hughes' study of the language use of a sample of 4-year-old girls, fifteen of whom were defined as working class and fifteen as middle class, both at home and in their nursery classes (Tizard and Hughes 1984). The study demonstrated that working-class girls in particular were given little opportunity to engage in sustained adult–child discourse in nursery classes. The girls received more frequent sustained and challenging opportunities for talk in their own homes. Although the patterns of adult–child talk at home can illuminate teachers' understandings of the cognitive and social benefits of one-to-one dialogues, my view is that it is unreasonable to expect teachers to operate in this way in nursery and infant classrooms. Schools are simply not able to be like homes. Teachers are managing not one or two but many young children during their day. However, that is *not* to argue that teachers should not try to improve the quality of their discourse with pupils.

A much more extensive study of children's language development has been based at Bristol University as part of a fifteen-year longitudinal research study (Wells 1987). Gordon Wells emphasizes the reciprocal roles of adults and children when they are talking to each other. Children do not simply imitate the language of those around them, but as Noam Chomsky (1976) argued, they are actively involved in generating their own versions of speech. Nevertheless the language of the community around them shapes the conventions of both language production and language use that the child will adopt. Wells points out that most adults intuitively moderate their language to the level at which the child can respond – when parents do so we call this 'motherese' – by for example shortening their utterances, emphasizing particular words, repeating and paraphrasing what the child has said. He likens these instinctive adjustments to the linguistic capabilities of a child to the strategies an adult will adopt when teaching a child how to catch a ball. Wells also emphasizes, as Margaret Donaldson does, the importance of language use being embedded in contexts in which the adult and the child have shared experiences from which to draw shared meanings:

> What seems to be more important [than quantity] is that, to be most helpful, the child's experience of conversation should be in a one to one situation in which the adult is talking about matters that are of interest and concern to the child, such as what he or she is doing, has done or plans to do, or about activities in which the child and adult engage together. The reason for this is the fact that, when both child and adult are engaged in a shared activity, the chances are maximised that they will be attending to the same objects and events and interpreting the situation in similar ways.
>
> (Wells 1987: 44)

Storying

Wells also examines the role of 'storying' in developing children's thinking. 'Constructing stories in the mind – or storying as it has been called – is one of the most fundamental means of making meaning; as such it is an activity that pervades all aspects of learning' (Wells 1987: 194). There has been a growing interest in the power of metaphor and the narrative mode to encapsulate abstract ideas and make them accessible to children and adults. Rosen wrote, 'Every chemical reaction is a story compressed into the strait-jacket of an equation. Every car speeds down the road by virtue of the well-known engineer's yarn called the Otto cycle' (Rosen 1984). For children the function of narrative can be to enable them to move from the here and now of their immediate experiences, to the more distanced ideas about what happened then and what might happen next. In other words the narrative form is a potent resource to help children to move to abstractions.

Stories have the additional advantage of engaging the emotions. It has already been suggested that emotional engagement is an aspect of learning which has been underrated and under-researched in early years education. Infant teachers know instinctively that children learn and remember things best when they are having fun, gaining emotional as well as intellectual satisfaction from an activity, and most stories are enjoyable shared experiences in classrooms. What is novel is the idea that stories may also serve the function of empowering children to think in more abstract ways.

The oral tradition

There is a further interesting development in the power of language to help children's thinking which parallels research into the way in which oral cultures are maintained. For example the long and complex songs of Aborigines, which are passed down from generation to generation, appear to be remembered by units of sound rather than words. In oral cultures, crucial patterns of beliefs are fixed in the minds of the participating communities by the repetition of rhymes, rhythms, etc.

> Education in such cultures is largely a matter of constantly immersing the young into the enchanting patterns of sound until they resound to the patterns, until they become 'artistically' in tune with, harmonious with, the institutions of their culture.
>
> (Egan 1988: 98)

Perhaps shared nursery rhymes, finger rhymes, traditional tales, skipping and tagging chants, and traditional songs provide for the young child a sense of security in a shared past – something that is common to grandparents, parents, teachers, siblings, cousins – and we should be working more consciously within schools to nurture what is left of British oral traditions and to introduce all children to the exciting additional oral traditions being introduced into the United Kingdom by, for example, Asian and Afro-Caribbean cultures. There is evidence also that an awareness of alliteration and rhyme is a significant advantage for children learning to read (Bryant and Bradley 1985)

In social development children move from egocentrism to the ability to empathize with others

Social development and schooling

It has already been pointed out that teachers of young children rank social development as high amongst the aims they identify for early years education, and yet in general they are not clear about how these complex processes of learning to be 'sociable' in a range of contexts work. However there is some interesting research evidence about the way in which children learn to understand and operate social conventions. Far more emphasis is being placed on the significance of the social contexts and mores within which a child develops as we are beginning to understand that the child is held within the culture of the family, community, school and society – nesting one inside each other like the casings of a Russian doll.

When children enter school they are faced with a new set of social conventions and relationships for which even the experience of a playgroup or nursery school may not have prepared them (see Cleave *et al.* 1982). The intimacy of a small family setting will certainly not have done so. The strategies the teacher adopts to socialize school entrants into appropriate behaviours will be discussed in Chapter 3.

There is evidence that children use 'scripts' (Nelson 1977) to understand routine events in their lives in the same way that adults do. Both adults and children can find the strangeness of entering into a novel set of routines fairly stressful. Think about the last time you moved house, or changed jobs. It is the very fact that you cannot predict what will happen next that is so unnerving. What time are the tea and coffee breaks? When will the gas board official come to read the meter? Where can I park my car, or buy a stamp, or find a milkman? What do my workmates/neighbours expect of me? There is plenty of evidence that coming to terms with the strange rituals of classrooms is stressful for children starting school. Nelson claims that children quickly establish for themselves an idea of the likely sequence of events that make up a school day. Within this mental map, they are then free to concentrate on unfamiliar or unexpected events and the significance of these for that particular moment. However, it is clear that for many immature and anxious children, any departure from what they come to see as the normal classroom routine can throw them into a state of distress – hence the tears over hall times or the arrival of a supply teacher.

Learning to be a social being

Apart from trying to come to terms with the conventions of an institution geared to the needs of many, rather than a family life geared to the needs of a small group, the child also has to learn how to be a social being. The conventions of making friends may be unknown to a child. One important set of skills is strategies for entry to a group. Rubin (1980), in his book *Children's Friendships*, describes this account by Corsaro of a 4-year-old gaining access to a group in a nursery school:

> Two girls, Jenny and Betty, are playing around a sandbox in the outside courtyard of the school. I am sitting on the ground near the sandbox watching. The girls are putting sand in pots, cupcake pans, bottles and teapots. . . . Another girl, Debbie, approaches and stands near me observing the other two girls. Neither Jenny nor Betty acknowledges her presence. Debbie does not speak to me or the other girls, and no one speaks to her. After watching for some time (five minutes or so) she circles the sandbox three times and stops again and stands near me. After a few more minutes of watching, Debbie moves to the sandbox and reaches for a teapot in the sand. Jenny takes the pot away from Debbie and mumbles, 'No'. Debbie backs away and again stands near me observing the activity of Jenny and Betty. Then she walks over next to Betty, who is filling the cupcake pan with sand. Debbie watches Betty for just a few seconds, then says:
> 'We're friends, right? We're friends, right, Betty?'
> Betty, not looking up at Debbie and while continuing to place sand in the pan, says, 'Right'.
> 'I'm making coffee,' Debbie says to Betty.
> 'I'm making cupcakes,' Betty replies.
> Betty turns to Jenny and says, 'We're mothers, right, Jenny?'
> Jenny replies, 'Right'.
> The three 'mothers' continue to play together for twenty more minutes, until the teacher announces clean-up time.
>
> (Corsaro 1979: 320–1)

Using careful observations of this kind Corsaro built up a picture of the way in which children learned to gain access to activities and to establish friendships. Children had to learn to overcome initial rejections, here illustrated in Corsaro's fieldnotes by Debbie's refusal to submit to Jenny's rejecting strategies designed to exclude her from the group around the sandbox. Children also had to learn how to *be* a friend. They had to learn how to give and take in sharing toys and attention. They had to learn how to manage conflict, not only how to express their own feelings but also how to empathize with the feelings of others. In many cases they learned by trial and error and by observing what worked and what did not work in making and keeping friends amongst the models offered by their peer group, but it appears to help if adults encourage children to reflect consciously on what they have learned. The role of the adult in supporting social development is to demonstrate conventions, to explain the processes involved and give feedback of both a positive and negative kind in encouraging children to develop the skills of making and keeping friends.

Gender issues in social development

There is evidence from classroom-based research (Mullin *et al.* 1986; Clarricoates 1980; Spender 1982; Weiner 1985; Davies 1989) that the social conventions of gender-appropriate behaviour are reinforced by interactions between both peer group and adult–child in schools. Boys and girls tend to gravitate to single-sex groupings even at pre-school level. On the whole boys opt for boisterous, large motor play, operate more confidently in all aspects of outdoor physical play, and choose areas to play where adult (usually female) attention is not often directed (e.g. in the construction play or outdoor sandpit areas). Girls opt for more 'domestic' activities such as house play and for table-top toys where adults are more likely to be near at hand. Both genders devise strategies to exclude each other from same-sex groupings. Browne and France (1986) describe the adult talk and behaviour towards boys and girls which reinforces sexist stereotypes in 'Only cissies wear dresses: a look at sexist talk in the nursery', but the issue of teacher strategies in relating to children from different race, class and gender will be addressed in more detail in Chapter 4.

The development of morality

Finally, interest is beginning to be shown in the way in which young children learn about morality. Until recently research into the development of moral reasoning was based on refinements of Piaget's study (Piaget 1932). Piaget pioneered the method of eliciting children's responses to stories which presented some moral dilemma. He asked the children what they believed was the right thing to do in such a situation. Children's ideas about lying, destroying property, etc. and about punishments and fairness were taken from the discussions about the stories. Piaget also used games of marbles to elicit children's beliefs about rules. He demonstrated that children move from a morality of constraint, where strict and unchangeable rules derived from adult authority were imposed on them from outside, to a morality of autonomy, where there was no longer a blind obedience to outside authority, where punishments were considered to be for righting wrongs rather than expiation, where rules may be modified by democratic processes within a group and where justice must take account of extenuating circumstances.

Building on Piaget's work, Kohlberg (1976) also used the method of presenting children with moral dilemmas couched in stories. He identified six stages of moral development, but overall he believed that children moved from a *Pre-Conventional level*, characterized by a concern for personal interests, the avoidance of punishments, and obedience to authority based on fear rather than respect; to a *Conventional level*, where laws and duties are seen as necessary to maintain stability in society and where it is winning approval from one's immediate social group that is important (most adolescents and adults stay at this level); to a *Post-Conventional level* where laws are respected because of a belief in universal moral principles such as liberty, equal rights and the dignity of human life.

The methodology used by Piaget and Kohlberg has been criticized for providing children with adult views of moral dilemmas and, as in Donaldson's critique of Piaget's work on the development of scientific and mathematical thinking, for constraining children's opportunities to demonstrate what they know and understand in their own terms and contexts. Feminist critiques have also argued that the hierarchy of stages of morality presented by male researchers rank justice above compassion and love (see Gilligan 1982) and argue that from a female perspective it is not enough to *understand* what is right and wrong. One must also *care*.

Turiel (1978 and 1983) has explored children's understanding of morality and social conventions and demonstrated that even young children can differentiate between important moral rules such as not hurting people and less important social rules such as whether one should wear clothes to come to school or practical rules such as cleaning one's teeth. Haste (1987) describes the processes by which children learn to decode 'the grammar of social relationships' by interacting with others as individuals but within the culturally defined norms of groups. Primary teachers rate social learning and the gaining of a sense of morality high amongst their aims for primary education: Ashton *et al.* (1975) found that teachers ranked third 'The child should be beginning to acquire a set of moral values on which to base his own behaviour, e.g. honesty, sincerity, personal responsibility.' Increasing concern about the breaking down of 'traditional values' has resulted in the promotion of both 'Christian' values and 'citizenship' as possible ways of fostering 'good' behaviour. However, despite this there is very little school-based research, teaching materials or guidelines for infant schools to support teachers of young children in putting these aims into practice.

Every child is an individual learning in his or her own unique way

The Plowden statement, 'At the heart of the education process lies the child', and the catch-phrase 'child-centred education' are often used by teachers of young children to defend their decisions about teaching strategies, approaches to classroom organization and curriculum planning. In the late 1980s these tenets were used rather desperately to argue against the imposition of a subject-based National Curriculum upon young children (see Blenkin and Kelly 1994).

Although every child (and indeed every adult) does bring a unique set of experiences and understandings to each new learning situation and gradually constructs his or her own view of the world, it *is* possible, and as far as the teacher is concerned *essential*, to see that there are patterns in the development of learning across children's responses and behaviours. Unless teachers of young children acknowledge and articulate these generalizable patterns, they are faced with an insurmountable task in planning and implementing a curriculum which fosters learning in a class of up to thirty-five children. Of course, it is important to retain insights into the particularities of each child as a learner and to respect their individuality, but it is equally important to acknowledge their similarities.

Teachers learning about children's learning

For teachers of young children, time spent in close observation of their pupils engaged in learning should be a regular part of how they organize their teaching time. In most cases infant teachers have the advantage, because of the way they organize their classrooms and their teaching styles, of being able to work at close quarters with their pupils. Ideally they should become skilful at constructing their own theories about children's learning from the myriads of specific teaching and learning episodes to which they bear close witness every working day.

An infant teacher who had trained herself to work in this way, using a range of techniques – including a video camera – to collect information about teaching and learning episodes, wrote:

Children learn if they are given meaningful tasks where they can see a purpose in the activities. I know it is also important that they should be working in a fairly relaxed atmosphere so that they are not afraid to have a go at things, not afraid of making mistakes. But I've also recognised that there is a sense in which they take their cues from me – from my facial expression, my body language, the tone of my voice. So if I show that I have higher expectations of what they can do, then they will respond to those. I know also that they need to be able to access resources and equipment without having to keep asking me – they shouldn't have to have that kind of dependence on me. They need to be able to get on with each other. That also saves me a lot of time. But I've learned the hard way that that does not happen without us working at it. They have to learn how to work together. It doesn't just happen. Then they need lots of practical situations to try things out.

(Anning 1987)

Another infant teacher who had observed children's learning in a similar way wrote:

I see the process of children's learning as:

(a) responding to an initial stimulus
(b) being given some idea by an adult of how to go about a task – for example some skills demonstrated or materials explained – to enable the children to do something
(c) being given a clear goal
(d) time to enable all the input to work in the child's own head so that maybe he can produce something related to the stimulus or theme which is uniquely his own.

She added:

The time could appear to be spent non-productively. For example a child going away to quietly work with Lego may be planning and thinking. Some teachers find this difficult to justify as learning time, but I don't.

(Anning 1987)

It is these 'common-sense' theories, developed through a critical reflexiveness towards what they already know, that provide teachers with the insights to address other people's theories, including psychological models, in a more confident and receptive way. There is, as we have seen, so much fascinating research into young children's learning now in progress. In reading about the research and at the same time closely observing children's learning behaviours in their own classrooms, teachers may address themselves to the gap between theory and practice identified on pp. 21–3.

For example to counter an argument either for or against a Behaviourist or Developmental model of children's learning with such clearly defined general principles as those articulated by the two infant teachers quoted above *must* be more effective than simply to repeat vague slogans about child-centredness. To understand how children learn to be social beings must help teachers to structure learning activities in the classroom or to respond sensitively to incidents in the playground so that they can guide children towards effective strategies for forming and sustaining friendships. This is the kind of professionalism that many primary teachers are now developing. It has been sharpened by increasing demands to assess, record and report what children have learned since the introduction of the statutory requirements of the National Curriculum (Gipps 1994).

The process of developing this kind of professional knowledge can be represented in diagrammatic form as in Figure 2.

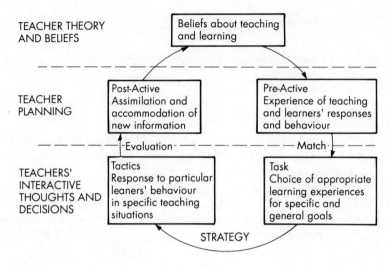

Figure 2 A cyclical model of teacher thinking

Source: Anning 1988: 144

Teachers generate their theories through a continuous process of reflection in action. They plan on the basis of their past experiences of children learning. A specific classroom behaviour they encounter feeds back into and refines further their general understanding of children's learning behaviours. They modify their teaching strategies for their next set of plans. It is a cyclical process.

It is towards the implementation of their professional knowledge into classroom teaching strategies, represented in the bottom sector of Figure 2, that we now turn.

3

Teachers teaching

The status of early years teachers

The kinds of strategies that teachers of young children use are the subject of a great deal of confusion and misunderstanding, amongst both practitioners and commentators on early years schooling. In the world at large they are often the source of the kind of amusement typified by the English actress Joyce Grenfell's unforgettable sketches of a harassed infant teacher at work. She portrayed vividly the bizarre rituals of a teacher trying with stern but smiling fortitude to control a class of young children. But what is rarely acknowledged is the level of professional challenge that is inherent in the infant teacher's task. Teachers must ensure that classes of up to thirty-five children make progress in the conventional school learning of literacy, numeracy and knowledge about the world. At the same time they must induct them into the conventions of school culture.

Yet it is still not uncommon for secondary-trained teachers to be offered jobs teaching infant classes, presumably on the basis that anybody (particularly if they are female) can teach young children. An infant-trained teacher would rarely be offered work in the secondary sector, unless they were to work with children with special educational needs – in itself a dubious slur on that particular expertise at secondary level. It is also not uncommon for secondary-trained tutors in university, polytechnic and college education departments, whose teaching experience may in fact have been restricted to grammar schools only, to be training students to work with young children. The requirements of accreditation as training agencies, since 1994 under the control of the Teacher Training Authority (TTA), have specified that tutors of students in initial training should have substantial, recent and relevant school experience of working in classrooms with the age range of children for whom they are training students. However, most ex-secondary school tutors training students to work in primary schools elect to do their 'recent and relevant' experience with junior age ranges, where understandably they feel more at ease. Moreover, the decimation of training college departments in the 1970s, many of which had impressive tutor expertise in the education of 3–8-year-olds, has had unfortunate long-term consequences for teacher supply. In 1971 there were 148 public sector institutions where teachers were trained; by 1984 these had been reduced to 54. Many of the courses closed were BEd routes into teaching, the traditional source of early year teachers in the UK. The emphasis in initial training at primary level has shifted inexorably to 'subjects' as the need to prepare newly qualified teachers to 'deliver' the content of the National Curriculum has taken priority. For example, courses are required to demonstrate 150 hours of English, mathematics and science tuition to all primary trainees. Courses in child development and training in understanding of physical development have been squeezed out. Experienced trainers of infant teachers acknowledge the problem and yet they are reluctant to lobby for a radically different training programme for teachers of 4–8-year-olds for fear that this will ghettoize Key Stage 1 teachers and limit their promotion prospects.

It is a long haul to get the expertise of early years teachers recognized and given the status it deserves. But to some degree it must be acknowledged that early years practitioners themselves have been to blame. They have been reluctant to articulate their professional knowledge. Early years cliques have tended to feed on their own shared understandings. This was partly a defensive reaction to the low status in which they felt that their expertise was held by other educators. On the whole infant teachers were not encouraged to study for higher degrees, and so they lacked the skills or confidence to analyse the complex strategies they were using in classrooms. As a consequence, what little research has been done in infant classrooms has been by researchers with little 'inside' knowledge of teaching very young children.

In a sense even the quality of people who opt to become early years teachers is perhaps a self-selected type, through the combined processes of schools career counselling and the interviews for entry into initial training programmes. A 'type' of school pupil, student or young teacher who demonstrates strong views, who dresses slightly unorthodoxly or who is academically able would be unlikely to make it into the nursery or infant school system. For instance in King's (1978) study of infant school cultures, the headteachers whom he interviewed had definite views on the ideal infant teacher type:

> Her classroom was clean and tidy, although decked with the children's products. She completed her administrative tasks correctly: marking the

register, collecting the dinner money, distributing notes for the children to take home. She came early in the morning and did not leave until school finished. She came in before term started. She gave a good performance in assembly. The quality of her craftwork was high. She showed professional pleasantness, affection and equanimity; she had a 'very good manner' and 'likes her children'.

(King 1978: 73)

The 'typical infant teacher' is thus characterized as a conformist and compliant type. There is no reference to her (and she is universally seen to *be* female) intellectual ability or professional knowledge, other than in relation to the most mundane routine activities.

Once a young teacher enters early years education, he or she is quickly socialized into the cultural norms of certain well-established routines of teacher behaviours. In referring to Figure 1 (page 19) I argued that these routines are far more influential on young teachers' daily strategies in classrooms than the ideologies presented to them in programmes of initial training or in staffroom talk.

At the same time, because primary school teachers tend to be strongly imbued with a sense of their professional competence as inextricably bound up with their sense of self as competent people (see the seminal work of Jenny Nias 1989), their awareness of the gap between the ideologies they claim to espouse and the strategies they actually use creates enormous tensions and feelings of guilt. When 'outsiders' have identified the gaps between their theories and their practice, teachers have reacted with genuine pain. It *is* important to acknowledge the debilitating, emotional reactions of the teachers of young children to the kinds of negative criticisms they have received from research findings. Yet, in my experience, it is only when teachers face up to the gap between their 'espoused theories' and their 'theories in use' (Argyris and Schön 1976) that they begin to make sense of their habitual teaching strategies, recognize their strengths as well as their weaknesses and become realistic in their analysis of what is possible in infant classrooms.

The dilemma language

The 'dilemma' language, demonstrated in the absorbing account of the American husband and wife team, Ann and Harold Berlak (1981), who came to England to explore 'informal' primary education as it was practised, seems to be particularly useful to primary teachers as a tool for analysing their strategies in classrooms. Infant teachers face dilemmas created by conflicting roles in responding to the need both to instruct children and yet at the same time to control their behaviour in the classroom, and in reconciling the demands of external agencies – both parents and other professionals – with their own professional judgements about what is expected of them. These three areas of potential conflict – teacher as instructor, teacher as agent of control, and teacher as respondent to external pressures – and the effects on their teaching strategies, will be discussed in turn.

Teacher as instructor

To intervene or not to intervene?

One of the most obvious dilemmas for teachers is to reconcile their role as direct instructors with their role in indirectly nurturing the learning of young children. The conflict in roles can be traced directly back to the different traditions of schooling, the elementary and the progressive (delineated in Chapter 1) and the polarization between a Behaviourist and a Developmental view of children's learning (identified in Chapter 2). On the one hand, teachers see their role as being responsible for teaching children the kind of knowledge that is deemed desirable by society and, on the other, they see their role as guiding children through a voyage of discovery towards their own personal knowledge.

Many infant teachers claim that they prefer to adopt a 'progressive' approach to education and espouse a non-interventionist stance towards promoting young children's learning. They prefer children to find things out for themselves, preferably through first-hand, practical, play activities. Their role is simply to structure the learning environment so that children can take advantage of the opportunities to learn that are provided within the school day. Yet at the same time they feel compelled to intervene in children's learning in a very direct way in the teaching of literacy and numeracy.

Observations of teachers working in infant classrooms have identified two clear consequences of this schizoid approach to teaching young children. It is clear that teachers tend to spend most of their time interacting with the children who are engaged in 'basic skills' activities. They appear to be responding partly to pressures from outside the school to concentrate on children's acquisition of literacy and numeracy. There is plenty of evidence that parents value these aspects of beginning schooling above all others – where the stated priorities of teachers are quite different.

In a study of 4-year-olds in schools in Rochdale, Wigan and Calderdale based at the Children's Centre at Leeds University (D. Bennett 1987) the infant teachers interviewed rated as high among their aims for educating the children: developing personal qualities such as self-confidence and independence, and positive attitudes to learning such as enjoyment, a sense of achievement, and satisfaction from learning. They also ranked the development of moral judgement, language and social skills as important. However, ninety-six parents of the 4-year-olds expected their children to learn reading, writing and arithmetic.

Comments were made like 'letters, reading, counting, they're important' . . . 'practice things, maths, reading, writing' . . . 'do a few odd sums
but not take aways' . . . Of the parents, only three made statements like
'I'm content if he's happy and wants to learn' . . . 'sure and confident' . . . 'able to develop at his own pace', three spoke of obedience
and discipline and one of continuing nursery education. The majority of
parents wanted their children to go to school, 'she's bright, I want her
pushed a bit' . . . 'ready and eager to learn' . . . 'It's time . . . the first seven
years are the time to learn'.

(D. Bennett 1987: 21)

A more recent study of parental attitudes to infant schooling led by Martin
Hughes at Exeter University (Hughes *et al.* 1994) confirmed that parents were
concerned with their children's progress in the 3Rs as a high priority; but
when asked, 'What makes a good school?', they put overall emphasis on the
quality of staff and relationships between parents, teachers and children,
the ethos and atmosphere of the school, rather than academic results or
facilities and resources. There are of course equally strong pressures from
within the educational system on teachers to instruct children in the 3Rs.
Until a national system of testing was set up in 1988 through the Schools
Examination and Assessment Council (SEAC), most primary schools formally
tested children only in reading and numeracy. Some tests were imposed
by local authority requirements – often at points of transfer – for example
at 7 and 11 when children moved from infant to junior and from junior to
secondary sectors. But teachers also know that their colleagues within schools
make judgements about 'good' teachers on the progress of their pupils in
'the basics'. It is not surprising then that these are the aspects of school
learning towards which teachers direct their attention. Nor is it surprising
that they adopt didactic approaches to teaching the basics. They are, after
all, repeating patterns they have learned at their own primary school teachers'
knees! And those primary teachers in their turn were reflecting the persistent
traditions and aspirations of the elementary school tradition.

Yet we have seen that infant teachers are also strongly influenced by the
ideologies of progressive education. So the second major effect of the teacher
intervention or non-intervention dilemma is that they adopt a decidedly
laissez-faire approach towards teaching the rest of the infant curriculum –
what Robin Alexander (1984) has called Curriculum II – the humanities,
arts, physical and moral development. (Science and technology sit unhappily
between the two approaches as pressure to teach these relatively new areas
of the infant curriculum has been imposed by the dictates of the National
Curriculum – see Chapter 5.)

The non-interventionist stance towards teaching Curriculum II is expressed
in the lack of overt teacher time given to interacting with children when
they are engaged in topic work, or creative or practical play activities. These

areas of the curriculum are often relegated to 'choosing time' and serve the function of keeping groups of children 'busy' while the teacher can get on with the 'real' work of teaching the basics. Teachers justify this dispro- portionate division of their time by claiming that children need the time and opportunity to express themselves creatively, to learn from playing with each other, and to learn from self-chosen, first-hand experiences. In this way they struggle to reconcile the conflicting imperatives of teacher-directed and child-centred approaches to teaching and learning.

The complexity of teaching strategies

The simplistic descriptions of primary teachers as formal or informal (N. Bennett 1976), or didactic or exploratory (DES 1978a), or into the four teacher types – individual monitors, class enquirers, group instructors and style changers – identified in the Oracle research (Galton et al. 1980) do not take into account the complexity of teacher thinking and action in classrooms.

How do infant teachers describe their own behaviours? It seems that they find it difficult to do so. When Jennifer Nias (1988) asked six primary teachers to define informal teaching they found the exercise impossible. They *were* able to describe formal teaching and to state that this was one of the repertoire of teaching strategies they used (sometimes more than they wished they did). So turning her original question on its head, Nias then asked the teachers to give an account of a teaching situation where they had *not* been teach- ing formally. In this way, by concentrating on specific episodes rather than general explanations, she was able to encourage teachers to describe informal teaching. They were then able to identify characteristics of the teaching/ learning episodes described which were common to the accounts. Informal teaching occurred when children adopted a teacher's original teaching stimu- lus and made it their own; when the children were engaged in purposeful and personally meaningful activities; when they worked collaboratively; and when they used the teacher as a resource rather than an instructor.

It is possible, working in this teacher-sympathetic way, to help teachers to identify and describe their teaching strategies. In the research project undertaken with six primary teachers cited at the end of Chapter 2 (Anning 1987), two infant teachers commented in detail on the evidence of teaching and learning episodes recorded in their classrooms. They were absolutely clear about why they had used certain strategies. For example a recurrent theme was the need to identify when to intervene directly in children's learn- ing processes and when to hold back from intervention.

One teacher, Wendy, believed that her role was to provide an under- lying structure for children's learning. She would therefore deliberately teach technical vocabulary, demonstrate new apparatus to the children, and teach strategies for accessing information from books, dictionaries, textbooks, etc. Sometimes this direct instruction would be as she sat and worked closely with a group, sometimes she would pull the whole class together for a ten-minute burst of direct instruction, and sometimes the instruction would be in the context of an exchange with an individual child engaged on a task. However, she argued that beyond the initial direct guidance she gave, the children should then be encouraged to develop their own strategies for extending that learning.

She was aware that the moment at which the teacher intervened was critical. She described her strategy while working with two very able 6-year-olds on a task which involved them transferring information they had collected about children in the two parallel top infant classes from chart to graph format:

> I hadn't used the word graph at any time, but that's what I was trying to get them to do, but I really didn't want to say to them, 'This is how you can make a graph.' I wanted them to try to come to the conclusion themselves that if you're making a graph like that, that you need to do it in a vertical way – to show the difference between each particular thing that you are measuring. And the thing was that I said to them – they put out their cubes horizontally on the table – and I tried to get *them* to make some decision about placing them in a better way. But it didn't come straight away. So I didn't – I just left it at that because I didn't want to say, 'Oh no, *this* is the way you're going to do it.'
>
> When the children obviously hadn't come to what I considered the right sort of placement for cubes for a graph I just decided to continue. And I said, 'Oh all right, let's just leave it. We'll talk about that later.' Then there was quite a bit of silence really because the children did seem to be working it out for themselves. I chipped in when it wasn't going quite right.

In another recorded activity, Wendy was working with a mixed ability group of 6–7-year-olds on arranging a list of the names of children in the two top infant classes into alphabetical order. She described her strategy when the children first encountered two names beginning with the same letter:

> They found the two names that both began with 'A' and I said, 'Do you think it matters where I put them?' I think I was trying to – instead of just giving them a rule straight away – I was trying to make them realise the *need* for a rule if you know what I mean. In that way they would realise that you've got to do something about it – and hopefully they would then remember *what* to do about it, rather than just be told. And I wanted them to try various strategies themselves, hopefully to see if they could somehow get something out of that. You know, to build on what they knew and did rather than me just throw in something entirely new to them. I wanted *them* really to come up with the answer. I didn't want to come in straight away and correct them. Because I've often

found that if you leave it long enough it evolves anyway; and if it's come from the children then they tend to remember it, rather than me, having me tell them.

The directive strategies she used were, on the surface, very mechanistic. They included focusing children's attention on key aspects of learning during the task. For example commenting on her strategies in the maths activities, she said:

> I noticed dozens of times I kept recapping on what we'd done before. At one point I said to the children, 'Right, let's look what's happening here.' Again I brought them back to, 'Now what is it we're trying to show? And what are those cubes?' Just so that they would not forget the purpose of what we were doing. I came back again with 'What does this cube mean?' so that they did understand what we were dealing with. It wasn't a cube as a cube. It was just a family. It was representing something else.

This seems to me a perfect illustration of the Donaldson argument that young children can and should be empowered by adults with access to symbol systems in the early years of schooling. As Donaldson pointed out, the learning activities which give opportunities for children to move towards abstractions should be embedded in their realities. In this example, the children were working on a shared, practical activity, dealing with data about their friends in the school, with the skilful 'scaffolding' of a teacher who was concerned to push them towards new levels of intellectual competence.

Another strategy Wendy used was consciously to introduce the children to a new vocabulary of abstractions:

> The word 'represent', now whether they'd come across that before I don't know, but I noticed towards the end of the session I wasn't actually saying, 'What does it mean to you?' I was saying, 'What does it represent?' And they came back with it straight away – so they picked that terminology up.

She also cued children into 'correct' responses when that was necessary to keep the processes and pace of learning moving. In the language activity she explained:

> I did notice my use of inflection when I said to the girls, 'Where are you up to now?' And they said they were up to 'B'. So I said, 'Oh well, what does that mean?' It was quite obvious to anybody listening that what I *did* actually mean was, 'Well, you're nowhere near it yet.' And I presume – I think they did actually pick that up. There were quite a few occasions when it was quite obvious from my voice that they hadn't got the right answer so far.

However, underlying all these basically mechanistic strategies was a constant awareness of the children's likely emotional responses to what she
was doing and saying. She knew that she wanted children to develop independence in learning situations, and in order to become independent they
had to become confident enough to tackle new learning activities, and she
was able to identify clearly the key strategies she used to create an atmosphere in the classroom where the children would 'have a go' without fear
of failure. For example she used facial expressions and body language to
communicate her support, particularly when children appeared to be anxious:

> I noticed I smiled a lot at them. It must have been quite early in the
> recording, I think Shane was in the middle of explaining something
> and I was just nodding and smiling as if to say, 'Yes, you're on the right
> track. Go on,' because he's quite nervous really, Shane, and he needs
> that sort of thing. . . .
>
> I did in fact sit quite close to Tom. I normally sit close to the one who
> needs my physical presence really – I actually put my arm round him.

She used humour to defuse tension, particularly to support children who
were struggling to find the solution to a problem or who had made an obvious mistake, and she treated children in quite different ways depending on
their likely emotional responses to risk situations:

> I was worried that John might get a bit upset if I put him under pres-
> sure for too long. So when it was his go, I left him for a few minutes.
> But he just wasn't moving at all. His hand was frozen over the shapes.
> Then I felt I didn't want to embarrass him any more, so I said, 'Do you
> want to do it or do you want me to help?' Perhaps left he could have
> done it – but the situation at that point seemed too much. On reflection,
> I think it was the only thing to do. Looking back it didn't appear to do
> him any harm because when it came to his turn again he went straight
> in and did it that time. . . .
>
> I did notice that my attitude was not the same to all of them in that
> I tend to put more pressure on Shane. Where he was trying to explain
> something at one point, I did say, 'Yes, carry on,' you know, 'Keep
> going'. Whereas with Tom I'm perhaps more gentle for instance . . . I
> definitely put more pressure on Shane. He was explaining what he'd
> done, and I suppose he was under quite a lot of pressure from me to
> explain correctly what he'd done. It wasn't enough – I didn't just accept
> that he'd got the answer right – whereas probably had Tom got it right,
> I'd have shown a lot of pleasure at that. With Shane I felt, 'Yes, OK.
> You've got it right but . . .' He needed – was able – to explain it as well.
> And therefore I expected him to do that for me. . . . Another thing, I
> noticed when I gave the task to Shane I said, 'I'd like you to do this
> . . . blah, blah, blah', but when I asked Tom to do a task I said (soften-
> ing her voice), 'Would you like to . . . ?' which was again this slightly kid

glove attitude I've got towards Tom. I suppose it's all the time, you know, giving him encouragement. My interaction with Tom was very gentle all the time.

What these extracts from an experienced infant teacher's account of her strategies demonstrate is that there are many layers of meanings underpinning the minute-by-minute decisions she is making in the classroom. Research which simply records teacher actions using a coding system, or defines teacher strategies simply on the basis of an analysis of transcripts of their talk, or relies on questioning teachers about their intentions and actions without constant reference to real classroom episodes against which to compare their explanations – all these approaches to understanding classroom processes give only partial information. The complexity of teacher decision-making is illustrated in Figure 2 (p. 46) and to slice across the layers of teacher theory and beliefs, teacher planning and teachers' interactive thoughts and decisions at any one point gives a distorted view of the way in which skilful teachers operate in action. But the problem is that working intensively with teachers in order to encourage them to articulate their multiple realities is very time-consuming and expensive. It also requires trust between the observer and the observed, and researchers have to work hard to establish that kind of trust against a history of the teachers' resentment of the negative feedback they have suffered from 'top down' research programmes in the past.

What is also clear is that there *are* patterns common to infant teachers' strategies. Once they have become aware of these patterns, research findings have more chance of 'getting under their skin'. In my experience it is only then that teachers begin to turn to theoretical models with much more commitment to make sense of them.

Models of pedagogy

Jerome Bruner's *Towards a Theory of Instruction* (1966) still seems to provide a useful and usable model of pedagogy for teachers. What is particular about Bruner's work is that he argues his thesis through from an analysis of children's learning, to a model of classroom pedagogy and then to a curriculum framework.

He sees children's learning as moving between three modes of representation: enactive, iconic and symbolic – knowing something through doing it, through a picture or image of it, and through some such symbolic means as language; and all learners move from one mode to another throughout their lives. He argues that the child should be active in discovering important principles – such as the ability to classify and generalize – from practical examples.

Mastery of the fundamental ideas of a field involves not only the grasping of general principles, but also the development of an attitude toward

learning and inquiry, toward guesses and hunches, toward the possi-
bility of solving problems on one's own. . . . To instill such attitudes by
teaching requires . . . a sense of excitement about discovery – discovery
of regularities of previously unrecognized relations and similarities between ideas, with a resulting sense of self-confidence in one's abilities.

(Bruner 1960: 20)

For if we do nothing else we should somehow give to children a
respect for their own powers of thinking, for their power to generate
good questions, to come up with interesting informed guesses . . . to
make . . . study more rational, more amenable to the use of the mind
in the large rather than mere memorizing.

(Bruner 1966: 96)

The role of the teacher is to 'scaffold' the child's learning by gearing the
activities, resources and interactions to the level of competence and maturity
of the child. The teacher must constantly revisit ideas, spiralling upwards to
build endlessly on children's previous understanding, and must, therefore,
be aware of what learning the child brings to a task. Bruner argued that
'much of what we do and say in school only makes children feel that they
don't know things that in fact they knew perfectly well before we began to
talk about them'.

Tizard and Hughes (1984) give a perfect example of this unproductive kind
of strategy in *Young Children Learning*. A 4-year-old child, June, approached
her teacher with a piece of paper:

Child: Can you cut that in half? Cut it in half?
Teacher: What would you like me to do with it?
Child: Scissors.
Teacher: With the scissors? (Child nods.) Well, you go and get them,
               will you?
Child: Where are they?
Teacher: Have a look round. (Child goes over to the cupboard, gets
               some scissors.) Where do you want me to cut it?
Child: There.
Teacher: Show me again, 'cause I don't quite know where the cut's got
               to go. (Child shows the teacher where she wants the paper
               cut.) Down there? (Child nods; teacher cuts child's piece of
               paper in half.) How many have you got now?
Child: (No reply)
Teacher: How many have you got?
Child: (No reply)
Teacher: How many pieces of paper have you got?
Child: Two.
Teacher: Two. What have I done if I've cut it down the middle?
Child: Two pieces.

Teacher:	I've cut it in . . . ? (Wants child to say 'half'.)
Child:	(No reply)
Teacher:	What have I done?
Child:	(No reply)
Teacher:	Do you know? (Child shakes head.)
Other child:	Two.
Teacher:	Yes, I've cut it in two. But . . . I wonder, can you think?
Child:	In the middle.
Teacher:	I've cut it in the middle. I've cut it in *half*! There you are, now you've got two.

(Tizard and Hughes 1984: 194–5)

This transcript also illustrates the 'flatness' of dialogue which characterized many of the nursery class conversations recorded by the Tizard and Hughes team. Teachers dominated talk, simply by the sheer volume and length of utterances they contributed to the 'conversations'. Their talk was also characterized by a string of questions – a 'teaching' device intended to stimulate thinking.

Questioning has been a habitual teaching device since Socrates recommended it, and most of us can remember the agony of trying to monitor, under stern directions from tutors on our teaching practices, which of our questions to children were 'open' and therefore 'appropriate' or 'closed' and 'inappropriate'! Such superficial analysis is unhelpful. It is possible to ask open questions in a decidedly closed way, or closed questions in a way that requires the respondent to think in a divergent way. In the Tizard and Hughes study the teachers' questions seemed to be designed either to assess at a very simple level what the child already knew – 'What colour is your jersey?' – or to promote their linguistic or cognitive competence – 'What do you think will happen if we plant these seeds?' But the conversation between June and her teacher illustrates the dangers inherent in this approach to teaching young children. The child, as Bruner suggested often happens in schools, is made to 'feel that they don't know things that in fact they knew perfectly well'. June had asked her teacher to cut the paper 'in half' in her initiating turn in the conversation. From the moment of initiation her contributions to the talk were reduced by the teacher's style of interaction, designed to elicit the 'correct' answer (which June had in fact already given), to one- or two-word utterances. Such exchanges clearly do not empower children with 'a respect for their own powers of thinking'. If the emphasis is genuinely to be on 'starting where the child is' teachers must learn to listen to children and engage in dialogue rather than cross-examination (Edwards and Mercer 1989).

Forman and Cazden (1985: 344) compare the linguistic conventions of the child's 'home' world with those encountered in formal schooling. The example is illustrated by the child learning to play peek-a-boo:

The mother initially enacts the entire script herself and then the child takes on an increasingly active role eventually speaking all the parts initially spoken by the mother. The contrast between such learning environments and the classroom is striking. In school lessons, teachers give directions and children non-verbally carry them out; teachers ask questions and children answer them, frequently with only one word or phrase. Most importantly, these roles are not reversed. Children never give directions to teachers and questions addressed to teachers are rare except for giving permission.

Teacher as agent of control

The teacher's view

In order to function as instructors it is inevitable that teachers exercise some form of control over the social behaviour of children in their classrooms. For many teachers, trained in the traditions of child-centredness, there are real dilemmas presented by the control of children in reconciling the needs of the individual with the needs of the class. Teachers set a high value on the quality of their relationships with pupils as individuals, but in organizing all the children into routines which allow teaching to take place, they are forced to coerce individual children into 'norms' of acceptable school behaviour. The profound uneasiness which teachers feel about this dichotomy is often expressed at the end of the first week of infant school teaching practice when idealistic postgraduate students, white-faced and exhausted, will blurt out, 'I don't want to behave like a dictator or policeman! But that's exactly what I hear myself doing.' They have, in their naivety, identified a critical issue – the potential abuse of power that is inherent in teacher–pupil relationships in schools. In order to reconcile the uneasiness they feel about the unequal power relationship, experienced teachers of young children moderate the exercise of their power by clearly identifiable strategies designed to soften the processes of establishing their authority.

The child's experience

Recent studies of the 'rites of passage' as children make the transition from home to school have highlighted some of the inevitable discontinuities in their experiences of home and school life. Barrett (1986), in a report on the responses of reception class children to school commissioned by the Assistant Masters and Mistresses Association, described the difficulties children beginning school have in coming to terms with rituals such as milktime, playtime, procedures for going to the toilet, lining up and assemblies. For young children used to operating within the easy-going routines of home or playgroup, these are mysterious rites – and adults rarely explain to them *why* they should conform to the novel patterns of behaviour required of them. They may also find some of the classroom activities somewhat bizarre. What sense can a young child make, for example, of being offered a waist-high container of sand or water, assorted containers, a command to put on a mysterious garment described as an apron, and a constant rhetorical question '*How* many children are allowed in the sand/water?' whenever they set out intrepidly across the classroom to join in the ritual? Most significantly, children have to learn how to operate as one of a large group of people when their previous experiences may have been limited to socializing only with small groups of family or friends.

A more extensive study of the transition from home to school (Cleave *et al.* 1982) which formed one part of a National Foundation for Educational Research project, 'Continuity of Children's Experience in the Years 3 to 8', looked at the 'sources of shock' experienced by children entering sixty-three infant classes from a range of pre-school settings: childminders, play-groups, day nurseries, nursery classes and schools. The study identified potential sources of shock as:

1 The setting – the scale of the building, the range of movement required by access to toilets, school hall, playground, etc., and the constraints on the child's movement around his or her own classroom territory.
2 The curriculum – the daily programme, the range of activities, the amount of choice the child has in how to spend his or her time.
3 The people – contact with older, bigger and noisier children (particularly on the school playground), competition for teacher attention, organizational constraints imposed by unfamiliar adults such as welfare assistants, teachers on playground duty or the headteacher.

The team concluded:

Three ingredients are essential if shock is to be reduced to a minimum:

1 Changes and the introduction of new experiences must be *gradual* rather than sudden.
2 People, places and things must to some extent be *familiar* rather than totally strange.
3 The child must have a sense of *security* rather than instability.

(Cleave *et al.* 1982: 210)

The teacher's role in the socialization of pupils

What then are the processes by which teachers socialize young children into acceptable school behaviour? King (1978) described some of them in his wry account of life in infant school classrooms. He based his descriptions on observations in three infant schools over a three-year period. The children came to know him as 'The Man in the Wendy House'! He described the strategies the teachers used to impose their middle-class cultural views of appropriate school interests and behaviours on their school populations, while at the same time preserving their 'ideology' of the innocence of childhood.

> Their methods of control were typically oblique, particularly with younger children. Their preference was to make requests rather than to give orders, to reward good behaviour rather than punish the bad. These actions were consonant with the idea of the children being innocent. They were capable of being naughty but did not have naughty intentions. When I put this analysis to teachers they confirmed it with phrases like, 'Well, yes, you can't really blame them, can you?'
>
> (King 1978: 50)

The teachers monitored children's behaviour by constantly scanning the classroom and making eye-contact with or directing disapproving looks at children who were stepping out of line. They also used 'public and private voices' to exercise control. A public comment like, 'I can see a group over there not working', would have a 'ripple' effect on other children in the class-room, as would specific comments to a child such as, 'Have you put the date on your paper, Paul?' Reference control was used when some external author-ity was invoked. Typical invocations would be, 'Now, nice and quietly down the corridor. You know Mrs Brown [the headteacher] does not like noisy children', or 'Put the apron on. What would Mummy say if you come home with paint on that nice new jumper?' Sometimes control was couched in a game, 'Boys close eyes. Girls creep out, quietly get your coats. Don't let the boys hear you!', or a mechanistic quietening-down routine, 'Hands on heads. Fingers on lips. Lock hands in laps.' Private voices were used when an individual child or small group were being addressed and were generally much softer in tone as well as volume.

In order to impose classroom rules, the teachers discouraged behaviour that was labelled 'silly' and rewarded children for being 'sensible'. King quotes typical teacher comments which made their frames of reference explicit through the use of well-chosen adjectives and adverbs:

> Now I can see the *sensible* people because they are *busy* working already.
> Go into prayers *quietly* and *sensibly*, sing as *nicely* as you can.
> I want Paul to sit by me because he has been so *nice* and *helpful*.
> Gary you are being *silly* and *noisy*. No, I'm not smiling, I'm sorry.

Politeness was insisted upon:

> *Child:*   Can I go to the toilet?
> *Teacher:* Pardon? (She has heard what he said.)
> *Child:*   Can I go to the toilet, please?

Teacher: Just remember those two very special words.
Children: (in chorus) Please and thankyou.

The processes of peer group socialization

Jane, the second infant teacher in Anning's research project (Anning 1988), was aware of the value of particular children with high peer group status in supporting her control strategies in the classroom. She described the behaviour of a child whom she had taught previously in the nursery, and who now formed part of a reception class:

> I recognise – I think it's perhaps because I've taught him for two years – I recognise Christian's phrasing in mine. Particularly in the classroom. And I can hear – it's almost that he's saying the word, but when I'm just sort of thinking it – but it's the word I want to use, you know. . . . It's happened since we've been doing 'time', and Christian has picked up on it even more. We can go into PE and they'll be half an hour for PE. They've five pieces of apparatus to go on if they're all doing their tasks properly and not being silly. And we have gone into the hall when it's taken a long time for them all to get changed, a long time to line up, being silly in the line, silly in the hall – and they've probably done two pieces of apparatus and Christian has then said, 'You know *why?*' to them. 'Because now we've only got . . .' and he's the first one to look at the clock now when we go into the hall. He'll say, 'Look, we've got to be quick because we're late coming in because we've been silly', you know, he's worked it all out. And gradually more and more are beginning to do it and become aware of it. That's – I feel they've learnt a lot.

Jane was honest enough to admit that she used a form of emotional blackmail as one of her range of control strategies:

> The only time I deliberately make the children feel uncomfortable is when they are behaving objectionably. And then they know who they are, and I do it then for a different reason – so that I can get them to modify their behaviour so they can have me, Mrs H, as she is when they are behaving normally. When they are behaving in an objectionable way, then they must do something to get me to be *nice*. And I only need a facial gesture some time. I don't need to use words.

In turn those same key children, who knew Jane's moods, would try to prevent this uncomfortable tension in the classroom from surfacing:

> Christian, when I begin to do that, when he sees this thing of me falling apart, will say loudly, 'This is ridiculous, you're all being very silly, aren't they, Miss?' And he'll spell it out before it happens. And then one or two others will pick the cues up – and gradually they do it for me – and I don't have to do anything except stand and look disapproving.

The linguistic conventions of control

Mary Willes (1983) describes the highly specific uses of language associated with establishing classroom routines. These rule-governed language conventions have to be learned by the young child. The structures reflect the power vested in the adult position of authority and, because they then transfer to teaching and learning episodes, form a substantial obstacle to the kind of 'open' dialogue that characterizes the pedagogy Bruner suggests is conducive to encouraging children to be confident and independent learners. The teacher sees her role as keeping the discourse flowing. She has the right to decide on changes of subject, to interrupt children, to ignore inappropriate contributions. Children learn that they are expected to provide brief responses (particularly in so-called class 'discussions') so that others do not get fidgety; to keep silent in teaching situations unless nominated or invited to bid for teacher attention; and to try to make guesses to get as near as possible to the 'correct' answer in the teacher's head when they are asked a direct question. Sinclair and Coulthard (1975), who designed a model of discourse analysis for classrooms, asked 'How does the five year old who speaks when he wants to become the ten year old who waits to be nominated?' If the conventions described by Willes are established at the point when children are at their most vulnerable, as 'relatively inexperienced members of the speech community', that is at point of entry to school, it is not surprising that when teachers attempt at a later date in junior or secondary classes to get children to negotiate for a more 'equal' pattern of discourse, the children are resistant to change. The same patterns even persist into higher education where in seminars or tutorials students assume that tutors will sustain the dialogue, and tutors, socialized into distrust of silences, will 'fill up the vacancies of attention', with instructional talk.

Nor is it surprising that attempts to elicit children's views of the role of the teacher have confirmed that they are very much aware of the power of teachers as authority figures. Willes (1983) tried initially to elicit children's views about how they perceived the relations between teacher and taught, and their grasp of the linguistic conventions that expressed those relationships, by observing them in free play with a Fisher Price Playschool. The children did tend to play out 'school routines' like registration with the four small pupil dolls and one teacher doll. However, to gain more systematic information, Willes designed a storybook, illustrated by photographs, of some normal events in a morning at school. The children were asked to fill in gaps, in an oral or written cloze procedure, at various points in the book. Over the time-span of three terms, it was clear that the children were increasingly aware of the school routines and accompanying conventions of school talk. In adjusting or 'settling down' to school, they had learned 'to accept their place as very junior members of an elaborate social hierarchy' (Newson and Newson 1977: 45).

Young children also quickly pick up on 'fear of wrong doing' in this hierarchical school culture. When Barrett used a similar technique of showing 5-year-olds a series of photographs of classroom events during their first few weeks in school, their responses indicated dependency and anxiety:

Girls can't do it – perhaps she's drawing a ship.

A boy doesn't know what to do. He is sucking his pencil. He cannot do his work. He must tell his teacher.

I don't know how to do it – I didn't know how to paint or mix the colours properly.

I didn't like to write when I came to school. I couldn't make a snail. I couldn't draw a picture. It was too hard. I was too little.

I feel miserable when I can't do it. I'm frightened I might get it wrong.

These fears were expressed by children whose teachers had tried hard to make the transition to school a happy experience – by staggering the school entry, starting children off on part-time attendance, involving parents closely in the initial entry to school. Yet the children still felt anxious about the demands of the school activities. It is sobering evidence of the children's distress and worrying when we know that learning is not likely to be effective when the learner feels stressed or anxious.

Pupil power

However, power is not solely vested in the adult in the classroom. Andrew Pollard (1985, 1988) has provided some fascinating analyses of the power of children's culture in primary classrooms. He argues that children are not nearly as passive in the negotiation of classroom processes as has been suggested in previous studies of classroom life.

Child culture and child friendship groups generate norms, values, rules, understandings and a sense of social structure which is extremely complex and sophisticated . . . and these provide a means by which children make sense of and cope with the adult world when it impinges on them.
(Pollard 1985: 245)

Pollard argues that both the pupils and the teacher have dominant 'interests at hand'. Figure 3 indicates what these interests are.

He argues that the teacher and the children negotiate, from their standpoints of different concerns and interests, towards a 'working consensus'. The teacher will negotiate for acceptable noise levels, attention to tasks, movement around the classroom, clearing up the classroom – while the children will negotiate for time to 'easy ride', legitimate reasons for moving around the classroom to talk to friends (pencil sharpening is a favourite ploy), avoidance

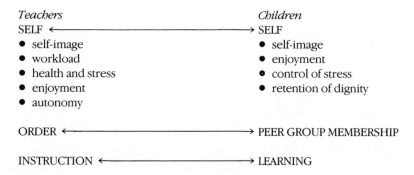

Figure 3 Primary and enabling interests of teachers and children
Source: Pollard 1985: 156

of tidying up activities ('Miss, can I go to the toilet? I'm *desperate*'). Most children are willing to comply with the working consensus – they do not particularly like hassle – though some children may challenge the system either by subtle strategies of evasion or by overt rebellion. These isolated instances of deviance will be explained away by teachers as a child who is 'going through a phase', possibly because of some trouble at home, or the result of immaturity, 'something he'll grow out of', or in extreme cases as a child beyond the normal range of 'naughtiness' expected in classrooms and therefore referable to the educational psychologist. But the combined power of a class of children, who have decided to reject a teacher's authority because they are bored, frustrated or angered by his or her behaviour, can be very effective. It can drive a supply teacher out of the school after one day, never to return, or devastate an inexperienced student; and, of course, it is fear that they will not be able to cope with the combined power of their pupils that makes student teachers resort to 'policeman' or 'dictator' tactics.

In Nias' sample of six experienced teachers, on the other hand, it was significant that they claimed that they were able to work in a collaborative rather than authoritative way with pupils only when they felt 'relaxed', 'easy', 'not frightened any more', 'able to be themselves'. 'In other words a classroom climate in which teachers feel secure appears to be a necessary condition for the establishment of self-directed, purposeful learning on the part of the pupils' (Nias 1988: 133). The task for teachers is to negotiate a climate where they can talk openly and honestly with children about the need for shared responsibility for the mechanics of managing and organizing a classroom, for getting through a reasonable amount of work each day, for having fun, for admitting when things have gone wrong. Lynne, one of the teachers in Nias' sample, wrote:

> What teaching this way means for me is that I'm happy. I feel cared for.
> I don't feel as if I'm acting. I don't feel stressed or bored. I never look

at the clock. I don't have to fight for control – and I have the satisfaction of knowing that I do the job better, that I'm a better teacher. . . . I expect it to be a two-way thing – for example, if I've been away ill, I want them to ask me how I am. . . . If I think they're trying it on, I'll tell them why I think it's crappy . . . It's important that they do something as well as they can, then they can get the satisfaction from it. It's *their* work but I tell them what I think about it.

(Nias 1988: 135)

We need studies of classrooms where this kind of working consensus between the teacher and the children has been achieved – where children are producing high standards of work and where teachers are functioning effectively. A start has been made by Peter Woods (1993) in his study of 'critical events', periods of particularly effective teaching and learning in primary schools. What is clear is that infant teachers cannot operate a pedagogy which is based on principles which encourage children to take responsibility for their own learning if they at the same time are discouraging children from taking responsibility for their own behaviour.

Teacher as respondent to external pressures

Societal and cultural values and teachers

Teachers bring to the classroom a set of values that have been acquired from their own personal histories as well as from the professional contexts in which they have worked. The values they hold have a profound influence on their behaviour as teachers (see Figure 1, p. 19). It has already been suggested that a particular type of person enters the teaching profession. Most teachers' family backgrounds are middle class or skilled working class, though of course their subsequent careers, personal situations, or higher education may have broadened their life experiences. Nevertheless, there is evidence that teachers present a set of values and aspirations to pupils which reflect white, British, middle-class assumptions, even when they are at pains to prevent this happening.

In the 1970s and 1980s a series of studies in primary schools identified aspects of teachers' attitudes towards class and race, and more recently towards gender, which affect the way teachers behave towards children.

Class

Nash (1973) addressed the 'expectancy' problem (research reviewed in Pilling and Kellmer Pringle 1978: Part IV), which had become a key issue in educational research in the vanguard of destreaming in primary schools and the transition from selective to comprehensive secondary education. His concern was to explore how far teachers' attitudes towards their pupils influenced pupil self-concept and performance in schools. He worked with eight junior school teachers and from them elicited the most common constructs they held about their pupils as learners – hardworking/lazy, mature/immature, and well-behaved/poorly behaved. He then observed interactions between the teachers and their pupils, and it was clear that the teachers treated the children differently according to their perceptions of them. The evidence upon which the teachers made their judgements was not always accurate. In some instances, for example, the teachers wrongly attributed children to a particular social background. Slower and less likeable children were perceived as coming from poor homes, though objective data indicated that their background was similar to other well-regarded children in the class. The teachers claimed that they 'knew each child well', but 'knowing' in this sense appeared to be very much within the school context and cultural expectations. The teachers also claimed that they were scrupulously fair and treated all pupils the same. Nash's evidence suggested that teachers clearly preferred some children above others, and their behaviour towards them reflected their preferences.

Another study was carried out with the headteacher and infant staff of a primary school by Sharp and Green (1975). They explored the gap between the 'theories' of progressivism implicit in the teachers' talk and the realities of their classroom practice. They found that teachers spent more time interacting with the 'ideal' pupils who were usually defined as coming from 'good homes'. Their success as effective 'progressive' teachers was measured against these successful school learners' progress. On the other hand failure to learn was attributed to 'bad home backgrounds' rather than to factors within school. Ironically the children who were most in need of direct teacher attention were most likely to be sent off to play or to practical activities to keep themselves occupied until they were 'ready' to learn. Thus the gap between those succeeding and those failing on school tasks began to widen.

King (1978) found that teachers' assessment and typification of pupils were based on three aspects of pupil behaviour – their compliance with teacher rules, their relationship with other children and their progress in learning – but in making judgements teachers were also influenced by assumptions about children's home backgrounds. The way they interacted with pupils was profoundly influenced by these typifications. Thus King wrote,

> The posing of the family–home background theory was made easier, if not actually made possible, by their child-centred practices, which presented them with the 'evidence' of the children's homes and families through their writing, drawing and talking. Taking an interest in the whole child legitimated knowing about his or her life outside the classroom. Thus the child-centredness permitted the family–home background theory and was protected by it.
>
> (King 1978: 146)

The deficit view of working-class children had been legitimized in the massive programmes of compensatory education in the 1960s (see Chapter 1). In the 1970s the spectre of teacher expectations determining pupil progress loomed large and at the same time the myths about 'working-class' homes being without books, culture or indeed 'language' began to be dispelled. Yet there is worrying evidence that teachers continue to make judgements about pupils based on sketchy understanding of their home backgrounds. It is also clear that the judgements are not simply based on assumptions about class, but are the result of a subtle and complex interplay of attitudes towards class, race and gender. These attitudes affect the way in which teachers respond to pupils in classrooms, and this in turn affects the way pupils perceive themselves as 'good' or 'bad' pupils and as successful or unsuccessful learners.

Race

Research into teachers' attitudes towards race have shown marginal changes in the past two decades. In Elaine Brittan's (1976) study of 500 teachers in twenty-five primary and secondary schools, where the school population of ethnic minority children ranged from 18 per cent to 24 per cent, 94 per cent of the teachers claimed to support the principle that 'schools have a responsibility to promote good race relations among pupils'. They agreed that assemblies and religious education syllabuses should reflect minority faiths, and that some curriculum changes should be made to accommodate the countries of origin of ethnic minority children.

However, many also expressed a strongly assimilationist line, claiming that 'immigrant children should merge in with the English pupils'. Little and Willey's *Studies in the Multi-Ethnic Curriculum* (1983) reported that most teachers were impatient with the small but vociferous lobby of professionals committed to multi-cultural education for all schools. They saw the issues as 'irrelevant both to them and to their pupils'. Teacher attitudes displayed 'the whole gamut of racial misunderstandings and folk mythology . . . racial stereotypes were common and attitudes ranged from the unveiled hostility of few, through the apathy of many and the condescension of others, to total acceptance by a minority'. In the 1970s and 1980s pressure began to grow from minority groups to examine the possible effects of negative teacher attitudes and low expectations on black children's school achievement. In 1979 the government set up a Committee of Inquiry into the Education of Children from Ethnic Minority Groups. The Rampton Report (DES 1981b), *West Indian Children in Our Schools*, was published in 1981, followed by the Swann Report in 1985, from which this extract is taken:

> It will be evident that society is faced with a dual problem: eradicating the discriminatory attitudes of the white majority on the one hand, and

on the other, evolving an educational system which ensures that *all* pupils achieve their full potential.

(Swann Committee 1985: 2.6, 768)

Yet racism still persists in primary schools (Troyna and Hatcher 1992). Cecile Wright (1992) studied three First schools and one Middle School. She found that teachers criticized African-Caribbean children (especially boys) more than other children and that they had negative stereotypes of South Asian children, attributing poor linguistic and social skills to them. Asian children experienced regular name-calling and physical abuse from their white peers. Teachers were aware of this racist behaviour, but unsure about how to tackle it.

Gender

During the 1980s attention was focused on the differential treatment of girls and boys in classrooms. The Sex Discrimination Act 1975 included education in its scope, and the Equal Opportunities Commission was set up to monitor the principles of 'equality of opportunity' for all. Local authorities have responded by producing guidelines on equal opportunities. But paper policies never quite match up to classroom realities, and research has identified some crucial differences in the way in which teachers perceive boys and girls and the way in which they interact with them (Clarricoates 1980; Spender 1982; Whyte 1983; Weiner 1985; Mullin *et al.* 1987; Tutchell 1990). Teachers differentiate between girls and boys in control and organizational strategies. Competition between boys and girls is encouraged by infant teachers as a way of urging children to work harder or behave better. Registers are called separately; boys and girls are expected to line up separately; to wash their hands separately; sometimes to play in separate school playgrounds.

There is plenty of evidence that boys dominate teacher time and talk. When Dale Spender tried to compensate for this known imbalance by deliberately trying to distribute her attention evenly between girls and boys, in ten taped lessons with secondary age children,

> the maximum time I spent interacting with girls was 42% and on average 38%, and the minimum time with boys was 58%. It is nothing short of a substantial shock to appreciate the discrepancy between what I *thought* I was doing and what I actually *was* doing.

(Spender 1982: 56)

Most infant teachers are equally shocked when they realize, through observations or the use of tape recordings, how boys dominate classroom talk. Despite the fact that adult power is held by a predominantly female workforce in infant schools, boys learn how to dominate favoured 'male' space and resources such as computers and brick play, outdoor equipment, and key playground areas.

From the outset of schooling, girls are orientated towards the demands of the teacher, rather than the task. While boys seek attention through aggression and rule-breaking, girls seek approval through conforming to pupil norms. Although girls' intellectual achievement is in general better than that of boys, they retreat from sex-competition, lack confidence and react more negatively to perceived failure. They comply with the male orientation of resources, tasks and norms and in doing so 'learn to lose'.

(Whyte 1983: 32)

It is, however, also true that boys receive far more negative feedback from their teachers. This may explain in part why more boys than girls demonstrate aggression and deviance throughout the school system. If you are constantly being reprimanded publicly for noise, movement around the classroom, and aggressive behaviour, it seems likely that you will assume that these characteristics are expected of you by teachers and will oblige with the appropriate behaviours. It is also self-evident that not all boys conform to the 'macho' stereotype; nor that all girls conform to the stereotype of passive compliance. The attempt by a team of researchers from Northern Ireland (Mullin *et al.* 1987) to explore categories of 'visible' and 'invisible' children in infant classrooms, and only within that overall system to begin to locate gender differences in behaviours, seems a more promising approach.

Effects of teacher expectation on pupil progress

Most teachers feel guilty when they become aware of research findings into the 'self-fulfilling' prophecies of teacher expectations and pupil progress. They have learnt to adopt self-censoring strategies when they talk publicly about issues of race, class and gender. For example the label 'working class' is more often substituted by euphemisms such as 'does not have a supportive home', though in fairness to teachers this has been demonstrated to be a more tangible source of determining school failure than generalizations made on the basis of parental occupations and income.

Where is the hard evidence of the effect on pupil progress of infant teachers', often unconsciously, classist, racist, and sexist attitudes? In their study of thirty-three ILEA infants' schools, Tizard *et al.* (1988) tried to tease out the effects of home background, parental aspirations and teacher attitudes on the school progress of working-class white and Afro-Caribbean boys and girls. Attainments at school entry were highly predictive of attainments at the end of infant schooling. The factors at home which appeared to influence attainment at school entry were parents' educational qualifications and the amount they helped children with school work at home, particularly the experience they gave children of books. Over three years black boys made the least progress in reading, and black girls the most progress. Boys made more progress in maths.

The effect of teacher and school factors was much less clear. The team hedge their findings with caveats, but they acknowledge that

> teachers' expectations and the range of children's curriculum coverage, and, to a lesser extent, whether children were seen to have behaviour problems, to be under-achieving, and to be a pleasure to teach, were associated with children's school attainment and progress. Teacher expectations and curriculum coverage were themselves associated, and it was suggested that the range of curriculum coverage activities given to individual children may be one way that teachers' expectations operate in the classroom.
>
> (Tizard *et al.* 1988: 142)

This issue will be explored in the discussion of the infant school curriculum in Chapter 4.

One label that is consistently used by teachers to explain school failure is single-parent status of a child's family. What is the evidence of this link? Osborn and Milbank (1987) examined the effects of changes in home life to which children in the longitudinal Child Health and Education Study were subjected between the ages of 5 and 10 on their educational attainment and behaviour at 10. They concluded that single parent status *per se* did not affect the school progress of the children, though a change for the worse with all the associated socio-economic changes in the family unit's lifestyle (the continuum being measured from the optimal situation of both natural parents present to the least desirable, from the child's point of view, of the child being placed with foster or grandparents) did increase the risk of conduct disorder and hyperactivity. On the other hand, an increase in family size, especially of two or more children, did reduce a child's test scores. It is important that teachers are made aware of these kinds of data. 'Family' types are as varied as the number of children in a class, and we should be wary of making assumptions about the 'ideal' two-parent, two-children, nuclear family and school success.

Teacher values and controversial issues

It is impossible, perhaps even undesirable, for teachers to be neutral in the values they bring to educating young children. In this sense they are both guilty and innocent. But particularly worrying for nursery and infant staff is how to deal with classroom incidents that reflect children's awareness of complex social problems gained through television news coverage, soap operas like *EastEnders*, videos, newspapers and adult talk. How do teachers deal with ethical and moral issues with young children? There has been little support for teachers in the teaching of moral education and little research into the moral development of children (see pp. 42–3).

In 1986 *Child Education* (Anning *et al.* 1986) funded a small-scale exploratory study of the strategies nursery and infant teachers used when confronted with examples of children playing out, for example violent clashes between police and strikers or miners, teachers striking, terrorism, overt sexual behaviour, sexist stereotypes, or when children manifested overt racism, religious intolerance or bullying.

The strategies teachers used were categorized as involvement or extension, direction or manipulation, and delay or diversion.

Involvement or extension

In involvement or extension strategies (27 per cent of the total categorized), teachers listened to, joined in with or explored in talk the children's feelings about the incidents without expressing their own views. For example, when the children were playing 'cops' versus miners:

> If the children were playing (in a violent way) without involving too many others I might simply join them and listen. After all, this seems to me a clear example of children playing through anxieties. After a while I might add a few things such as, 'Why are you calling the policemen pigs? How do you think they might feel? What do you think the policemen tell their children when they get home?'

When the home corner was a space-ship:

> *Boy:* And I'll be the astronaut. Give me the back-pack. You can't be the astronaut.
> *Girl:* (holding on to it) I am.
> *Boy:* No. . . . You're a girl.
> Girl still holds on tightly to the back-pack. At this point I intervened, asking the girl, 'Well, what do you think?' The whole group talked briefly about whether or not girls could be astronauts. 'If nots' had to be justified with 'why nots' and the argument was easily resolved.

Direction or manipulation

In direction or manipulation strategies (41 per cent), teachers made their views very clear, with or without giving reasons, or while appearing to accept children's ideas, gave preference to those which accorded with their own, or manipulated the children's feelings. For example when the children announced they were 'on strike':

> I would point out that when in school the teacher works and that as the children are there too they must tidy up otherwise the classroom cannot function. I would not attempt to discuss the politics of strike action with very young children.

When children were heard making racist remarks:

> A visitor (coloured) walked into the school and the children aged 6
> and 7 years remarked, 'Here's a blackie,' and were generally rude. I
> dealt with it immediately, quickly and firmly, saying sternly, 'I think you
> have said some very silly and hurtful things. I don't want to hear anybody
> say silly things like that again.' I made it clear I strongly disapprove and
> would not tolerate it.

When the children said they were glad about the bomb planted in a Brighton
hotel which had nearly killed Mrs Thatcher:

> I asked them, 'How would you feel if your mummy had been bombed?'

Delay or diversion

In delay or diversion strategies (32 per cent), the teacher made no immediate
effort to become involved but either ignored the incident or attempted to
distract the children's attention. For example when children were simulating
sex in the house corner:

> I knocked on the door and said, 'It's Postman Pat. I've got a letter for
> you.'

When children were making racist remarks in a class discussion:

> I would probably try to ignore 80 per cent of this discussion as too
> much recognition may encourage more comments.

Individual teachers' strategies

It was difficult to detect consistency in the strategies described by each
teacher, because it was clear that the teacher's own value system dictated
the response made to each separate incident. However, some teachers offered
general views about dealing with controversial issues such as:

> One of the problems in dealing with controversial incidents like this
> with young children is that most of the time they are echoing views
> and remarks of parents. One does not want to undermine the stability
> of home–school relationships but at the same time has to try to broaden
> the attitudes of children. With older children in primary schools it is
> possible to encourage independent thought because they already have
> examples of occasions when they disagree with parents' views. In gen-
> eral, I think one has to act immediately to prevent volatile situations
> from getting out of hand. But one should also be aware that issues
> such as racial and gender stereotyping, tolerance and violence should
> be dealt with in the infant curriculum. I see little educational benefit
> in the approach voiced in responses such as, 'We don't have that sort of

behaviour in this school,' since it is merely pushing the problems out of sight only to re-emerge later.

Other responses were from teachers who, still hanging on to the myth of childhood innocence, appeared to want to do precisely this:

> I think there can be a danger of 'blowing up' casually repeated remarks (heard at home?) to represent an attitude which is clearly not present in the classroom. Mindless comments about ethnic groups copied from an adult could be part of everyday conversation without affecting a younger child's great friendship with a 'Paki' for instance.

It is this sort of ostrich-like response which caused some of the ILEA teachers in Tizard's study to claim that there was no racist behaviour in their schools when the children could describe specific incidents of verbal and physical abuse (see Tizard *et al.* 1988: 157). A more helpful approach is for teachers to face up to the harsh realities of children's lives and provide a supportive and humane climate in which children can begin to establish their own moral framework. Perhaps whole-school approaches can be helpful in establishing some consistency and 'common sense' in dealing with controversial issues, while at the same time allowing for individual differences in values held by staff and pupils. An ILEA infant school headteacher described a 'whole-school' approach to dealing with conflict:

> Our strategies overall to deal with conflict include much work in discussions where children are encouraged to explore conflict, motives, feelings, possible resolutions. Drama is the main teaching strategy which puts children into conflict, problem-solving activities and allows them the safety-net of distance. We have a responsibility to protect a child from racism, sexism, or any name-calling, bullying, etc. We also hope to develop moral awareness using suitable stories – and sometimes 'unsuitable' – for discussion. Conflict in the playground we talk about extensively. The school has adopted two key words, 'caring and sharing', to particularly be aware of when in their playground space. We have a positive policy for aggression problems and this has been blessed by parents. Nearly 100 attended a meeting this term to discuss the policy and add to it, and to bless the built-in deterrents. The parents discussed their difficulties of telling children to 'hit back', especially when they played out (holidays, evenings, etc.). We talked about the fact that children and adults accept different 'rules' in different situations and they could recognize that at school certain 'rules' may be acceptable that seem unacceptable at home. I'm not happy that children should hit back when playing out, but there is a line when 'Home rules OK', and I am simply not able to support the children out of school. One can hope that 'school' values in this case might develop at home.

The final sentences of this statement make an important point. Teachers cannot be expected to set the world right in the face of societal pressures. However, they *may* be expected to be aware of the need to offer alternative models of moral frameworks to children. I would also argue that they *must* be aware of how their own value systems can operate, perhaps unconsciously, to the detriment of children's progress in school.

There is a woeful lack of in-service work devoted to this vital area of teachers' professional development. A final comment from a teacher who responded to the *Child Education* survey expresses with clarity the difficulty many teachers feel:

> So much is dependent on the ethos of the school and the relationship with parents which is built up over a long period. It is important that children feel secure in knowing there is room for many views. The teacher is more of a mediator and must never press their own views in the classroom but act as a catalyst in order that children have opportunities to mature in play, discussions and living together in a unity which allows for differences. The humanity of everyone must be accepted – including the teacher. We're all fallible.
>
> I have an overall high level of concern about the decline of real values in society (social, moral and spiritual), and particularly how politicians and top powers seem to have double standards in these areas. This presents educators with a problem. To many children real care and empathy can be a new experience – to some a completely 'foreign language'.

Teacher strategies and the curriculum

As we have seen from the issues explored in this chapter, the strategies used by infant teachers are underpinned by multiple layers of thinking and feeling. It is particularly galling when this kind of practical intelligence is undervalued within the teaching profession. But the responsibility for redressing the Joyce Grenfell image must lie partly with the teachers who work with young children. The teachers quoted in this chapter have begun the demanding process of articulating their thinking.

Equally demanding for teachers is the ability to define the curriculum they offer to 4–8-year-olds in a way which is rigorous but at the same time genuinely compatible with their preferred ways of working in classrooms. The infant school curriculum will be the focus of the next chapter. The changes brought about by the National Curriculum for Key Stage 1 will be explored in Chapter 5.

4

The curriculum

The curriculum is one of those slippery words, like 'the integrated day' or 'group work', that are widely used by educators but often mean different things to different users. In this chapter the word will be used in the broad sense of John Kerr's definition as 'all the learning which is planned and guided by the school, whether it is carried on in groups or individually, inside or outside the school' (Kerr 1968: 16). Discussion of the curriculum in infant schools will be grouped under the following headings: 'The organization of the classroom', 'The structuring of learning in the school day' and 'The content of the curriculum'. We will argue that there was a well-established, if not well-articulated, infant school curriculum before a statutory National Curriculum for 5 to 7-year-olds, Key Stage 1, was imposed in 1988.

The organization of the classroom

The physical layout

The physical layout of most classrooms in infant schools in the UK conforms to a recognizable pattern. There will be a carpeted area which often doubles as the book corner and the site for registration, whole-class instruction, stories, etc. There will be curriculum 'areas' more or less identifiable, either through the storage of 'subject'-specific resources or, more emphatically, by workshop-type spaces, for maths, language and 'messy' activities. Tables will be grouped together, usually scattered around the middle area of the classroom, to allow for groups of up to six to eight children to sit together for 'seat work'. There may also be 'play' areas such as the home corner or role play area (for example a shop, a garage, a clinic), a carpeted area for construction play, and sand and water containers. There will probably be an interest table reflecting the current theme chosen by the teacher as the focus for topic work, and the classroom displays of children's work, predominantly art based, will also reflect that topic. Other teacher-produced wall displays will serve a didactic purpose: a number line in the maths area, lists of the most commonly used words for the children's writing activities in the language area, a *Child Education* poster related to the current topic.

The physical layouts of classrooms have reflected the beliefs and ideologies that infant teachers espouse and assumptions about 'best practice' as defined by successive official documents such as the Hadow Report (Board of Education 1931), the Plowden Report (CACE 1967) and the HMI surveys of primary schools (DES 1978a; 1982a). Golby (1988) describes classrooms as the 'curriculum in waiting'.

> What is in the classroom, and where it is, is so in every case for a reason, or set of reasons. Like the classroom itself, a human invention that came into being at a certain time through an act of educational imagination.
>
> (Golby 1988: 28)

The practical areas are there because teachers believe that children learn by doing. The tables are pushed together because children should work in groups, not as a class. The displays are there because they are said to reflect what is currently 'turning the children on'. The messages are as clear as those announced by the rows of uniform desks facing the blackboard at the front, and the imposing teacher's desk raised high on a platform, of the elementary school classroom.

But what is really happening when teachers and pupils are functioning as teacher and taught in the kinds of physical contexts described? Close observation of the use of the infant classroom environment, set out like a stall for learning, will probably reveal that areas are used rather differently from the way the rhetoric would lead one to expect. It is likely that the book corner is rarely used by the children as a space for quiet and sustained reading (Southgate *et al.* 1981). Instead the comfortable carpet is likely to provide the boundaries for wriggling children at story-times or the ubiquitous 'mat' time when they are awaiting instructions for the next session. The home corner or, in some cases, the 'messy' areas may be out of bounds for children until after dinner and may therefore remain empty around the periphery for long periods of the day while children squeeze themselves into a crowded middle area of the classroom getting on with the 'real' work of the basics. As for the children working together in groups, the evidence is that group work is very rare in junior (Galton and Williamson 1992) or infant classrooms (Bennett *et al.* 1984).

Observations of where the teacher spends most time will probably identify that he or she is based predominantly in the middle area of the classroom where the 'seat-based' work takes place, making occasional brief forays into the play and practical areas. Non-teaching assistants – parents, nursery nurses, secondary school pupils on 'Life Skills' placements – reverse this pattern of movement. There may be then a bleak picture of mismatch between the physical manifestations of the stated intentions of infant teachers in the layout of the classroom, and the realities of how the learning environment is actually used.

The Primary Needs Independent Evaluation Project (1986–90), based at the University of Leeds, focused in one of their formative evaluation reports on the Leeds City Council funded Primary Needs Programme on classroom organization (Alexander *et al.* 1989). The report surveyed the physical arrangements and management of learning in the classrooms of thirty-eight primary teachers and monitored their responses to an LEA course on 'good practice' in classroom organization and layout. The LEA policy was defined as 'flexible teaching strategies within a quality environment rich in stimulus and challenge'. A detailed study of the classrooms, beliefs and practices of ten of the teachers provides some useful information on the variety of ways in which teachers organize their classrooms as well as how they respond to prescriptions about 'good practice'.

Mrs C was teaching twenty-seven 5–6-year-olds. Her classroom had labelled storage spaces for maths equipment, textbooks, a library and reading materials. An annexe at the back of the room, which also served as a cloakroom, was used for painting, although the child-level sink was at the opposite end of the classroom. She taught one area of the curriculum at a time. In the mornings, the children worked in ability groups on maths and language activities – mainly workcard or workbook based and linked to the maths and reading schemes – with occasional groups doing art activities with the non-teaching assistant. Children who had finished their 'basics' in the morning were expected to read. In the afternoon the children were allowed to sit in friendship groups to work on their topics.

Mrs C claimed that she felt that her practice already conformed to the LEA view of 'good practice'. After the course she had, however, 'made workbays' in her classroom.

> Soon after this, she had put her cupboards back against the wall because she didn't work an integrated day, and in any case the new arrangement had taken up too much space in a classroom that was already too small. However, the course had made her realize that it was better to keep the equipment and resources for each subject area together.
>
> (Alexander *et al.* 1989: 272)

She gave clear justifications for her style of organization and management of learning. She argued that the children in the catchment area of the school were difficult and needed the stability of a tightly structured day. She felt that the children would be confused if more than one curriculum area was being practised at a time, and besides she liked to monitor closely what everyone was doing. She also believed that children of 5 and 6 did maths and language best in the mornings when they were fresh.

In contrast Mrs D's classroom had areas set aside for language activities, a reading corner, a maths area which included a post-office/shop, and a home corner. Two tables served the function of space for 'overflow table-top work'; play activities such as sand and woodwork were outside the classroom. Her class of twenty-six vertically grouped 5–7-year-olds were allocated by age to three groups – reception, middle and top infants – and subdivided further for maths and language activities. Children worked in their groups simultaneously on maths, language or 'activities'. Her response to the LEA course had been that it had confirmed her belief in the value of mixed curriculum teaching and group work. After the course she had reorganized her classroom into curriculum-specific bays and concentrated on making resources more easily accessible to the children. Although Mrs D believed that vertical grouping gave her the opportunity to concentrate on working intensively with groups, she admitted that the lion's share of her teaching time was directed at the younger children.

The effects of classroom layouts

It was clear that neither of these teachers had been encouraged to study the *effects* on children's learning of changing around furniture, re-siting resources or re-allocating floor space to different curriculum priorities. There was simply an *assumption* that such changes resulted in 'better' practice. Such assumptions need to be substantiated by hard evidence. Teachers need support in the techniques of monitoring movement about a classroom, in the design and evaluation aspects of efficient siting and use of resources and floor-space. For example how can they justify space given to bulky equipment such as sand and water containers, which theoretically enhance children's learning of scientific and mathematical concepts, if observations such as those of Tizard *et al.* (1988: 58) indicate that sand and water are rarely used for teaching or learning?

In a sense Mrs C, although she did not conform to the model of 'good practice' defined by her LEA advisers, was responding with basic common sense to her ultimate rejection of 'workbays'. Her reasons, given her views on the most effective strategies for teaching in her classroom, were sound enough. Mrs D paid lip service to the value of practical activities and art work as the third aspect of curriculum priorities. But in fact it is significant that the sand and water and other practical activities were sited outside the classroom, where it is assumed any sustained interaction from her would be almost impossible. Whose response was the more honest – Mrs C's or Mrs D's?

A positive finding of the Prindep evaluation was the benefits of the LEA funding extra staffing in Leeds primary schools. This has allowed teachers to work together to try to resolve dilemmas in the management of learning. Leeds teachers agreed that one of the significant benefits of working collaboratively was the opportunity to 'clarify instructional goals and decide on organizational procedures for achieving them' (Alexander *et al.* 1989: 229). However, other aspects of the Prindep Report critical of Leeds primary classrooms observed were later hijacked in the course of political and media hostility to flexible working patterns and group work and fuelled demands to return to 'traditional' classroom methods and whole-class teaching.

One of the major concerns of teachers is to encourage young children to concentrate on activities without 'flitting' from one unfinished task to another. There is evidence that children are distracted not by noise levels around them but by visual interference. In the Cleveland LEA nurseries described in the references to schemas in Chapter 2, teachers and nursery nurses have experimented with child-height screening to enclose work areas for sand, painting, construction, water, emergent writing, etc. Children are encouraged to concentrate on activities with perhaps one or two other pupils for extended periods of time. The screening ensures that the adults are able not only to observe these sustained learning episodes without distracting the children, but also to be aware when it is appropriate to intervene. An impressive feature of Montessori school classrooms is that children may pick up a small floor- or table-mat to ensure themselves some personal space to work out a play activity without fear of disruption. Some classrooms now provide screened-off, private areas for personal writing. This is a more sensitive strategy than to expect children to concentrate on a writing activity with the distraction of six or seven of their peer group writhing and chattering at a table around them.

Perhaps we also surround children with too much visual brilliance. There are schools which dazzle rather than provoke thought with their displays. The walls are dripping with extravagant and largely teacher-directed friezes. Mobiles swing wildly from every available ceiling space. One longs for the relief of a blank wall. The same sense of over-kill may characterize the number of resources available to children in some classrooms. The Montessori system offers children a controlled choice each day from a range of colour-coded resources stored in baskets or containers on shelving. This adult structuring of activities may be helpful rather than restrictive to young children. Sometimes what is exhausting about supermarkets is the sheer enormity of the choice on offer! Perhaps some classrooms have the same effect on pupils.

The point is that the physical layout of a classroom should be based on systematic analyses of teaching and learning behaviours, rather than on blueprints of the visible features of so-called 'good practice'. But the Prindep team observed that little attention had been given in the Leeds LEA course

on Classroom Organization to monitoring the effectiveness of teacher and
pupil interactions:

> practice becomes talked about less in terms of operational detail than
> in terms of broad sentiments and commitments; less in terms of learn-
> ing *processes* than in terms of what is called 'the environment of
> learning'; a kind of conceptual skirting around of the very act which
> is at the heart of education.
>
> (Alexander *et al.* 1989: 291)

We have already explored many of the critical issues related to classroom
interactions in Chapter 3, but there are other issues to do with grouping
arrangements, the organization of pupil and teacher time, curriculum differentiation and coverage which also need to be explored beneath 'the
visible surface of practice' and it is to evidence of these aspects of classroom
realities that we now turn.

The structuring of learning in the school day

Patterns of organization

The classroom organization of most teachers of 4–8-year-olds, in infant, first
or primary schools, falls into one of three broad types.

1 The *skills and frills* approach – characterized by Mrs C's classroom – is
  basic skills in the morning, with children working as a class but on various
  levels of tasks in maths or language; and art, topic work including the
  humanities, science and technology, practical play activities or 'choosing
  time' in the afternoons.
2 The *rotation system* is when groups of children are moved around several
  basic curriculum areas – usually maths, language and 'activities' which
  might include art practical work related to a topic or theme, and 'play' –
  during the day on a roundabout system.
3 In the *integrated day* children work throughout the school day, usually
  individually but sometimes in groups, at a variety of curriculum tasks at
  their own pace and level.

Within all patterns of organization, set class times for subjects like physical
education and music or school television broadcasts will be dictated by
access to timetabled hall space, television rooms/spaces, a piano and possibly
a specialist music teacher.

Pre-National Curriculum there was limited evidence from HMI surveys and
research projects about the way in which infant teachers structure the school
day. In the 1978 Primary Survey (DES 1978a) teachers were categorized as
having two broad approaches: mainly didactic or mainly exploratory.

A didactic approach was one in which the teacher directed the children's work in accordance with relatively specific and predetermined intentions and where explanations usually, though not always, preceded the action taken by the children. An exploratory approach was one in which the broad objectives of the work were discussed with the children but where they were then put in a position of finding their own solutions to the problems posed and of making choices about the way in which the work should be tackled. The scope and timescale of the tasks involved were likely to be flexible and the path of the work was likely to be modified in the light of events; explanation by the teacher more often accompanied or followed action taken by the children.

(DES 1978a: 26, para 3.19)

Three-quarters of the teachers of 7-, 9- and 11-year-olds in the 542 primary schools surveyed employed a mainly didactic approach. Fewer than one in twenty adopted a mainly exploratory approach. One-fifth of the teachers were said by HMI to have 'employed an appropriate combination of the didactic and exploratory methods, varying their approach according to the nature of the task in hand'.

In the HMI survey of eighty first schools (DES 1982a) classroom organization and methods were defined as 'well suited to the children' in all the classes of sixteen of the schools. HMI went on to define what they meant by 'well suited':

In these schools there was a satisfactory balance between the opportunities provided for the children to find things out for themselves and more formal teaching. A good balance was kept between the activities initiated by the teacher and those chosen by the children. Individual, group and class teaching was arranged according to what was being taught and the needs of the children, rather than from a belief that one arrangement was superior to another.

(DES 1982a: 49, para 3.11)

In thirty-five of the schools such satisfactory methods were used in one or more of the classes, but in twenty-nine of the schools the children were either 'over directed' or 'given too little help in organising their work'.

In fact it is significant that in neither of the two HMI reports is much attention given to classroom organization and the management of learning. The terms used in the report are very vague, and there is little indication of the complex similarities and differences within and between classrooms in primary schools. Curriculum content on the other hand is given a great deal of attention in both reports.

In Bennett and Kell's (1989) study of 4-year-olds in classrooms, the infant teachers described their organization as 'integrated day', 'structured activities' and 'individualized learning'. These terms were used loosely, and the authors chose to give a flavour of the variations in patterns of organization by quoting directly from some of the teachers' accounts of their way of working:

> An integrated day generally – a combination of class, group and individual work. I tend to put more emphasis on language, maths and science in the morning and craft work in the afternoon. The four year olds work to the same kind of pattern but their 'work' time tends to be for shorter periods and their free choice time tends to be more.

> The children structure their own day, choosing activities out of those available. Certain work has to be done each day.

> I have basically a thematic structure. I plan a term and then have weekly planning with built-in spontaneity.

> An integrated day. I have a choosing board and the children select from the activities that are on offer – in tune with the nursery approach.

But these are simply descriptions of how the teachers in the study *claimed* that they organized their classrooms. There has been little systematic observation of the realities of infant classroom organization. The Oracle data on teacher and pupil types (Galton *et al.* 1980) is often generalized to infant practice on in-service courses or in reviews of educational research; but in fact all the Oracle data was drawn from observations in junior classrooms.

The project on *Extending Beginning Reading* (Southgate *et al.* 1981) provided some evidence of practice in the classrooms of 7-year-olds, though the data gathered focused on the teaching of reading. In Southgate's study the teachers devoted between twenty and one hundred minutes per day to listening to children reading. However, the child usually read to the teacher for only two- to three-minute periods, and this process was likely to be interrupted every thirty seconds. In teaching throughout the day the teachers switched their attention on average thirty-two times in each twenty-minute period of instruction. There was depressing evidence of 'the infant queue' where children would stand by the teacher's desk to read, or to have work marked, or to be given help when they were stuck or waiting to move on to a new activity. In some cases there would be dual queues, with one relatively fast-moving queue waiting for words to be written in wordbooks or for written work to be marked, while a second slower-moving queue of readers trailed through the task of reading aloud to the teacher as he or she frenetically marked and checked. If advisers and headteachers have conspired to spirit teachers' desks away in an attempt to dispose of 'the infant queue', the result has often been a perpetually moving queue with the teacher at its head, graphically described by Golby (1988) as 'a comet's tail of children with spelling books at the ready'.

Individualized learning

The data from Southgate *et al.*'s (1981), Bennett *et al.*'s (1984) and Bennett and Kell's (1989) research pointed to the difficulties that teachers were having in their attempts to implement a policy of individualized learning. In order to cover the basics, teachers frequently relied on mathematics and reading scheme workbooks, worksheets and workcards to keep young children 'busy' on individualized seat-based activities. The teacher's role then became reactive. Having briefly introduced a task to a child, or a group of children, his or her attention was often diverted to the learning or custodial needs of other children. The teacher was rarely able to observe the processes by which children completed the tasks assigned to them. The teacher often withdrew to sit at a desk, table or chair, only interacting with a child again when the child sought help, or when the task was completed. It was difficult for the teacher to operate a diagnostic approach to checking and evaluating the finished work. In many cases the teacher simply responded with a quick 'Yes, yes, yes', a string of ticks, with maybe a more searching response to any error the child had made. This pattern of feedback had the unfortunate consequence of children learning to expect teachers to comment only when they had done something wrong, but to give scant attention, other than a cursory 'well done', to their successful strategies.

When the Oracle team continued their research on managing children's learning in classrooms, they tried to elicit children's views of their expectations of teacher feedback. They presented some middle school children with a cartoon depicting a teacher marking a child's piece of written work at her desk and asked the children to write what the teacher was saying. The vast majority attributed negative comments to the teacher such as, 'Go and do it again,' or 'Pay attention' (reported in Galton 1989: 73). We appear to be inculcating children with an expectation of negative feedback from teachers.

It is clear from all the research studies quoted that the problems of trying to implement the Plowden doctrine of individualization are overwhelming for teachers of young children. Teachers are imbued with a sense of urgency to get the children literate, numerate and able to record. If they try to share their time out on an individual basis to a class of twenty-five to thirty-five infants, each child will have a very limited amount of direct teaching time. Consequently children have to operate independently on tasks for long periods of the day. When young children are engaged in practical activities, this can be a perfectly acceptable demand to make on them. But the problem is that children are required to 'work' on the basics as isolated individual learners, albeit seated alongside others of their peer group engaged on parallel tasks, without adult support. They are required to 'read' workcard instructions beyond their capability, or to record mathematical operations within mathematics workbooks before their writing skills have developed. Consequently children spend much of their time 'coasting' in a fairly desultory way simply because they are overwhelmed, bored or frustrated by the tasks they have been assigned.

Bennett and Kell (1989) give some poignant examples of 4-year-olds in infant classrooms trying to respond to tasks beyond their capabilities. Mary was one such 4-year-old:

> The teacher's intention is sorting numbers by colour to provide experience in writing numbers. The activity is drawn from SPMG *Infant Mathematics Stage 1*. The teacher's instructions were 'Now go and get your maths book' and 'do the next page.'
>
> 11:30 Mary has taken her workbox from the table and takes out *Infant Mathematics*, Heinemann Ed. Book Stage 1 . . . Sorting. Matching 1 and 2 (SPMG) Page 10 – write 2. Mary has traced 2 – several times at the top of the page. Under this there are four sets of pictures (of, for example, 2 trees with a box alongside, where Mary should write 2).
>
> Mary has written a reversed 3 beside each set of two. Auxiliary walks over and asks what she has written. Mary does not reply.
>
> 11:38 *Auxiliary:* 'I'll go and get a rubber and rub them out.' She does so. Mary does another shape exactly as before, followed by another in the next set below. Auxiliary counts the pictures with her. Mary counts correctly. Auxiliary draws 2. Mary draws. *Auxiliary:* 'Copy those again.' Rubs out Mary's 2s at the top of the page. Mary copies over the shapes. She starts from the bottom in each case. They end up looking fairly accurate. *Auxiliary:* 'Now do the sets where you got them wrong.' Mary goes back to the picture sets and does them wrong again. (She starts each number from the bottom as she did when tracing the numbers at the top of the page.) This time she rubs them out herself before Auxiliary sees them. Mary is nearly crying with frustration. She knows she has them wrong but just cannot get them right. Auxiliary re-appears from other side of table and tells her not to worry.
>
> 11:45 She tries again and gets one right and two wrong. Shrieks with frustration and hits Auxiliary on the arm to attract her attention. Gets two wrong again. Stands up and covers face with hands shouting 'Oh! Oh!' Scribbles on second square where she should write 2. Auxiliary comes and sits next to her. She smiles sympathetically at Mary and says, 'I like that one', pointing to the only correct one.
>
> Mary shouts to the teacher who happens to walk past the table, 'I can't do it. It keeps going wrong!' She has tears pouring down her cheeks. Teacher doesn't appear to really look at her. She says, 'Never mind. It doesn't matter as long as you try.'

She ticks the work and tells Mary she can put her book away now.

(Bennett and Kell 1989: 68)

When the researcher questioned the pupil and teacher later about this activity, Mary was adamant that she could not do 2. 'I couldn't do it. It was too hard. I didn't like it. I don't like the books.' The teacher on the other hand rated the activity a success, arguing that the child got on with it, and it was a bit of her own work, and concluded 'She seems to like doing her maths book.' When asked what Mary would be doing next in the light of the day's work she replied, 'The next page'!

Other children are less conscientious when assigned tasks beyond their capability. Ray, for example, had been asked to make a Mother's Day card. He had been given a template, without any explanation as to what it said, with Mummy written on it. The researcher's observations were:

9:05 The teacher gives him the Mummy template and he starts to do this. Ray and Harry argue about what the template says: 'Daddy, Mummy . . .' Ray insists it says Daddy. They talk about Mummy and something to do with Readybrek. They start to tease another boy about his name, making up a new surname. Ray laughs. Starts colouring in again: 'We are working hard.' He moves the template and colours in the same letter as before, 'y' only, at the bottom of the page. He carries on in the same way starting to write in the template. It moves and he starts somewhere else. His paper has all disconnected lines on it.

9:55 Ray and Harry creep away, bending double, but they come back when the teacher moves. *Ray:* 'Harry, you want to go to the toilet, shall we both go?' (He went just now.) The teacher comes and talks to Harry. She writes his name. She looks at Ray's paper. *Teacher:* 'Haven't you done any shapes, Ray?' She goes and Ray gets another shape – a diamond – and draws that more successfully once. He does more colouring in. Using a pencil he draws in the 'y' in the template. He takes the template, the wrong way up and draws in it, then gets up, goes down the room, comes back, draws a bit. He makes a few round shapes with tails on, then tries the template again doing 'mmy' before moving it to the bottom of the page and doing 'my' again. Now he is working on the other side of the paper. He stops to talk again. Meanwhile another boy takes the template and starts doing it carefully. Ray wants the template back but is able to find one on another table.

(Bennett and Kell 1989: 73)

In the pupil and teacher interviews after this activity, Ray could not explain anything about Mother's Day and thought that the template was a pattern. The teacher said that she was quite pleased with Ray's work.

These detailed observations of young children at work raised important issues, first about the inability of teachers to gain accurate information about pupils' learning unless they are able to observe the child on task, and second, about the mismatch between children's capabilities and the tasks assigned to them by teachers. In his detailed earlier study of the learning environment and experiences provided by sixteen able (as defined by LEA advisory staff) teachers of 6–7-year-olds, Bennett *et al.* (1984) claimed that more than half of the language and mathematical tasks observed in the study were mismatched.

> Overall there is a remarkably consistent picture for the two areas of the curriculum. In number 43% of tasks were matched (40% in language), 28% were too difficult (29%) and 26% too easy (26%). In both areas of the curriculum, high attainers were underestimated on 41% of the tasks assigned to them, low attainers were overestimated on 44% of the tasks. Middle groups got a diversified experience in number but tended to be overestimated in language.
>
> (Bennett *et al.* 1984: 45)

Bennett also raised important questions about the lack of clarity in teacher's intentions for setting tasks (Bennett and Kell 1989). Sometimes the stated intentions of the teachers were simply not reflected in the activity designated. For example a child spent twenty minutes colouring in an extremely large circle when the teacher's stated intention was shape recognition. Tracing around a tree was the task set when the stated teacher intention was learning from left to right orientation.

Some tasks were set with multiple intentions, but rarely were children made directly aware of the *purposes* of any activity. In fact, the nightmare task of trying to give brief but clear instructions to a whole class of young children seated on a carpet, as often happens at the beginning of a working session, means that teachers habitually resort to focusing on procedural rather than cognitive issues as they set children off on activities. Bennett pin-pointed this discrepancy in his earlier study in 1984. In setting writing activities, for example, he noted that teachers would claim that their intention was to get children to write creatively, but invariably the final instructions to the children would emphasize correct spelling and neat handwriting. Children picked up these none too subtle messages when they were set writing tasks.

> They were clear about what would please their teachers. They recognised and were able to rate neatness as an important criterion and strove to finish another page to fulfil the quantity quota.
>
> (Bennett *et al.* 1984: 104)

Group work

If the individualization of learning proved to be an illusory ideal, what about the alternative strategy of group work? Many infant teachers claim that they operate 'group work' in their classrooms; but what do they really mean? There are three common interpretations.

1 Six to eight children sit together around a table, working alongside each other, but essentially engaged in individualized tasks.
2 The teacher sits and concentrates on teaching one group of children at a time, throughout the day for sessions lasting between several minutes to, for example, the complete block of time between registration and playtime.
3 Children are encouraged to work collaboratively on shared activities.

In the first interpretation, a method of seating children can hardly be defined as group work in operational terms. Nevertheless, the criteria for grouping the children will almost certainly have an effect on the processes of learning. Teachers offer a variety of criteria for forming groups. The most obvious is ability, particularly in reading, but sometimes in mathematics. In Tizard's study of ILEA infant classrooms (Tizard *et al.* 1988) approximately half of the reception class teachers (of 5-year-olds) grouped children for teaching purposes, 55 per cent for maths and 48 per cent for language, mainly on the basis of the children's judged ability levels. Although 61 per cent of the top infant teachers (of 7-year-olds) used group teaching, their criteria included separating children who did not work well together or accommodating friendship patterns. In Bennett and Kell's (1989) sample of seventy-one infant teachers about half used ability grouping, but one in four said they used mixed ability groups and one in six used friendship grouping. In mixed age classes they also grouped the children by age or date of intake.

We have already identified that teachers are aware of the dangers of self-fulfilling prophecies. Infant teachers often try to disguise the fact that children are grouped by ability in their classrooms. Groups are given colour, animal, or flower labels – 'I want the chipmunks over in the maths area this morning with me, whilst the squirrels do art work with Mrs Brown, and the possums can get their Ginn workbooks out.' The animals are, of course, of a cuddly nature! Teachers have a range of euphemisms to describe their low ability groups to visitors: 'The ones that need a lot of support sit on Green table.' 'The slow children go out with the non-teaching assistant for extra reading in the mornings.' Children, however, are not so coy, and usually have a pretty shrewd idea of how they are ranked by teachers within the classroom.

Some children can stay within a grouping system, defined within weeks of school entry, throughout their primary schooling, particularly if the criterion used is reading ability. Patterns of dependency and dominance can build up amongst a small group of children who habitually work together. It is quite obvious in some cases that the absence of one dominant child from a table for a day will change the levels of work of the entire group, either for the better or worse. A dependent child who transfers at 11 to a secondary school system, where in many classes pupils are required to work in silence without peer group support or friendship, can be devastated by this abrupt change in working conditions.

Because of their anxieties about self-fulfilling prophecies many primary teachers prefer to use mixed ability grouping for teaching, but this can cause them all kinds of operational difficulties. Mixed ability teaching for ideological reasons may *not* prove to be an effective strategy for teaching purposes. Wendy, the teacher of 6–7-year-olds in the project referred to in Chapter 3 (Anning 1987), described the problems of pacing activities in a mixed ability group. In a task which involved children in putting names into alphabetical order, she had to slow down Shane, a child defined as of high ability, in order to accommodate the learning needs of the whole group:

> I said to the children, 'Now what comes first?' Shane actually came in straight away with the answer, but I didn't think it was wise at that point to say, 'OK, that's it.' I felt that. So I did actually ignore him and kept on saying it in the hope that I'd pick up the other children as well. My strategy to cope with that was to ignore Shane when he came through with the right answer quicker than I felt the other children latched on to it.

In another example, Jane, a reception class teacher in the project, admitted that she had seated 'a good reader' in a mixed ability group working on word recognition at a point on the table where the flashcards would be upside down for her (whereas they would be the right way up for the less able children) in order to stop the able child giving all the answers!

Wendy also worked with a mixed ability group on a task which involved introducing the concepts of machines and operators, using Bulmershe equipment. She had to intervene frequently to explain new ideas and procedures to the lower ability children. When she reviewed the tapes of the activities, she could see the contrast between the dynamics of this group learning situation and those of the matched ability group engaged on the graphical representation task (see p. 54). She commented:

> If you have a group of children who are all one ability, I suppose the match of the task is better isn't it? So you start off talking; but then you can back off, because it's something you expect them to pick up on. Maybe this is a drawback of having a mixed ability group for this kind of task – I had to keep chipping in.

It is, I think, also significant that the exhilarating pace and progress in learning apparent in the graphical representation task, was the result of a *pair* of children of matched ability working together. Anybody who has suffered the frustration of being required to work on a shared task in small groups, perhaps six to eight, of fellow professionals at conferences or on in-service courses, will bear witness to the slow progress that is often made! Working in pairs is often more productive. It seems common sense that this should also be true of children's working preferences. Researchers have indicated how little collaborative work of any kind there is in primary classrooms (Tann 1981; Bennett *et al.* 1984; Bennett and Kell 1989; Galton and Williamson 1992) and a contributory factor could be that children resist group work simply because the mechanics of working collaboratively can be so irksome. The middle school children whom Galton (1987) interviewed expressed some of this irritation. They rated the image of a group of children working together without the teacher present, but with a tape recorder strategically placed in the centre of the table, as their least popular classroom situation. The 8-year-olds gave such reasons as 'My friends make me silly', or 'There's no teacher' or 'You're worried if things go wrong.' The 12-year-olds interviewed were more positive about working with their peer group. They made such comment as 'It's good to work things out without the teacher' or 'You can have a laugh when you discuss', or more strongly, 'I would like to work with my friends and discuss things on our own because when you work with teachers they *always* stop you' and 'One could learn more from each other when there is no teacher to nag.'

This last comment draws attention to another important issue. Teachers do not really trust children to learn from their peer group despite the kind of evidence cited in Chapter 2 of the significance and value of children's learning from each other. The fact that a tape recorder was left in the centre of the table in the image presented to the children in Galton's study is not without significance. Children know that teachers feel the need to check on peer group learning. In Galton's study the children articulated very clearly their frustration at having the 'ownership' of peer group collaboration hijacked by the interference of the teacher. They told him that often, just as their group were beginning to find a way of tackling a shared activity, the teacher would join the group and suggest an alternative set of strategies. The teacher gives one set of messages through his or her instructions and another through subsequent sabotaging of the children's collaborative efforts. A child expressed his resentment:

> You feel a bit upset. You have put all that work into it and then the teacher suddenly changes it. You don't feel it is your piece of work. You feel as if it's the teacher's. When you have done everything to it you think that's my piece of work and no-one else had done owt to it, but when the teacher's done something to it, it don't feel as good.
>
> (Galton 1987: 309)

On the other hand, the advantages of teachers working closely with a group in the role of *instructor* are clear because ironically it *does* then become possible for teachers to individualize learning. So, for example, Jane described the way in which she individualized a task within a small group activity for an immature learner, Brian. The task was to recognize the written form and sequence of the days of the week:

'T' in Tuesday has occurred before and I know these particular children will identify 'T' possibly with a character in the reading scheme which they've both used on colouring sheets. They've coloured this particular figure which is a little boy called Tommy. They've come across Tommy in one of the Trailer Books to the Link Up Scheme, and I do know that if I mention or show a picture of this boy Tommy, they will identify the letter 'T' more easily, 'T' for Tommy, and then they'll probably be able to transfer this learning to Tuesday and Thursday.

I've drawn some sketches of things we do together as a class on different days to help them with the days of the week. I've included Brian's peg on one of them; I thought I'd do all this deliberately to see if he would notice his name. He can write his name – really very well – so I thought I'd see if he does notice it. The other clue was he had the tortoise on his peg, you see, and I thought well if he doesn't get his name, he'll get the tortoise – which he did. The only thing I'd done wrong was the colour of his towel!

Jane's close involvement with a group working on the task meant that she could cue the children in to links with previous learning, as well as personalize the resources. In another activity, designed to encourage children to be more independent in their attempts to spell words, Janine, an above-average 5-year-old, was attempting to write the word 'kitchen'. Jane remembered that the child had recently drawn a witch for Hallowe'en:

She was quick to recall another 'itch' word, because I said, 'What were you drawing round?', and I mentioned the two things specifically to see if she could recall the other one – and she did, so that made my job easier. . . . I had pointed out the 'itch' bit – I'd told her what it said – when she drew the witch the previous day.

Sometimes the teacher has to guide children towards appropriate links. In the 'machines and operators' activity, Wendy referred to several examples of children making associations between past and present learning. When she first introduced them to the word 'operator' she noticed that the children 'kind of shuddered' and put this down to the fact that it reminded the children of 'operations'. Ryan, a child who had arrived recently from Northern Ireland, was having great difficulties with mathematics *and* the Salford accents! Wendy commented:

Ryan was unsure about the word 'operator'. He said, 'Do you mean like the apparatus in the hall?' and then, 'But do you mean it starts with "a" like Angela?', and although that had nothing to do with the task, at least it showed me that Ryan had learned other things that he didn't know a few months ago.

Another child tried to make sense of the task by comparing the word 'machine' and the emphasis on the thickness and thinness of logi-blocks to a real machine. 'Kevin said, "Ah, you mean like in a machine, it goes in thick and then gets squashed and comes out thin".' Wendy noticed that as Kevin was trying to make sense of this abstract process by comparing it to a real machine, he was actually working the ideas out with his hands – miming squashing and shaping shapes. Other children in the group repeated these machine-like actions when it came to their turn to change a logi-block by shape, size, colour or depth.

But occasionally inappropriate links are made. When the children were asked at one point to focus on the changes in the colour of the shapes, Suzy whispered into the teacher's ear, 'Is it like the song – Red and Yellow and Pink and Blue?' In this instance Wendy gently guided Suzy into a more appropriate strategy for selecting the next logi-block.

These examples illustrate a way in which individualized learning can be accommodated within small group instruction. The *task* is assigned by the teacher, but she encourages and supports a variety of *individual strategies* for pupils to adopt in tackling the task, and the teacher's responses are based on an intimate knowledge of the children's lives and learning experiences.

It is difficult to imagine how such close awareness of individual strategies and previous learning episodes might be used in whole-class teaching; but there is evidence that class teaching can also be used effectively with young children despite the negative connotations of elementary school rote learning that the words conjure up.

Class teaching

Whilst working in Western Australia, I witnessed more class teaching than I had seen in years of working in and visiting early years classrooms in the UK. Some of it was desperately bad – 6–7-year-olds being bombarded with information, followed by instructions to work from the blackboard at tasks which involved a lot of copying. But some of the teachers used class teaching, between sessions of group work related to the sessions, so effectively and with such panache, that the young children in their classrooms groaned when it was time to go out to play! I think there is some truth in Gage's (1985) belief that since class teaching is so deeply entrenched in teachers' repertoires of techniques, it would be more useful to find out how to improve class teaching than simply to send it underground when LEA advisers or Ofsted inspectors were doing their rounds. Gage writes:

> Within the art form called classroom teaching there is also a great variation in quality. What I see as promising is research that accepts the basic parameters of classroom teaching: teacher-centeredness, whole-class organization, subject matter orientation, and much recitation interspersed with short lectures, discussions, tutoring and seat work. Such research will study the infinite variations possible within this stable art

form, the variations that make the difference between superb, average
and atrocious classroom teaching.

(Gage 1985: 49)

Galton (1989) summarizes research on the effectiveness of direct instruction (see also Rosenshine 1987; Good and Brophy 1986). Of course, direct
instruction can refer to work with an individual, a group or a class of pupils.

> These reviews stress the importance of structuring the learning experi-
> ence – by proceeding in small steps at a rapid pace, and using frequent
> questioning – and of providing opportunities for overt, active practice,
> with plenty of feedback and corrections during the initial stages of learn-
> ing new information.

(Galton 1989: 105)

In the USA direct instruction has always been more acceptable, but teachers
in the UK baulk at some USA practices. For example, Bereiter and Engelmann's (1966) fierce methods of direct language instruction of disadvantaged
young children (later developed in the 1970s into the DISTAR Learning
Programme for pre-school children (Engelmann *et al.* 1972)) horrified many
British teachers in the 1960s. In contrast, UK early years teachers have habitually used whole-class times for listening to stories, music, physical education, television or radio broadcasts or 'news times'. They may also claim
that they use whole-class discussions to stimulate language development.
However, systematic analyses of class 'discussions' (Willes 1983; Edwards
and Westgate 1987) reveal that the teacher dominates the talk in class discussions in order to retain control. A small percentage of children, often
those that place themselves strategically in the main sight lines of the teacher,
make brief contributions to the 'discussion'. The word discussion is simply
not appropriate.

I feel that it is hard to justify the use of intense teacher questioning during
whole-class instruction. We only have to think of the memorable paragraph
in Holt's (1984) *How Children Fail* when he reported asking children how
they felt when he asked them a question. A child bravely responded, 'We
gulp.' 'I asked them why they felt gulpish. They said they were afraid of failing, afraid of being kept back, afraid of being called stupid, afraid of feeling
themselves stupid' (Holt 1984: 70). Feeling 'gulpish' within the confines of
a small group activity can be difficult enough for children, as a sensitive
teacher like Wendy acknowledges (see p. 55). Feeling 'gulpish' in a public
arena such as class teaching time is something to which I believe we should
not subject young children.

But drawing young children together at various points of the school day,
in what has been described as a 'wave' model (Chazan *et al.* 1987: 32), for
short bursts of direct instruction may be appropriate for vocabulary extension,
consolidating knowledge of letter sounds, practising simple mental arithmetic,

introducing new information related to a class topic, demonstrating hand movements for letter formation – in fact, for a whole range of fairly routine activities.

In the next chapter we will return to the issue of whole-class teaching in the evaluation of changes monitored in Key Stage 1 classrooms in the UK since 1988.

The content of the curriculum

From the time of the relaxation of the control of the elementary school curriculum in 1926 to the Education Reform Act of 1988 there was a great deal of autonomy in the decisions primary school teachers made about curriculum content, although it was clear that the assumptions of parents, LEA officers and the government exerted pressure on schools to conform to expected patterns of provision. This autonomy ceased with the implementation of the prescribed content of a National Curriculum specified in the Education Reform Act 1988, which will be discussed in Chapter 5. However, it is important to look at pre-1988 practice, both the paper models and practical realities of curriculum provision in infant schools, since those practices certainly influenced the way the National Curriculum was taught at Key Stage 1.

Principles underpinning curriculum models

There are broadly three approaches to justifying the content of a curriculum offered in schools – as passing on 'desirable' knowledge, as servicing the needs of society, and as responding to the developmental needs of children.

Passing on knowledge

HMI identified six broad educational aims for primary and secondary schools in the government White Paper, *Better Schools* (DES 1985a). These aims, also recorded in the HMI document *The Curriculum from 5 to 16* (DES 1985b), are

  1 to help pupils to develop lively, enquiring minds, the ability to question and argue rationally and to apply themselves to tasks, and physical skills
  2 to help pupils to acquire knowledge and skills relevant to adult life and employment in a fast changing world
  3 to help pupils to use language and number effectively
  4 to instil respect for religious and moral values, and tolerance of other races, religions and ways of life
  5 to help pupils to understand the world in which they live, and the

interdependence of individuals, groups and nations
6 to help pupils to appreciate human achievements and aspirations.
                                                            (DES 1985b: para 1)

HMI identified the following areas of learning and experience: linguistic and literary, mathematical, aesthetic and creative, physical, scientific, techno-logical, moral and spiritual (DES 1985b: para 33).

These headings reflect a view that there are logically distinct forms of knowledge, each with its own distinctive but interlocking central concepts and specific methodology to which all pupils should have access (see Peters 1966; Hirst 1974). Despite the reluctance to accept the confines of what they regard as 'secondary school style subjects', primary practitioners used the HMI framework in early years documents on curriculum planning. In the Inner London Education Authority document on *The Early Years: A Curriculum for Young Children* (ILEA 1987) the eight areas were further defined.

1 Linguistic and literary
   ● about symbolic representation
   ● about listening, talking, reading and writing
2 Mathematical
   ● about recognizing and solving problems
   ● about sorting and classifying, and identifying relationships and patterns
   ● about pure numbers, measures, logic and sets, and their application to
     other areas
3 Aesthetic and creative
   ● about symbolic representation, imaginative play, art and craft work,
     display, drama, movement and music
   ● about creating things for themselves and appreciating the creations of
     others
4 Physical
   ● about body awareness, co-ordination and control
   ● about spatial, manipulative and motor skills
   ● about imaginative use of the body
   ● about health and its maintenance
5 Scientific and technological
   ● about problem-solving
   ● about changing and controlling the environment
   ● about ourselves and living things
   ● about physical surroundings
   ● about forces, movement and energy
6 Moral
   ● about awareness of self and others
   ● about right and wrong, fairness and justice
   ● about being a member of a group and wider community
7 Spiritual
   ● about significance of life

- about sense of awe and wonder
- about myths and legends
- about religious experiences reflecting many faiths

8 Human and social
  - about how we live and the world of work
  - about relationships with each other and the environment
  - about events and actions in the past and their relationship to the present and the future
  - about physical and human conditions.

The ILEA authors emphasized the need to maintain a cross-curricular perspective in planning an early years curriculum. They argued 'these separate subject strands usually remain undifferentiated, but they are none the less important in planning to ensure we provide breadth and balance in the curriculum' (ILEA 1987: 8).

Many infant teachers argue that 'knowledge does not fall into separate compartments' (CACE 1967: 187) and claim that they integrate all aspects of the curriculum in their teaching. In fact, the evidence from research into curriculum coverage in primary schools pre-dating the National Curriculum indicates that maths and English were taught as discrete areas of the curriculum, often using commercially produced schemes. Other aspects of the curriculum were often subsumed under the labels topic, project or theme-based work.

It seems clear that though children may not differentiate between 'subjects' in their learning, for teachers a framework such as that provided by the HMI aims, ensures that they plan a broadly based curriculum. In fact, 'integration' did not go unchallenged as a panacea for primary curriculum and implementation. There was criticism in the 1978 Primary Survey (DES 1978a) that an integrated approach led to many children experiencing a disconnected series of learning opportunities which lacked rigour and cohesion. In the 1980s headteachers were encouraged to appoint curriculum 'consultants' amongst their staff to provide support throughout the school for aspects of the curriculum in order to work towards balance, cohesion and progression in planning (Campbell 1985).

The needs of society

The second way of rationalizing curriculum content is that it should reflect the needs and demands of society; a social-imperatives approach. For example the emphasis on the world of work, market forces and science and technology in the DES documentation of the Thatcherite years reflected an instrumental view of education as providing the state with 'value for money' by preparing pupils for the world of work. According to a social-imperatives view of the curriculum, education is seen as being controlled by powerful

dominant groups who use the transmission of knowledge in schools to perpetuate privileges and hierarchies (Young 1971; Lawton 1980). The analyses
of Sharp and Green (1975) and King (1978) identified these processes at work
in infant classrooms, where the authors claimed that a middle-class, bourgeois
culture was operating against the interests of working-class communities.

The needs of the child

The third approach is to take the nature, interests and patterns of development
of the child as the basis for selecting the content of the curriculum. Blenkin
and Kelly (1987) argued that a Developmental Curriculum takes 'common
developmental principles' rather than 'common subject content' as the basis
for planning the curriculum. 'The emphasis is placed on children's learning
through experience or their growth in competence rather than on the learning of the knowledge and skills themselves' (Blenkin and Kelly 1987: 46).
They argued that

> The developmental curriculum . . . emphasises feeling as well as logical
> thinking . . . and values a wide spectrum of symbolising activities, not
> just words and numbers. . . . It is important, therefore, that the oppor-
> tunities we offer to children in the early years classroom are multi-
> sensory and allow for the representation of thought and experiences
> through such modes as the visual, auditory, tactile, graphic, linguistic,
> motor and logical-analytical.
>
> (Blenkin and Kelly 1987: 42)

W. A. L. Blyth (1984) presented a case for an 'Enabling Curriculum' based on
the concerns and interests of young children. He argued that 'In the course
of planning the experiences that a school can contrive, it is easy to overlook
those that are already present in children's lives' (W. A. L. Blyth 1984: 24).
He rejected the over-used instructional objective/subject based model of curriculum planning. He argued instead for the content of the primary school
curriculum to be based on six broad areas of experience which are central
elements of children's lives and relate to their lives outside 'the school box':

1 growth, health and movement – because the growing child is faced with
   daily consequences of rapid changes in their physical development
2 communication – through the modes of speech, dance, music, drawing, model-making, etc.
3 interpretation of the world – through, for example, scientific understanding or the humanities
4 vision and imagination – through play, drama, storying, etc.
5 feeling, expression and imagination – through the arts, literature
6 values and attitudes – a planned sequence of moral and social education.

(W. A. L. Blyth 1984: 53)

Curriculum guidelines

Unifying the distinct strands of curriculum content, whatever the theoretical frameworks they use, is a daunting task for the primary teacher who is responsible for teaching the whole class the whole curriculum. The enormity of the task was set out in paragraph 12 of *The Curriculum from 5 to 16*:

> The curriculum should aim to be broad by bringing all pupils into contact with an agreed range of areas of learning and experience. It should also be balanced in that it allows the adequate development of each area. In addition, each major component should have breadth, balance and relevance and should incorporate a progression in the acquisition of knowledge and understanding. The various curricular areas should reinforce and complement one another so that the knowledge, concepts, skills and attitudes developed in one area may be put to use and provide insight in another, thus increasing the pupil's understanding, competence and confidence.
>
> (DES 1985b: 7)

If we examine the paper versions of curriculum planning used in primary schools before the introduction of the National Curriculum, there was evidence of variable provision of school-written guidelines to support teachers in this formidable task. HMI (DES 1978a) found written guidelines for maths schemes in 85 per cent of the schools they surveyed, and 88 per cent had English schemes. In their survey of first schools (DES 1982a) HMI found that only 75 per cent had maths schemes and 78 per cent language schemes. Science, art, physical education and music guidelines were represented in between 36 and 44 per cent of schools in the two surveys, and drama in 18 per cent. In fact many teachers openly admitted to 'doing their own thing' in interpreting school schemes of work even if they were provided. So faced with the task of selecting curriculum content, how did infant teachers set about planning?

Curriculum planning

McCutcheon (1980) studied the planning of twelve elementary teachers in Virginia using classroom observations, interviews with teachers, transcripts of meetings and analyses of the teachers' written plans. British teachers will instantly relate to the findings. Daily planning was written by teachers as an aid to memory; lists of activities that were crossed off, as with shopping lists, as they were completed. Most teachers agreed that they listed objectives only if required to do so by the principal (in the UK context substitute headteacher, adviser or school practice supervisor). One teacher wrote: 'Objectives are implicit in the activities. I know what the activity is for, but it doesn't make sense to write so much down.' The continuous processes of 'mental planning' were described by the twelve teachers as occurring any time, either during the school day or while walking down the aisles of supermarket stores. The teacher continued: 'The subconscious does a lot of sorting for you. You can think of many things almost simultaneously. The sorting is rapid, not logical or sequenced, and is different for different lessons.'

The teachers defined the purpose of this relentless process of reflective thinking (see Figure 2, p. 46) as to help lessons run smoothly or to anticipate and 'short-circuit' what might go wrong. In planning ahead, they referred back to previous experiences of teaching similar content and structuring similar activities – what worked and what did not. In other words, teachers are constantly rehearsing classroom routines in the same way that we as individuals rehearse our personal encounters or daily work or travel routines as we clean our teeth in the mornings. The neat and tidy notion of the standard objectives model of planning: (1) specify objectives (2) select learning activities (3) organize learning activities and (4) specify evaluation procedures (Tyler 1949) may be reassuring for the tidy minds of administrators and headteachers, but it does not match up to the way teachers prefer to plan. Nor does a neat objectives model of planning take account of the contextual changes to which teachers must continually respond – an absent colleague means that you suddenly have six extra children to educate for the day; the community policeman calls; a wet playtime scuppers plans to set up art activities for the afternoon. As with rehearsals of the dramas we are anticipating in our personal lives, the scripts we plan for classrooms never quite turn out as we expect!

It also seems clear that teachers have always used curriculum content rather than aims and objectives as the basis for their planning. Many primary school teachers still use the ubiquitous 'topic web' to manage the complexity of the National Curriculum programmes of study. They take a central concept like 'colour' or 'ourselves' or a class visit to a castle, shopping centre or farm, etc. and map out related areas of interest or possible curriculum-based activities. For student teachers, inexperienced in the art of 'topic webs', this can result in some extraordinarily contrived links. But for experienced teachers the loose overall structure appears to provide a useful, if somewhat rough and ready, framework for their planning. What content-based planning does not allow for is a consideration of the skills and learning processes that children should be systematically acquiring.

If we go right back to the beginning and ask ourselves, 'What is worth teaching and learning for 4–8-year-olds?', we are likely to identify the *what* of the curriculum, including information, concepts and practical skills. These might be grouped under the HMI broad areas of learning and experience, as in the ILEA (1987) document, or in the current climate of a subject-based National Curriculum, under subject headings. But of equal importance is how

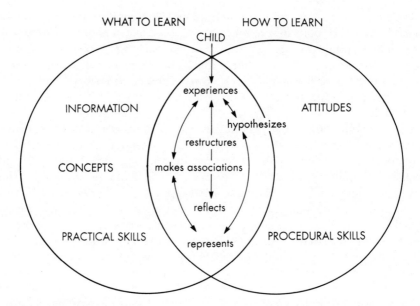

Figure 4   A content and process model for the infant curriculum
Source: Anning and Gates 1989: 26
Note: I am indebted to Judith Gates and LEA and HE colleagues who helped to design this model at a *Child Education* sponsored conference on the Early Years curriculum in York as the subject-based framework of the National Curriculum was about to be introduced at Key Stage 1.

children should be encouraged to develop attitudes such as curiosity, empathy, self-confidence and procedural skills such as problem-solving, observation, goal-setting, learning from mistakes – the *how* aspects of learning. If the 'what to learn' is represented alongside the 'how to learn' in a Venn Diagram (see Figure 4), in the intersection of the sectors we can represent what children actually do in classrooms. They experience, either through practical or reflective activities, make associations, hypothesize, reflect upon or represent in various ways the experiences they have. The learning processes identified in this intersection reflect the new insights from research into the way children learn discussed in Chapter 2. Through these processes children are continually restructuring their own particular understanding and knowledge. A model of planning such as this one which includes references to both curriculum content *and* processes, and at the same time recognizes how children learn in classrooms seems a more useful starting-point for planning than a list of 'aims and objectives,' and recognizes that all three approaches to justifying the content of the infant school curriculum – passing on knowledge, reflecting the needs of society and recognizing the learning needs of the child – are of equal importance.

Table 1 The proportion of time children were observed in different activities (continuous observations of ninety 6–7-year-old children)

	Working time in class (%)	School day (%)
Working time in class		
Art/craft/construction, etc.	21	10
Writing	20	9
Maths	17	8
Oral language	23	10
Reading	4	2
Being allocated activities	4	2
Permitted 'free play'	3	1
Not assigned/wandering/other	4	2
Procedure (e.g. fetching books)	2	1
Uncodeable	2	1
Total	100	46
Other time		
Work activities		
Music/PE/rehearsals, etc.		4
Assembly		3
TV/tape recorders		1
Other school work, out of class		2
Total		11
Non-work activities		
Outside play/dinner-time		28
Lining up/tidying up, etc.		5
Toilet visits, etc.		4
Register/dinner money/milk, etc.		3
Uncodeable		3
Total		43

Source: Tizard *et al.* 1988: 51

The curriculum in practice

Finally, what happens when the paper planning of teachers is translated into learning activities in infant classrooms? We know that infant teachers always expected and ensured that children spent up to two-thirds of the school day on maths and language activities (Bassey 1978; DES 1982a; Bennett *et al.* 1984; Tizard *et al.* 1988; Bennett and Kell 1989). For example, there was a detailed analysis of the curriculum experienced by infant children in the Tizard study (see Table 1).

Once we have recovered from the dismay at registering that 43 per cent of the children's day was spent in 'non-work' activities, we can turn to the

Table 2   Free play activities observed in top infant classrooms

Free play activities	% of free play activities (N = 28)
Role-play (home/hospitals/shop)	46
Small figure play (doll/farm/fort/cars, etc.)	21
Sand play	14
Board games	11
Uncodeable	7

Source: Tizard et al. 1988: 58

'work' categories. Overall the children spent 64 per cent of their time in 3R activities – 17 per cent of their working time in maths, 20 per cent in writing and 27 per cent in other language activities such as reading, discussion and story times. The team speculated that the surprisingly small amount of time designated to reading (4 per cent of class time) was a reflection of the emphasis placed in the schools on parents listening to children reading at home. In view of recent disquiet over a reported decline in reading standards of 7-year-olds, leaked by educational psychology services in some LEAs (*Times Educational Supplement* 1990) this is worrying evidence. The three most common forms of writing were related to language workcards or workbooks, descriptive writing (describing a topic or picture) and story writing, though news and handwriting practice were also quite common. The great majority of maths tasks were in number – usually concentrating either on underlying number concepts, or on the formal operations of addition, subtraction, multiplication and division. Other areas of maths, with the exception of time, weight and length, were rarely observed, and no children were seen working on volume and capacity. (Many infant teachers simply find these too messy to set up and clear away.) In the late 1980s, time spent on scientific activities was so minimal (e.g. activities such as tasting a variety of food for a topic on 'food'; testing water absorption for different materials) that they were recorded under 'Other school work' in Table 1.

Where was all the play that we are led to believe is so central to the infant school curriculum? Sand play occurred infrequently and water play was nonexistent. Of the 195 constructional and creative activities observed, about half involved drawing, crayoning or tracing. Painting and claywork were only relatively infrequently seen. 'Free' play was extremely rare, accounting for 1 per cent of the school day. A breakdown of the twenty-eight free play activities observed shows that most were imaginative role-play or doll play of one form or another. The breakdown is given in Table 2.

These then are the kinds of curriculum realities that faced infant-aged children in their classrooms in the 1980s. Would the implementation of a subject-based National Curriculum drastically alter these patterns in the 1990s? It is to this issue that we turn in Chapter 5.

5

A National Curriculum for 4 to 8-year-olds

On 29 July 1988 the Education Reform Act became law. The Act legislated for far-reaching changes in the education system. The powers of LEAs were drastically curtailed and as levels of funding declined they were unable to offer the level of support through advisory services to which primary head-teachers were accustomed. Parents were given the right to choose the schools their children should go to, so long as the school had the capacity to accom-modate them. Under the terms of Local Management of Schools legislation, control of the budgets of schools was devolved to governors. The Act also provided for the governing bodies of schools with more than 300 pupils to apply, with the consent of a majority of parents, through a secret ballot, to 'opt out' of the LEA system and into direct DES funding as Grant-Maintained Schools. Only a handful of primary schools have done so, but the require-ment to raise the question of opting out annually at governors' meetings is unsettling. Legislation was introduced to ensure that all schools were inspected by Ofsted, Office for Standards in Education, formerly Her Majesty's Inspectors of Schools, every four years. Ofsted was 'detached' from the Department for Education and set the task of training large numbers of inspectors. It proved an impossible task to organize the inspection of all 18 000 primary schools within four years. By 1995, a significant backlog of schools awaiting inspection had built up. Models of teacher appraisal were set up across the country within LEAs. Infant schools became the guinea pigs for the introduction of a National Curriculum drawn up by a National Cur-riculum Council (NCC) based in York. Programmes of study and attain-ment targets for a curriculum for 5 to 16-year-olds – Key Stages 1 to 4, for ages 5–7, 7–11, 11–14 and 14–16 – were designed by working parties of 'experts' in each of the prescribed subjects. The three core subjects – English, mathematics and science – were introduced to Year 1 classes in September 1989.

Six of the foundation subjects (not modern languages) – technology, history, geography, art, music and physical education – were introduced over the next three years. Religious education was the responsibility of local Standard Advisory Councils on Religious Education (SACREs) with a requirement to conform to government guidelines. A range of dimensions (such as personal and social education), cross-curricular skills (such as study, problem-solving and communication skills) and themes (such as health education, citizenship and economic and industrial understanding) are also expected to be covered by schools. Statutory assessment requirements, including Standard Assessment Tasks for all 7-year-olds in the core subjects, were designed and piloted under the auspices of the Schools Examination and Assessment Council (SEAC) based in London.

For infant teachers the emphasis on the teaching of subjects left them feeling alienated and deskilled. They were required to teach a secondary school curriculum model to 5–7-year-olds. Within the working parties preparing each subject order, there were few representatives from the primary sector and even fewer from infant schools. Their membership was drawn predominantly from Higher Education or secondary schools. It was yet another example of the lack of recognition of the expertise of early years educators in the profession.

Fuelled by the ideology of an influential group of right wing educationists (Cox and Boyson 1977; Hillgate Group 1986, 1987) politicians took potshots at 'project work' and 'play'. A Minister with responsibility for Education, Michael Fallon, reported in the educational press, claimed that project work had turned primary schools 'into playgroups where there is much happiness and painting but very little learning'. Kenneth Clarke, then Minister for Education, derided 'child-centred' education as 'a lot of sticking together of egg boxes and playing in the sand'. The Hillgate Group (1986: 16) argued that market forces should be applied to educational systems: 'Schools will have to work to stay in business, and the worse their results, the more likely they will be to go to the wall.' John Major intoned his version of education at the 1992 Conservative Women's Conference: 'Knowledge. Discipline. Tables. Sums. Dates. Shakespeare. British History. Standard English. Spelling. Marks, Tests. Good Manners.' Ministers talked about sending 'commando-style units' to sort out failing inner-city schools. The discourse of this male, largely private school educated, dominant power group could not have been more different from that of early years educators.

Many primary teachers reacted angrily to the concept of losing their traditional autonomy in the choice of the content of the curriculum and with hostility to the notion of a subject-based curriculum framework. They argued that teachers in primary schools worked in an integrated way and not in subject areas, that young children did not see knowledge in separate subject compartments, and that their planning was based on themes, topics or projects rooted in the children's interests and immediate experiences (Blenkin and Kelly 1994).

As we have seen from the evidence presented in Chapter 4, in reality, the basics of language and maths were taught as discrete areas of the curriculum, often heavily dependent on commercial schemes. The third 'basic', science, hardly figured in the infant curriculum, other than as 'nature study' until the 1980s, when its development was rapid and largely successful. The humanities – history, geography, moral and religious education – were planned within the 'topic web'. Art had become the servicing agent for projects, with learning experiences, media and techniques introduced because of the requirements of wall displays or project folders. In general, the content of the physical education and music curricula was as self-contained as the maths and language curricula, though perhaps dance or movement sessions or the choice of new songs to be learned might have been loosely linked to the current topic – 'The Wheels on the Bus' for a project on transport; 'Squirrels Hiding Nuts' dances for a project on autumn.

Infant teachers' claims that children's interests dominated the curriculum may also be challenged. Whilst it was true that good teachers did initiate visits and introduce lively starting points to stimulate young children's learning and that planning was based on a genuine responsiveness to the kinds of things their class of children found interesting, many of their colleagues annually made assumptions that every new class of children they met were interested in bread, spring lambs, bunnies, catkins, tadpoles and the seaside – and always in that order! In fact, many children are deeply interested in all aspects of television (particularly the soap operas such as *Neighbours* and *Eastenders* and cartoons), clothes, football, pop music and dance, bikes, computers and technical toys (often based on comic, film or television characters), shopping, how things around the house work and why natural phenomena occur. How many of these children's interests were routinely reflected in topics? In an honest child-centred curriculum, perhaps they should be.

Education, however, is a deeply conservative process. Jean Rudduck (1986) expressed the dilemma well.

> The inertia of past meanings is a formidable barrier to change. In education, you cannot create a vacuum in which to grow a new set of meanings and practices; you cannot stop teaching for a year in order to work together in a different way. The show must go on. It is against such pressures that the task of change has to be undertaken.

Infant teachers, after initial angry reactions to the proposals for a National Curriculum simply knuckled down to making the best compromises they could between their preferred ways of designing and implementing the

curriculum, and the new requirements of the programmes of study specified by law. In 1989 a group of influential early years 'experts' reported
that 'A number of ideas which permeate these documents assent and affirm
the very principles on which the early years curriculum is founded' (Early
Years Curriculum Group 1989: 21). In fact, in maintaining their commitment
to an integrated approach to curriculum planning many school staffs became
much more rigorous in their long-term planning of themes and topics. In
a sense their bluff had been called. Issues of overlap and progression in
curriculum content were addressed perhaps for the first time as teachers
struggled to come to terms with the National Curriculum (DFE 1992; Bennett
et al. 1992).

As waves of separate Orders swept through Key Stage 1 classrooms,
with minimum consultation at grassroots level, it became apparent that
there was simply too much content to fit into school hours. Alterations
were made to the statutory Orders in the core subjects and technology in
1992 whilst teachers were struggling to put the original Orders into practice. Information from government-funded evaluations of the effects of
the reforms was carefully controlled (see Graham 1993). In the end, the
unpiloted, legislated National Curriculum was officially declared 'unmanageable'. A complete review was ordered, under the direction of Sir Ron
Dearing in 1993.

Each of the subject Orders will be considered separately. The final section
gives an overview of issues raised by attempting to 'deliver' the National
Curriculum at Key Stage 1 since 1989.

The core subjects

English

There has been a great deal of research and in-service training in the teaching
of language in primary schools. It is probably the one aspect of schooling
with which most primary teachers feel confident. The Working Party was able
to draw on these strengths in compiling the programmes of study for Key
Stage 1 for English. In the 1989 Order, after pressure had been exerted by
practitioners, equal weighting was given to three profile components –
Speaking and Listening (AT1), Reading (AT2) and Writing (ATs 3–5) – acknowledging that a holistic approach to teaching language was best.

An evaluation of the implementation of the English Order by NCC in 1991
drew on a survey administered by the National Foundation for Education
Research (NFER) and evidence from HMI inspections (NCC 1991). A group
at Warwick University were commissioned to investigate key issues in the
teaching of English, but even by 1992 the NCC had reported *The Case for
Revising the Order.*

Speaking and Listening

In Chapter 2, the works of Tizard and Hughes (1984) and Wells (1987) were discussed. They stressed the importance of building on children's competences in their home language by setting up opportunities in schools for genuine conversations about shared experiences. In the introduction to the original Programme of Study for Speaking and Listening, the importance of encouraging children to 'encounter a range of situations, audiences and activities which are designed to develop their competence, precision and confidence in speaking and listening, irrespective of their initial competence or home language' was stressed (NCC/WO 1989a: 13).

In the Non-Statutory Guidance, the emphasis was on learning through language as discourse between peers and adults, rather than on language taught by the teacher as expert. However, it was pointed out that speaking and listening activities should be planned, not simply left to chance, and should include access to stories and poems from different cultures, responding to audio and visual recordings, discussion and collaborative work, talking about shared class and home experiences, play and drama, giving and receiving simple explanations, information and instructions and asking and answering questions. It was made clear that pupils unable to communicate by speech were able to use technology, signing, symbols or lip-reading to speak and listen. Reference was also made to the role of 'bilingual speakers from the community or support services' to 'assist children, through the use of home language to a better command of English'.

The Warwick team was asked to investigate whether Key Stage 1 teachers were able to devote appropriate time to speaking and listening. They reported that 17 per cent of the English curriculum as a separate subject and 18 per cent within other subjects were spent on speaking and listening. The majority of teachers felt that they had an increased awareness of the importance of teaching this aspect of English (Raban *et al.* 1994). A preoccupation in the 1992 revisions was a greater emphasis on younger children becoming more confident users of Standard English and on their developing more effective listening skills.

In the 1995, third edition of the English Order references to media education and information technology were restored to the text and a greater emphasis on drama was signalled at all key stages.

Reading

In the 1989 Order, the approach to the teaching of reading stressed that reading activities should (NCC/WO 1989a: 15):

> build on the oral language and experiences which pupils bring from home. Teaching should cover a range of rich and stimulating texts, both fiction and non-fiction, and should ensure that pupils regularly

hear stories, told or read aloud, and hear and share poetry read by the teacher and each other.

Thus two important features of what was recognized as 'good practice' in the teaching of reading were stressed.

First, good practice builds on what children bring to the learning situation rather than disempowering them by presenting tasks that are divorced from their 'realities'. The seminal work of Frank Smith (1971, 1978) in Canada, Marie Clay (1979) in New Zealand, and Jessie Reid and Margaret Donaldson (1979) in the UK, emphasized the importance of facilitating children's access to reading by providing texts which recognized the common patterns of language used by and vocabulary familiar to young children and by encouraging them to use their own writing as a source of reading. The innovative Breakthrough to Literacy (Mackay *et al.* 1970) materials also encouraged this approach. In the UK, Reid and Donaldson argued that children should also be encouraged to make sense of the functional language all around them – advertisements, labels, street signs, posters – in their homes and in the streets.

The second and more controversial feature of good practice was that a diet of 'real' story and picture books was advocated as the best way to encourage children to gain and acquire independent reading habits (Bennett 1979; Waterland 1985). The teacher or parent was encouraged to offer a model of reading behaviour to the child. This approach was called 'the apprenticeship model' of teaching reading. The artificial, stilted texts and formalized conventions of the kind of reading schemes in common use in the 1960s and 1970s were discredited. It was argued that graded reading schemes offered children 'meaningless' reading tasks which they simply completed to 'please teacher'. Instead, children were to be encouraged to approach reading as an active, interesting and above all purposeful activity. The publishers quickly responded by producing reading schemes which looked like real books! Reading schemes were not mentioned in the 1989 Programmes of Study, despite the fact that many schools still use them as the basis of their teaching of reading, and many parents still wait anxiously to see which coloured book within the graded scheme system their children will emerge clutching at the end of the school day.

Reference was made in the programmes of study to the need to guide children to use 'the available cues, such as pictures, context, phonic cues, word shapes and meaning of a passage to decipher new words' (NCC/WO 1989a: 16). The subskills of reading, which in the past were habitually taught as isolated drills using flashcards, lists of words or phonics, were to be taught in the context of real reading activities. Children should also be encouraged 'to develop the habit of silent reading'. Emphasis was also given to reading for information, and the implication was that study skills should be taught to children from the earliest stages of learning to read. Non-sighted children would have alternative methods such as Braille to demonstrate their capabilities and those unable to read aloud might use signing.

The NCC evaluation of the implementation of the Order acknowledged that there was a lack of detail to support teachers in moving children from level 1 'begin to recognize individual words or letters in familiar contexts' to level 2 'read a range of material with some independence, fluency, accuracy and understanding' (NCC/WO 1989a: 7). In the revised Order of 1992 changes included more detailed references to the skills children need to be taught in learning to read; a narrowing of the gap between levels 1 and 2; and a greater emphasis on the use of reading schemes and phonics. The evidence from the Warwick Study was that this was more representative of how teachers were actually teaching reading at Key Stage 1. The Warwick Study identified that Key Stage 1 teachers were emphasizing building up a sight vocabulary at the initial stages of teaching reading and the use of phonic cues in Years 1 and 2. Unfortunately, much of this teaching of phonics was done as isolated exercises rather than within the reading of text (see Adams 1990; Clark 1994 for research evidence on the benefits of this approach to phonics).

Key Stage 1 teachers reported elsewhere (Evans *et al.* 1994) that they were spending less time 'listening to children read' as they broadened their approach to the teaching of reading in line with NCC requirements and as they struggled to pack in the content of all the other core and foundation subjects.

Recent research on early literacy reported by Clark (1994) and Beard (1995) has pointed out the importance of children developing a knowledge of the peculiarities of the English sound system and of teachers understanding better this aspect of teaching reading. This has been acknowledged in the revised text of the third version of the English Order which was introduced into schools after the Dearing Review in 1995.

In all three versions of the English Order, a prescribed reading list of 'classics' for each key stage caused a great controversy. Above all, it was formidably articulate English teachers, with a tradition of liberalism, who took the Government on in challenging the reforms and they resisted the idea of an NCC-prescribed canon.

Writing

There has been less research on the early stages of writing in schools, though both Smith in Canada (1982) and Clay in New Zealand (1975) moved on to study the development of writing skills, and in the UK Andrew Wilkinson (1986), Helen Cowie (1984) and Nigel Hall (1987) contributed to a growing understanding of how young children develop competence in writing.

In the 1989 Order, the programme of study for writing included three divisions – writing, spelling and handwriting. This approach sat uneasily alongside the holistic approaches to speaking/listening, and reading for pleasure/functional purposes. One suspects that the divisions were included as a sop to the demands for 'better standards' of spelling and handwriting in our schools. Explicit references to teaching and understanding of grammatical terms and the conventions of full stops and capital letters, albeit in the context of discussion about children's own writing, were included, but the Order put a surprisingly enlightened emphasis on teaching children to understand how language works, rather than on teaching the formal conventions of grammar. Knowledge about Language (KAL) became an increasingly important component of teaching English.

The general approach to teaching writing continued the theme of building on what children already know about print and encouraging them to experiment with communicating through 'emergent' writing (see Hall 1987) as well as through drawing and diagrams. As with the apprenticeship model of teaching reading, children were to be offered models of the writing process. They were to be encouraged to write both individually and in groups 'in different contexts and for a variety of purposes and audiences'. Children with special educational needs were to be encouraged to use technological aids wherever possible to enable them to complete programmes of study, and those whose disability made handwriting impossible were exempt from the handwriting aspects of the programme of study.

The Warwick Study reported that in writing teachers perceived that the gap between levels 1 and 2 was also too wide. There was confusion about the interpretation of Statement of Attainment 2a, 'produce independently pieces of writing using complete sentences some of them demarcated with capital letters and full stops or question marks' (DES 1992: 12). How many was 'some' supposed to be? Teachers reported that children had responded to their greater emphasis on teaching 'sentences' by writing less. They reported teaching more spelling and handwriting. However, the range of writing activities they were setting children had broadened as they responded to the Order.

The Working Party for the Revised Post-Dearing English Order raised the attainment criteria for level 1 in writing, reversing the 1992 Order 'emergent' writing perspective, to narrow the gap between levels 1 and 2, and integrated spelling and handwriting into the writing attainment target.

Mathematics

In the NCC Non-Statutory Guidance for Mathematics, mathematics was defined as 'a way of viewing and making sense of the world. It is used to analyse and communicate information and ideas and to tackle a range of practical tasks and real-life problems' (NCC/WO 1989b, 2.1: A2). The creative aspect of mathematics was emphasized. 'Mathematics also provides the material and means for creating new imaginative worlds to explore. Through exploration within mathematics itself, new mathematics is created and current ideas are modified and extended' (ibid. 2.2). This broad approach reflected the view of mathematics taken in the Cockcroft Report (DES 1982b) that children 'need to learn to think with mathematics rather than merely respond to routines'.

The programmes of study were set out under five broad headings – number, algebra, measurement, shape and space and handling data, with fourteen attainment targets altogether. The programme of study was not designed to specify 'a mathematics curriculum in action' but was to be seen as 'the common framework within which all schools construct their own policies and plans for mathematics'. However, it did provide a hierarchical framework with levels clearly specified for the teaching of mathematics.

Ironically in the Non-Statutory Guidance, it was pointed out that learning in mathematics is not a tidy and linear process but rather progression 'is to do with the way in which teachers explore, make sense of and construct pathways through a network of ideas'. Each child's progression through the network will be different, depending upon what previous knowledge and experience she or he brings to new learning experiences. The role of the teacher is 'to organise and provide the sorts of experiences which enable pupils to construct and develop their own understanding of mathematics, rather than simply to communicate the ways in which they themselves understand the subject' (NCC/WO 1989b: C2).

Current practice in infant school mathematics

How did the 1989 Order match up to evidence of the way in which mathematical experiences were then offered to children at Key Stage 1? Evidence offered by HMI in the Survey of First Schools (DES 1982a) was that only one-fifth of the 80 schools surveyed achieved 'a good balance between learning how to perform a calculation and using it in a practical setting'. In many of the schools there was an overemphasis on computation 'to such an extent that children lacked opportunities to apply mathematical ideas to everyday experiences and sometimes failed to understand the calculation they undertook' (DES 1982a: 20–1).

The NCC prescriptions sounded very fine, but the realities for teachers of being exhorted to teach mathematics through practical activities, and to base their interventions on a close understanding of the particular pathways to understanding each child might take, were complex and demanding. Extracts from teaching and learning episodes such as Wendy working on mathematical tasks (reported in Chapter 3) demonstrate that skilful teachers can and do cope with such complexities.

The temptation to which many teachers succumb, however, is to rely on a maths scheme to keep children 'occupied', with each child working individually at their own pace (see Bennett *at al.* 1984; Tizard *et al.* 1988). At the end of a session, there is then some recorded evidence of the children 'having done some maths'. In practical activity the evidence of learning often 'disappears' at the end of the session into a pile of plastic in a storage box. A teacher must be confident enough to live with such ephemeral outcomes. And of course children must be persuaded that there is maths outside a workbook. Maths workbooks are popular with children because on the whole the tasks set allow them to coast – or to copy from a friend – and, like all learners, they will settle for an easy ride if the opportunity is offered!

Since the introduction of the National Curriculum, concerns about the use of schemes have continued. 'Many schools used a commercial mathematics scheme, and there was undue reliance on them in most schools' (DES 1990a: para. 24); 'commercial mathematics schemes continued to be the dominant influence on work done in each Key Stage' (DES 1991a); 'a third of classes place an over-reliance on a particular published scheme and this has led to pupils spending prolonged periods of time on repetitive and undemanding exercises which did little to advance their skill or understanding, much less their interest and enthusiasm' (Ofsted 1994a: 23; reported by MacNamara 1995).

Children's strategies in mathematical learning

The Non-Statutory Orders suggested that children should be encouraged to use a variety of strategies in tackling mathematical tasks. 'Working in the head' should be encouraged, as well as pencil and paper and the use of calculators and computers to find solutions. In their study of mathematics in first schools, Desforges and Cockburn (1987) pointed out that within a group of children each may opt for a different route through a mathematical task set by the teacher. They might recall a similar task done recently and simply repeat a formula that appeared to be successful. They might even turn back to check earlier solutions in their workbooks. They might pick up on a solution offered by someone else in the group, or at worst simply copy the answers from a neighbour. They may memorize instructions given by the teacher at the start of the exercise, or simply decode the teacher's prompts as they are working through an activity. They may also decide to use an easier method than that suggested by the teacher, often adapting their behaviours or doctoring recorded work before it is taken to be checked so that they appear to have used the 'correct' procedures.

Sometimes children invent remarkable strategies of their own. Hughes (1986: 133) gave an irresistible example of 'an interesting finger counting strategy' from his observation of 6-year-old Mark at work:

He responded to the written problem '5 + 6 =' by laying one hand flat on the table, and saying 'Five'. He then laid a pencil down next to his hand. He put his other hand down on the other side of the pencil, and said, 'Six'. Finally, he added up all eleven items (ten fingers and a pencil), using his nose to count with! It was an extremely impressive performance.

Children's understanding of mathematical symbols

Martin Hughes was one of the researchers working with Margaret Donaldson on the reinterpretation of children's responses to Piagetian tasks in the 1970s (see pp. 23–6, Chapter 2). He pursued the idea expressed by Donaldson that children 'must become capable of manipulating symbols' (Donaldson 1978: 88–9), and that the role of the adult is to extend children's understanding of the power of symbol systems. Hughes' work (1986) paralleled research into children's emergent writing. He carried out a series of experiments with nursery and infant school children to explore both their ability to handle and represent the conventions of number symbols, and their ability to understand and use the far more abstract processes represented by mathematical signs such as plus and minus. Hughes discovered that young children used a range of strategies when they were asked to represent a number of bricks on paper. At pre-school level, 4-year-olds tended to use arbitrary and idiosyncratic responses – scribbles or 'letters' to represent the bricks. By five, children were more likely to make pictographic responses; that is drawing the number and position of the bricks almost as they saw them on the table, and in some cases actually drawing the bricks physically. At six or seven, children used either iconic responses – simple tally systems, circles or other objects drawn to indicate the number of bricks. Finally, children used symbolic responses – writing the numerals or the number words 'one', 'two', 'three', etc.

When Hughes went on to ask children to represent mathematical processes of addition and subtraction by taking from or adding bricks to those on the table, he was astonished to discover that no child in a sample of ninety 6–7-year-olds used the symbols '+' or '−' in their representations. 'And yet' (as Margaret Donaldson pointed out in the foreword to the book) 'three-quarters of these children were regularly using these symbols when doing addition and subtraction sums in school'. Hughes concluded that we need to be far more explicit in teaching children about the use and application of mathematical symbols. He devised a series of games using magnetic numbers and mathematical symbols attached to tins of objects to demonstrate mathematical operations. He argued that teachers should explicitly teach 'the formal code of arithmetic', and set up learning situations where children see the point of using the code to solve a problem or accomplish something which has a purpose for them. Such a purpose might be, for example, keeping account of the number of bottles of milk to be cancelled for absentees, or buying the ingredients within a set weekly budget for a baking activity and handling the additions and subtractions needed. The argument then is 'not to avoid mathematical symbols in a child's earlier experience. Rather one should capitalise on situations where children feel the need for symbols' (Buxton 1982, quoted by Hughes ibid.: 178).

Finally, it is important that teachers introduce children to the language of mathematics and model the use of technical vocabulary, as Wendy did when she introduced the concept of graphical representation of numbers (Chapter 3, p. 54). We cannot assume that young children understand what we mean by words like 'number', 'a set of', 'add', any more than they know what we mean by 'letter', 'sentence' or 'write'. Explicit explanations must be given.

Sometimes young children will buck the system, defying the 'logic' of adult strategies and explanations, as Mark did with his ingenious counting procedure. In the project involving six primary teachers at work (Anning 1987), 4-year-old Paul had been encouraged by his nursery teacher to sort Kugeli balls into sets by colour. He was rapidly tiring of the routine and becoming bored with the repetition of colour names and 'the same as' or 'not the same as'. He placed a black Kugeli ball amongst a carefully sorted set of yellow balls and stared defiantly at the teacher. 'Why have you put that black one with the yellow set?', she asked. 'Because he's the boss', replied Paul very firmly and stalked off.

The Mathematics Order was revised in 1993. The fourteen attainment targets were reduced to five, and in the post-Dearing review, to three. Primary teachers consistently reported that they felt insecure in delivering the mathematics curriculum (Bennett *et al.* 1992; Ofsted 1994a). Ironically, in-service support declined as LEA advisory services contracted and the twenty-day GEST courses (Harland and Kinder 1992) were reduced to ten days. Overall, the percentage of time spent on mathematics appeared to decline from 20 per cent of total curriculum time in 1990 to 18 per cent in 1993 (Campbell and Neill 1994). Ofsted (1994a) reported that the mathematics curriculum had broadened to include at Key Stage 1 the foundations of algebra, geometry, data handling, and some elements of probability but 'the learning time devoted to proficiency in basic arithmetic was reduced' (ibid.: 16). When children were working on arithmetic, the work was often presented as routine exercises and was undemanding. Children were often unsure about how to apply the mathematical operations they had practised to real-life problems. However, overall Ofsted reported that the quality of work in mathematics at Key Stage 1 was steadily improving.

In the 1995 post-Dearing revisions, the content was slimmed down to three attainment targets at Key Stage 1: Shape, Space and Measures; Number; and the important Using and Applying Mathematics were retained. At Key Stage 1, the main emphases were:

- Developing the appropriate mathematical language associated with number, shape and position.
- Learning to count in preparation for work on place value and working with larger numbers.

- Using the four operations of number in relevant contexts.
- Recognizing pattern and symmetry.
- Developing skills in meaning and estimating.

It was emphasized that talking about work has a higher priority than recording (reported in a review of the Dearing Proposal published in the *Times Educational Supplement* 13 May 1994 p. iii).

Science

Various initiatives were launched in the 1980s to improve the quality of science teaching in primary schools: for example the Progress in Learning Project (Harlen *et al.* 1977a, 1977b) and the Assessment of Performance Unit work in skills in science (APU 1984). Many LEAs took advantage of DES funding offered under the Educational Support Grants (DES 1984) and appointed advisory teachers in science to work alongside class teachers. Primary schools appointed Science Coordinators and sent them off on twenty-day GEST in-service courses to gain some confidence in devising a coherent school policy for science (Kinder and Harland 1991). Publishers began to produce science schemes for primary schools. in 1985, DES published a policy statement on the teaching of science – *Science 5–16: A Statement of Policy* (DES 1985c). By 1989, HMI reported considerable improvements in primary science teaching (DES 1989d) but science was still an uncharted area in many infant classrooms at that time.

The programmes of study in science

In the 1989 version of the National Curriculum Science Order (NCC/WO 1989c) there were two profile components – Exploration of Science with one attainment target and Knowledge and Understanding with (in Key Stage 1) fourteen attainment targets. As in the process profile component of the Mathematics Order, Exploration of Science incorporated procedural understanding, whilst the Knowledge and Understanding profile component incorporated conceptual understanding.

In 1991, in a revised version of the Order, Attainment Target 1 became Scientific Investigation, and Knowledge and Understanding was reduced to three attainment targets. In 1995, AT1 was renamed Experimental and Investigative Science and three other attainment targets were retained: Life and Living Processes, Materials and their Properties and Physical Processes.

The implementation of Key Stage 1 science created difficulties for infant teachers. In the first place, they had little experience of setting up and monitoring scientific 'explorations and investigations'. They approached 'practical activities' in the spirit of children 'learning by doing' in the hope that children would 'discover' scientific concepts for themselves. To a certain extent, this view was encouraged by the Non-Statutory Guidance for the 1989 Science Order: 'conceptual understanding can develop through continuous, well planned practical experiences'. But as Asoko (1995: 53) has pointed out:

> The activities themselves do not determine whether children use or learn science knowledge or operate in a scientific way. It is what is happening in their heads when they interact with the activities which matters. In order for children to be truly involved in scientific activity they need access to appropriate ideas and ways of thinking together with opportunities and encouragement to use these ideas. The teacher, therefore, needs not only to provide experiences but also to be prepared to capitalise on the opportunities they provide for introducing, or supporting children in using 'tools for thinking' in the form of selected science ideas and concepts.

Herein lies the second major difficulty: the lack of scientific knowledge, especially of the physical sciences, amongst a predominantly female, arts-based teaching workforce. This was identified as a source of difficulty by HMI as long ago as 1978, and has been frequently referred to since (Wragg *et al.* 1989; Bennett *et al.* 1992). It created genuine and understandable anxiety. In a sample of 901 primary teachers surveyed in the Wragg study, only 34 per cent felt competent to teach science compared to 68 per cent for mathematics and 81 per cent for English. A project set up to survey 450 primary teachers' knowledge base in science concluded 'the majority of primary teachers in the sample hold views of science concepts that are not in accord with those accepted by scientists' (Summers 1992: 26). It is a fine idea to set up open-ended learning situations which will encourage children to ask questions about science. But what do you say to the child who asks, 'Why do aeroplanes stay up in the sky?' or 'Do ants have hearts?', when you really have no idea at all what the answer might be? Of course, you might then dispatch the child to reference books to find the answers; but reference book explanations are often at a reading level way above the young child's capability. Moreover, 'scientific' explanations of complex phenomena, often intellectually demanding for adults, can be distorted by attempts to explain them at a very simple level. It requires a sophisticated knowledge of a subject to be able to interpret complex ideas in an intellectually honest but accessible way. Support for primary teachers has emanated from Ros Driver's work on children's learning in science (see Driver *et al.* (1994) for a summary). The research has taken a 'constructivist' view of children's learning in science. Children of all ages bring to schools' science activities a diversity of ideas and explanations about natural phenomena and the world around them. For example, when forty 5-year-olds were asked what they knew about air, most replied that 'air is everywhere'; a few had other ideas such as that air was also in water (because fish need to breathe) or that it came from clouds or the sky (Brook and Driver 1984). Driver argues that it is essential that teachers build up an understanding of children's conceptual maps of scientific phenomena if they are to be effective in extending their understanding of science. We have been offered the 'certainties' of three versions of a programme of study for Key Stage 1 in science on the basis of little evidence of how young children's learning in science progresses.

John Stannard (1988) gave an example of a young child trying to build upon previous learning experiences in science, this time from a school-initiated situation.

> Kevin is 6 years and 5 months old. He has been out with his class to explore the effects of echoes in a large pedestrian subway near the school, as part of a science topic about sound. He was very interested in how sound travelled and the explanations about soundwaves which his teacher had given. Some days later he came to her and said, 'I can tell you how people see.'
>
> *Teacher:* Tell me.
>
> *Kevin:* Well, you know how when you hear things, you get soundwaves in your ears and they bounce off things so that you can hear them . . . when you see you send sight waves out and they bounce back off things so you can see them.

After a short discussion and some demonstration by Kevin, who went round the classroom looking at things to show his teacher what was happening, the teacher suggested that he looked out of the window.

> *Teacher:* What can you see?
>
> *Kevin:* The playground, a tree, some people . . .
>
> *Teacher:* Tap the glass. What's it like?
>
> *Kevin:* Hard.
>
> *Teacher:* If it is all hard, how can you see through it? Why doesn't it make your sightwaves bounce back and stop you seeing past?
>
> *Kevin:* Oh.

Kevin did not seem to give it much further thought and soon had become reabsorbed in his other work. However, after lunch he returned to his teacher saying:

> *Kevin:* I know how you see out of windows.
>
> *Teacher:* How?
>
> *Kevin:* Well the glass is full of tiny holes that let the sightwaves past, but they are so small that you cannot see them.

This conversation is a modern version of the kind of exploratory talk pioneered by Susan Isaacs at the Malting House School in the 1930s. It is the kind of talk with which teachers feel comfortable. I doubt if Kevin's teacher wanted to offer a 'correct' scientific explanation to him since his own thinking has been at such a high cognitive level for a 6-year-old. The episode also illustrates the importance of allowing time for children to absorb information and transfer understanding to a new area of enquiry.

Teachers do, however, face real dilemmas about reconciling children's 'private' knowledge with the 'public' knowledge of science. At what point should they begin to substitute 'scientific' explanations for the 'alternative frameworks' devised from children's 'common sense' understandings and explanations? Or shall we know, instinctively, as parents do when their children begin to question the Great Father Christmas Lie, when it is appropriate to offer each child the stark reality of a 'scientific' explanation?

In 1989 Key Stage 1, teachers generally welcomed the structure offered by the science curriculum (Pollard *et al.* 1994) but regretted the continual tinkering with its content as three different versions were introduced into schools in 1989, 1993 and 1995. Ofsted evaluations of the quality of science teaching at Key Stage 1 (DES 1992; Ofsted 1993a, b) indicated a steady improvement. Additional support for primary teachers came from the SPACE publications (1990–4) and the *Nuffield Primary Science* materials (1993). However, the amount of time devoted to science was always less than that spent on the other core subjects, English and mathematics. Campbell and Neill (1994) reported 13 per cent in 1990, 15 per cent in 1991, 10 per cent in 1992 and 9 per cent in 1993. The post-Dearing recommendation was that science should be taught for 7 per cent of the total teaching time available at Key Stage 1, that is approximately 1.5 hours per week (compared to 3.5 hours for mathematics and 5 hours for English).

By 1993, 50 per cent of teachers felt that standards in science had been raised by the National Curriculum, though 44 per cent felt that it had had no effect. Standard assessments in science at age 7 years were withdrawn in 1993. In effect, science at Key Stage 1 became a foundation subject.

The foundation subjects

Technology

Technology was the first foundation subject to be introduced to 5-year-olds. The 1990 model was innovative though the working party had to grapple with the conceptual frameworks of secondary school CDT, home economics and business economics studies, art and design and information technology in order to create the Technology Order (NCC/WO 1989d):

> Technology is the one subject in the National Curriculum that is directly concerned with generating ideas, making and doing. In emphasising the importance of practical capability, and providing opportunities for pupils to develop their powers to innovate, to make decisions, to create

new solutions, it can play a unique role. Central to this role is the task of providing balance in a curriculum based on academic subjects – a balance in which the creative and practical capabilities of pupils can be fully developed and inter-related.

It consisted of four attainment targets – Identifying Needs and Opportunities, Generating a Design Proposal, Planning and Making, and Appraising – all with equal status. The key concepts of Designing and Making were perceived as an iterative process of reflection and action, but the way in which the attainment targets were presented encouraged teachers to plan activities in a linear sequence where pupils started by identifying a need and ended by evaluating the outcome.

For most Key Stage 1 teachers – mainly female, many with arts or humanities backgrounds – the language of the Technology Order was unfamiliar. Although there were well-established traditions of practical work in craft, construction and (at Key Stage 1) natural materials (sand, water, clay), there were many new skills and concepts for teachers to acquire; for example, the handling of tools and equipment to work with resistant materials and an understanding of structures and mechanisms. Moreover, the new subject technology sat uneasily between the pedagogic traditions of art where children were expected to find a personal path to creativity and science where they were likely to be 'taught' (Anning 1994). In-service support for primary teachers, especially for those teaching young children, was scarce and often focused on upgrading teachers' mechanical skills – teaching them how to construct axles or to use hydraulic syringes to operate toys – without explaining the fundamental principles of design and technology. Some excellent support materials came into schools in the guise of the 1992 non-mandatory technology SATs. The four SATs offered were carefully structured and teachers who followed the clear guidelines produced some good-quality class work, though the way in which teachers assigned pupil capability to levels in making assessments was often erratic (Ofsted 1993c).

The Technology Order, like the History Order, became the subject of political 'interference'. In the foreword to the 1990 version, the statement appeared: 'Whilst the contribution of technology to personal development of individuals is very important, of equal importance is its role in helping pupils to respond to the employment needs of business and industry' (NCC/ WO 1989e). In 1993, a Revised Order, heavily influenced by an engineering lobby, placed a new emphasis on Design and Make Tasks – 'making good quality products fit for their intended purposes'. There were two attainment targets – Designing and Making, and programmes of study specific to each key stage. It was easier for teachers to access but it was not a 'girl-friendly' model – food was omitted at Key Stage 1, textiles reduced to an aspect of material science and graphics marginalized at Key Stages 3 and 4 only. In 1995, a third Order was designed as part of the Dearing Review – it was slimmed down in content, especially at Key Stage 2; it was less fragmented; food was back; and Knowledge and Understanding were flagged as significant aspects of teaching technology. Despite the continual revisions of the curriculum, by the third year of inspection, HMI noted that 77 per cent of design and technology lessons observed at Key Stage 1 were 'satisfactory or better' though only 'a limited range of work was taught' (Ofsted 1993c). The School Curriculum and Assessment Authority (SCAA) published a 32-page booklet *Key Stages 1 and 2, Design and Technology: the New Requirements* (SCAA 1995), to help teachers implement the 1995 Order admitting in the introductory paragraph 'in its present form, Design and Technology is a relatively new and developing subject, changing rapidly both within and beyond education'.

There are a number of conceptual and pedagogic problems still to be resolved. Because teachers themselves are often unclear about the purposes of the practical tasks they set children (are they asking children to design and make a real object, a prototype, a mock-up, a model?) and about which skills or knowledge base should be taught and which 'caught' along the way, children are also confused. The SCAA booklet encouraged teachers to distinguish in design and technology planning between 'focused practical tasks, investigating, disassembling and evaluating simple products' and 'designing and making assignments'. It was made clear that teachers need to model or demonstrate skills such as measuring, marking out, cutting, shaping, joining and combining as well as children's ability to evaluate and design. Children also need to be taught about the characteristics of materials, how to use simple mechanisms and controls, an understanding of structures and an awareness of the quality of products and applications they meet in everyday lives. It is such an exciting subject for children it is to be hoped that Key Stage 1 teachers will persevere in trying to make it work in their classrooms.

Information technology was originally bolted on to the Design and Technology Order. Key Stage 1 teachers struggled with basic equipment, often jinxed by technical problems. Nevertheless, much of the work done on computers by young children – wordprocessing, handling databases, operating logo, art and design, and music composition packages – would have been unimaginable in the mid-1980s (see Constable in Anning 1995a). Acorn PCs are replacing BBC PCs, but there is still a problem of lack of resources, with children having limited access to computers (perhaps one machine shared between two classes of twenty-five–thirty children in each) (HMI 1991). Information technology now has a separate Order. In the Dearing Review, information technology capability at Key Stage 1 was defined as 'an ability to use effectively information technology tools and information sources to analyse, process and present information and to model, measure and control external events'. Information technology has been redefined as a 'basic skill' but there is desperate need for in-service support for primary teachers to boost their confidence in the use of computing as a 'natural' tool for learning

in schools. One solution may be for clusters of primary schools to get together to employ 'specialist expertise' in 0.2 segments of posts to make up
a full-time post to support generalist class teachers in work with computers
in their classrooms.

History

A damning report by HMI on the state of history and geography teaching
in primary schools, based on their inspection of 285 schools between 1982
and 1986, stated that 'most primary schools do not provide challenging historical and geographical work for their pupils. In too many schools, too little
time is devoted to these subjects; they are poorly planned and taught, and
assessment is superficial or non-existent' (HMI 1989c).

The report also suggested that teachers may be underestimating the abilities of young children in history partly because of the legacy of Piaget's
work on children's understanding of time (Blyth 1984; Little 1990: 320). HMI
argued, 'It is increasingly apparent that, for example, ideas associated with
change, chronology, location and distribution can be understood by young
children at an appropriate level if experienced in a practical way and within
a context which makes sense to them'. Poor standards were attributed to
limitations in primary teachers' own knowledge base and understanding of
history, and the dilution of the discipline of history within topic work.

There was little acknowledgement of infant school expertise within
the History Working Party. The programmes of study in the 1990 History
Order for Key Stage 1 were vague expressions of the need to develop the
beginning of a knowledge base centred on local or family histories and
the skills of historical enquiry. No specific period of history was prescribed
for study. The content was simply to include changes in the children's own
and other families' lives since World War II and 'the way of life of people
in a period beyond living memory'. There were three attainment targets:
Knowledge and Understanding of History; Interpretations of History; and the
Use of Historical Sources. Key Stage 1 teachers were given limited access to
in-service support to teach history and there was little published scheme
material or resources on the market, though museums, ever eager to increase
visitor numbers, are an increasingly productive source of support material
for schools' visits, and BBC broadcasts such as *How We Used to Live* have
been models of excellence. Research by Smith and Holden (1994) on 4–11-
year-olds investigating Victorian artefacts demonstrated that young children
were eager to make guesses and try to find out about the functions of
objects like button hooks and sack-grabbers. Children drew on knowledge
of artefacts drawn from television viewing, fairy tales or family reminiscences,
though the nature of the evidence upon which they draw and their con-
clusions could be idiosyncratic and they could find it difficult to distinguish
between fact and fantasy.

It is important for primary teachers to be sensitive when tapping into family histories. The 'standard' nuclear family with a clear genealogy may be a rarity in some communities and the experiences of families of minority groups may provide both rich and troubling evidence. Nevertheless, the oral histories of older members of the family, old toys, photographs, diaries, books, postcards can be potent sources of evidence about a past way of life. It is expected that children should progress 'from familiar situations to those more distant in time and place'. They would be expected to sequence a story about the past.

In the Dearing Revision, required 'units of work' on British history were slimmed down, but the political pressure to use the teaching of history in schools to support nationalistic fervour remains a controversial issue. At Key Stage 1 in the 1995 History Order, the three units of study have been reduced to two, cutting out the study of the immediate past and myths and legends. Children should be taught about changes in their own lives and those of their families and localities. They should be introduced to chronology and to different types of sources of information.

Geography

As with history, shortcomings in the teaching of geography through topic work were reported by HMI in 1989 (HMI 1989d). They reported a lack of rigour and an overreliance on the immediate locality of the school as the basis for geography teaching with an 'almost total absence of a national and world dimension' (1989d: 12). Unlike history, the Geography Order had no content-specific study units. Physical, human and environmental geography were described as themes. There were five attainment targets: Geographical Skills, Knowledge and Understanding of Places – the home area and region, the United Kingdom within the European Community, and the wider world – and the three themes. There was only one specialist primary geographer on the working party responsible for the 1990 Order. The language, especially for the Key Stage 2 Programme of Study, was too technical for most primary teachers.

The need to implement the Order encouraged interest in research into children's learning in geography. The requirement for children to study distant people and places challenged the received idea that children should learn from first-hand, direct experiences. Of course, many young children do travel regularly with their parents for holidays and develop concepts of climate, landscape, buildings and food from the countries they visit (see Wiegand 1991a, b). They also absorb a great deal of information from newspapers, television, story books, family photographs and films. However, one of the problems associated with children's access to media imagery is that of stereotyping – beliefs that all developing countries are poor and peopled by warring or famine-stricken populations or that all American Indians live in wigwams, ride horses bareback and wear deer-skin moccasins and feather head-dresses. It is important to deal sensitively with children's concepts of differences and similarities between places and people. A useful resource is Fountain's (1990) description of collaborative Global Education activities for 4–7-year-olds designed to help children to talk about and value the thoughts and feelings of others. Voluntary aid agencies like Oxfam and Action Aid have begun to produce resource packs to support less-biased views of distant places (see Hughes and Marsden 1994).

Work has also been done on children's understanding of maps and symbols for recording places. An understanding of plans and scale can be encouraged through structured play with model villages, then recorded in drawings. Children can be encouraged to record their routes to school or a shared outing to a local park (Spencer *et al.* 1990). Children are fascinated by maps and aerial photographs, but as Wiegand (1995) points out, adults need to help children to orientate them before they start to decode them.

Most primary schools now do their long-term planning in units of work and are likely to feature major geographical and historical foci at least once a year. Resources – photographs, videos, artefacts, dressing-up clothes, story and information books – are often stored centrally and accessed on an organized school-wide basis.

In the post-Dearing revised Geography Order, introduced into schools in September 1995, the Programmes of Study were drastically reduced. There was one attainment target called 'geography' but there still is a requirement to cover places, skills and the themes and to keep a balance between the study of local (and the known world) and global materials. At Key Stage 1, pupils are expected to carry out two investigations – one in the locality of the school and one in a contrasting location. They should study places and themes using, for example, photographs, pictures, pictorial maps and develop an appropriate technical vocabulary. They should learn how to use and follow directions, read and make simple maps and be able to identify geographical features such as seas, rivers and cities using a globe and maps.

Art

The Gulbenkian Report (Robinson 1982) presented cogent arguments for the entitlement of all children to quality arts education throughout their schooling. However, the fact that art and music, with physical education, were the last National Curriculum subjects to be introduced is an indication of their low status. Pre-National Curriculum, few primary schools had written guidelines for the teaching of art and music. Many teachers felt as insecure about teaching the arts as they did about teaching science. Their insecurity was compounded by inadequate initial training in the arts (Cleave and Sharp 1986; Sharp 1990; Clement 1993). Art coordinators tended to be Main Professional Grade status, likely to be female and likely to be Key Stage 1 teachers (see Alexander 1992: 35).

The Art Order was introduced at Key Stage 1 in September 1992. There were two attainment targets – Investigating and Making, and Knowledge and Understanding. A ratio of 2:1 in favour of practical was required for delivery and assessment of the programmes of study. Art, music and physical education, unlike other subjects, did not have a ten level of attainment framework for assessment, but End of Key Stage Statements of expectations of pupils' achievements.

What was the context for art education at Key Stage 1 into which the Order was introduced? Research evidence indicated that art in infant classrooms was rarely taught, but rather allowed to happen. It happened beyond the regular boundaries of the teacher's working space (Tizard *et al.* 1988; Bennett and Kell 1989; Alexander 1992), perhaps in wet areas in new or refurbished buildings or in cloakroom or corridor spaces converted as messy areas in older school buildings. Art activities were set up by the teacher but they were often supervised by nursery assistants or parent helpers, and were included within 'choosing' time, the 'play' rather than 'work' component of the day. Teacher attention was only sporadically paid to creative activities, particularly where there was a 'rotating groups' system of organization. It was rare to find a teacher planning methodically to cover a range of media over a term or year, or systematically teaching the use of tools and techniques other than in short introductory sessions. So, for example, children might be given general instructions about an art activity set out for that day during the start of the day 'mat time' – 'I want you to paint some lovely pictures about spring today' or 'Today we'll be making some buildings from the boxes on the table over there' or 'Choose some nice material to stick on the horses for our circus frieze'. But unless teachers timetabled themselves to spend time interacting with the children whilst they worked on the tasks, they were unable, for example, to teach basic techniques of colour mixing or which brushes were most appropriate for painting the sky and which for blossoms; or to discuss which boxes were the most appropriate shapes for making bungalows, flats, semi-detached houses, or to demonstrate techniques for covering boxes with paper so that children could then begin to think about the detailing of roofs, windows, doors, brickwork, guttering; or to help children find pictures of horses by a range of artists to look and see how they might convey the form and texture of those marvellous animals.

Many teachers still cling to the view that ability in art is something mysteriously innate and that teaching interferes with a creative process. However it is clear that if children are to make progress in the visual arts, they need to be taught the techniques of how to draw, paint, model, weave, pot. Children cannot be free to be expressive until they have mastered basic skills in representing their feelings and ideas in line, colour, texture or form. It seems illogical to make a distinction between teaching children to read and write and teaching them to paint and draw.

Children also need to be taught that to succeed in creating the effects they want may take many attempts. Even young children may have to go back several times to a painting or drawing or model before it is complete. A problem identified within the Art Interim Report (DES 1991b) was that children were being offered too many disparate, instant 'Blue Peter style' art experiences to produce an understanding of materials or the learning of skills or techniques.

As with technology, the teachers' lack of clarity about the purposes of art activities communicated mixed messages to pupils. Art often degenerated into a serving agency either for the window dressing of school or for the covers of project folders. Drawing in particular was used to keep Key Stage 1 children 'busy'. 'Doing a picture' after writing a story or science experiment was not valued, rarely commented upon by the teacher, but seen as a way of keeping 'bums on seats'.

The Art Order offered a framework for adopting a more thoughtful approach. However, it was introduced when teachers were already struggling with the requirements to teach the core subjects and technology, history and geography. Consequently, 54 per cent of Key Stage 1 teachers surveyed in the PACE project based at Bristol (Pollard *et al.* 1994) were found to be teaching *less* art in 1992. In Campbell's study of curriculum change, (Campbell *et al.* 1994) 36 per cent of the teachers he studied in 1993 believed they had allocated 'sufficient time' to art. Nevertheless, there is evidence that the Art Order has resulted in a more thorough approach to planning art activities, alongside opportunities for free exploration of media and techniques, and to more attention being paid to the teaching of skills and techniques. Teachers are still unsure about how to assess achievement in art. Often motivated by an impending Ofsted inspection, art coordinators are developing combinations of whole-class and schools' record keeping systems, complemented by dated folders or sketchbooks of individual children's dated work.

The biggest changes have come about with AT2, Knowledge and Understanding. This built on the seminal work in 'critical studies' of Rod Taylor based at the Drumcroon Centre in Wigan (Taylor 1986; Taylor and Andrews 1993). Opportunities have been devised to draw on the expertise of local artists and craftspeople under the auspices of Artists in Residence schemes funded by some LEAs.

Schools have begun to build up a stock of art books, posters, postcards, advertisements, and videos of artists at work, both popular and traditional. These resources provide support for teachers who feel 'inept' themselves at art, and therefore anxious about teaching it. Sadly, there is a tendency for many teachers to 'play safe' in developing visual literacy. All over the country young children are solemnly copying images created by white, dead, male European painters from their teachers' favourite postcards. For children in the 1990s their daily exposure to visual imagery is through television, comics, videos, computer games and the signs and symbols of the commercial world. It should be possible for schools to open up to children a whole world of visual literacy and encourage them to see art as a vital part of living culture, rather than something set apart in galleries for an élite section of the community.

In the Revised Art Order of 1995, the End of Key Stage Statements were reduced to eleven prose descriptions for the purposes of assessment. A direct relationship was signalled between these statements and the programmes of study. Strands, for example, 'gather resources and materials, using them to stimulate and develop ideas', were followed through at each key stage. There was an enhanced policy on art provision for children with special educational needs including appropriate provision for those who communicate through technological aids or signing or lip-reading, those who use non-sighted methods of reading or acquiring information or those who use technological aids for practical or recorded work within and beyond the school.

Music

The teaching of music in primary schools had its own idiosyncratic history. Singing dominated the curriculum, often taught by a pianist/specialist in the hall, or as part of 'hymn practice' for assemblies or for public 'events' such as school concerts – the annual rituals of harvest festival, the carol service, Mother's Day, each with its own distinctive traditions. Primary schools have relied also on school broadcasts to support generalist class teachers in teaching music, again with a bias towards singing.

Robust infant teachers grit their teeth and set up music corners resourced with instruments – commercially produced or made by the children – in their classrooms (usually as far away from the teacher's 'work' table as possible) for children to experiment with sound. There has been an established tradition of instrumental work – the ubiquitous descant recorder clubs at lunch times, whole-class percussion sessions as occasional alternatives to story times or individual instrumental tuition for interested or gifted children staffed by peripatetic brass, wind or string specialists. Some primary schools have successful orchestras and choirs which may have been initiated by a lone enthusiast at an arbitrary point in the school's history, but have been sustained by a series of replacement music specialist appointments because of parental expectations. LEAs often supported good-quality instrumental work in schools through free after-school or weekend tuition for children to play in regional bands or orchestras and through loans of instruments to children. Sadly, there has been a significant decline in these services in the last decade as LEA budgets have been cut.

Coral Davies (1994) provided an interesting review of research into young children's musical development. For example, children appear to develop schemata for songs by responding to the patterns of repetition and contrast in musical phrases that they hear all around them (Dowling 1984). Moog (1976: 115) describes those wonderful 'pot-pourri songs' children invent 'by putting together pieces of songs they already know. Words, melodies, and rhythms are mixed up, altered, taken apart and put together again in a different way, and then filtered in between stretches of original ideas.' Ironically, research into young children composing has focused on instrumental and environmental sounds rather than composing songs (see Mills 1991). Bamberger (1991) made a close study of one child's exploration of sound with instruments to try to explore 'the mind behind the musical ear'. Swanwick (1992) outlined a model of musical development: an initial sensory response to sound characterized by explorations of what the child can do with sounds; a second stage where children become more aware of the expressive nature of music; a third level where awareness of the structural elements of music develops; and finally, a growing awareness of their own and other people's music-making in a cultural context. Often in schools, a cultural awareness has been fostered by 'classical' music, relayed through ancient and crackly record players, force-fed to children as they file silently in and out of the hall for assemblies. More enlightened school policies have included inviting a range of musicians into schools to play live music to children and a policy of providing a rich cultural diet of music for children to listen to on good-quality sound systems.

Swanwick related his conceptual model to the four key stages of the Music National Curriculum. In the 1992 Order three areas of music were identified: performing, composing, and listening and appraising. Composing is probably the area where generalist primary teachers feel most inadequate especially if they do not 'read music'. But at Key Stage 1 children can be encouraged to invent simple symbols systems to represent and store their compositions. As they begin to play each other's compositions, the need for a universal system of notation will become apparent and then they can be encouraged to learn some of the conventions of musical notation. A scheme like Silver Burdett published by Ginn in 1989 can be a useful prop for generalist class teachers.

Dawson (1995: 118–19) argued that long periods of whole-class music tuition in hall periods are not the best forum for teaching music to young children. He recommended that Key Stage 1 class teachers should focus on short bursts of music teaching throughout the week to groups of varying sizes, including sometimes the whole class:

> There might be a two minute game developing pitch awareness, the listening to, clapping of, and feeling for a steady pulse, the adding of sounds to a story, the singing of a song linked to a topic or project, simply listening to sounds within and outside the classroom, explaining different qualities of sounds for a class assembly on 'contrasts'. Such and similar activities are the most effective patterns for music education at Key Stage One.

He also argues that the support of a consultant or curriculum leader is important (ibid.: 119):

This support may be technical advice, suggestions for suitable repertoire, assisting in the development of the class teacher's own music
skills and above all helping to build confidence.

A slimmed-down post-Dearing 1995 Music Order retained the Attainment Targets Performing and Composing and Listening and Appraising. The
musical elements of pitch, duration, dynamics, speed, timbre, texture and
structure were common to all key stages, but progression was defined clearly.
For example, at Key Stage 1 children should learn whether pitch is high or
low, but at Key Stage 2 they should learn about gradations of pitch and
chord. This clearer framework should help teachers to assess and record
children's progress. The end of key stage descriptors were 'simplified'. The
repertoire chosen for performing and listening was to include music in
various styles from Europe, the British Isles and a variety of cultures including
classical, folk and pop.

Physical education

There has been growing anxiety about the poor state of physical fitness of
many schoolchildren in the UK (Sleap and Warburton 1994). Access to safe
outdoor play in the inner cities or even on suburban streets is limited. In
nursery schools and classes it is possible to offer young children opportunities
to play on large outdoor equipment in the safety of fenced and supervised
spaces. However, for the 4-year-olds in reception classes, as for many Key
Stage 1 children, physical exercise within school may be limited to a couple
of hall times per week. The hall space has to serve many functions – for
school dinners, fund-raising activities, television broadcasts, rehearsal space
for school concerts, the venue for visiting theatre groups – the list is endless.
All these functions may further limit the time available to young children in
the hall for physical education and of course physical education outdoors
is restricted by the vagaries of the British climate. Yet Armstrong and McManus
(1994) argue that positive attitudes to exercise are laid down in the early
years. Pre-National Curriculum, it was usual for primary teachers to have one
large apparatus lesson each week, and at least one other timetabled session
focused on dance/movement, small apparatus equipment or outdoor games.
In dance, HMI found in 1978 that three-fifths of the teachers of 7-year-olds
were using BBC programmes as the basis for dance/movement lessons. In
using balls, hoops, beanbags, etc. teachers generally expected children to
practise in pairs or in small groups the skills of throwing, catching, kicking
and hitting. In floor work in the hall space, teachers concentrated on developing children's awareness and skills in body movements such as balancing,
jumping, hopping, etc. Finally, HMI suggested that 'full advantage was not
always taken of fine weather' to use outdoor space for physical education.
It seems sensible that the physical education timetable should vary with the

seasons in the UK, but many schools continue doggedly with the same routines of timetabled hall and outdoor games activities winter and summer alike!

Many schools had no written guidelines for physical education (DES 1982a). It was thus hard for teachers to challenge the more able children or to ensure progression across all ability levels. HMI wrote (DES 1982a: para 2.161):

> There was evidence of some children being insufficiently challenged; they were unresponsive, sometimes lethargic, sometimes noisy and uncontrolled, and there was a lack of progression in the work.

The 1992 Order specified six areas of activity though which children should be given the opportunity to learn physical skills: games, athletics, dance, swimming, gymnastics and outdoor/adventurous activities. In the Revised Order for Key Stage 1 of 1995, these were reduced to three – games, gymnastics and dance. The School Curriculum Assessment Authority's End of Key Stage 1 Descriptors were (DFEE 1995: 11):

> Pupils plan and perform simple skills safely and show control in linking actions together. They improve their performance through practising their skills, working alone and with a partner. They talk about what they and others have done and are able to make simple judgements. They recognise and describe the changes that happen to their bodies during exercise.

Though the Department for Education recommended that young children should experience an hour of physical education each day, achieving this target is unlikely with the constraints of getting classes of young children changed, with little or no non-teaching assistant help, and using closely time-tabled hall and playground spaces. Ofsted inspection schedules included a fairly rigorous framework by which primary schools could evaluate their physical education curriculum. In general, Ofsted (1993d) findings were that the Physical Education Order was delivered at Key Stage 1 mostly to satisfactory or better levels.

An area of contention was the extent to which children should be encouraged to take part in competitive team games. In the 1980s, sport in maintained schools traditionally done in out of school hours was decimated by the formula devised for teachers' contracted hours of work. In the 1990s, a vociferous sports lobby, backed by John Major, Prime Minister, argued for a 'revival' in school sport. A National Junior Sports Programme was set up with commercial sponsorship: 4–9-year-old children were provided with 'Top Play' games and activities, staffed largely by volunteers, though often based in schools' premises. Such initiatives may augment the time young children can spend safely in energetic physical play.

A further difficulty has been the lack of attention given to training in physical education and about children's physical development in initial training programmes – as little as four hours of training in some PGCE courses. The physical changes a child's body goes through between the ages of 3 and 11 are dramatic and their consequences for the kinds of expectations primary teachers should have of what children can achieve at the two key stages are of vital importance. Wetton (1990) has listed some important 'facts' to help teachers plan skill acquisition programmes: for example, control of larger-muscle groups precedes control of the smaller (whole hands before fingers); 84 per cent of children assessed at the age of 4 years are right-handed, but 5–8-year-olds are often willing to use either or both hands in motor tasks; 'footedness' is established by the age of 5 years and seldom alters; though boys are able to throw further than girls because of more chances to prac-tise, there are no gender-linked anatomical or physiological differences in motor-ability potential.

Sugden (1990) argued that all the skills children will ever have are present in a 7-year-old. Early years teachers have always ranked physical devel-opment high in their education aims. We need a clear knowledge base delivered to teachers though initial and in-service training about the way in which children's motor skills, physical competence and body management develop through maturation and the role physical education should take in enhancing these processes. There is also a particular need to offer training to class teachers for working with children with physical impairments – sight or hearing loss or restricted physical mobility – as more of these children join mainstream education.

Religious education

Pre-National Curriculum, under the terms of the Education Act 1944, religious education had been the only obligatory subject in the school curriculum, a legacy of the Church of England's influence in the provision of schooling. There was a conscience clause where teachers might opt out of teaching religious education and parents might opt their children out of receiving religious education in voluntary aided or maintained schools. Local authorities were required to provide an Agreed Syllabus in religious education.

In 1982, HMI reported that 'popular Bible stories, often in a random order' or 'stories associated with the main Christian festivals' formed the basis of 'the traditional approach' to religious education teaching in many first schools. Indeed, although religious education figured in teachers' cur-riculum planning, there was little evidence of religious education teaching in many classrooms, and assemblies often became 'the main vehicle for reli-gious education in school'.

The trend in schools was to broaden teaching religion into teaching about religions, particularly in areas of the country where many faiths were rep-resented within the school community. In some schools, assemblies became almost entirely secular in character – opportunities to create and sustain a school culture, to share work across age ranges and classes, to invite parents to class assemblies based around the children's current topic work.

Under the terms of the Education Reform Act 1988, religious education was termed a 'basic' rather than foundation subject. Local Standing Advisory Councils on religious education (SACREs) were required to review existing Agreed Syllabuses and ensure that they 'reflect the fact that the religious traditions in Great Britain are in the main Christian whilst taking account of the teaching and practices of other principal religions represented in Great Britain'. Membership of the SACREs was to represent 'such Christian and other religious denominations as, in the opinion of the authority, will appropriately reflect the principal religious traditions in the area'. Draft model syllabuses were distributed to schools in September 1994: Model 1 – Living Faiths Today and Model 2 – Questions and Teachings. Some Key Stage 1 teachers have welcomed the guidance of the models; others regard them as overly prescriptive (see Bellett 1995).

Daily acts of collective worship were obligatory, the majority to be 'wholly or mainly of a broadly Christian character'. It was possible for schools with, for example, a predominantly Hindu or Muslim population, to apply to the SACREs for exemption from this requirement; however, no reference was made to accommodating the beliefs of a predominantly non-religious community. Parental rights to withdraw children from religious education, and teachers' rights to opt out of participating in or conducting it, were retained.

The fact that our laws require us to teach religious education within a secular school system is something of a surprise to many outsiders to the British education system. The fact that it was the *only* subject we were required by law to teach under the terms of the Education Act 1944 was a source of genuine amusement. The Government has tried to address the need to raise moral standards and reaffirm family values through the school curriculum. The strengthening of religious education has been part of this crusade. However, for many Key Stage 1 teachers, religious education is arbitrarily planned – Noah's Ark when the theme is water, the Good Samaritan when there is an upsurge in selfish behaviour – or simply allocated to the assembly times. A 'multifaith' element might be lobbed in through a coverage of 'celebrations' of Diwali or Chinese New Year. Brendon Watson (1987) characterized this approach as 'a "Cook's Tour" of religions'.

An alternative approach is to use young children's daily experiences of religions – family christenings, story-book imagery of places of worship, a pet 'going to heaven', prayers chanted in assemblies – as the source for discussion and at the same time to plan systematically to broaden their knowledge base by teaching them the principles underpinning religious rites and beliefs of perhaps one or two world faiths such as Islam or Judaism, perhaps drawing on the expertise in local communities. It must be in the interests of world peace and harmony to encourage a tolerance of religious diversity from an early age.

Overview of Key Stage 1 curriculum reforms

As Key Stage 1 classrooms were at the sharp end of curriculum reform, funding was suddenly allocated to research in infant classrooms in order to study the effects of the Government's policy changes on practice.

The Primary Assessment Curriculum and Experience (PACE) project based in Bristol, begun in 1989, examined the effects of the 1988 reforms on British infant and primary schools (Pollard *et al.* 1994). At Warwick, as part of the Teaching as Work Project, the effects of the first two years of the National Curriculum on thirty-five Key Stage 1 teachers were studied in detail (Evans *et al.* 1994). In Leeds, an evaluation of the initial stages of SATs for 7-year-olds was funded (Shorrocks *et al.* 1993). In Exeter, the attitudes of the parents and teachers of 150 Key Stage 1 children in the first two years of reform were closely monitored (Hughes *et al.* 1994). At last we are beginning to get a clearer view of what goes on in infant classrooms.

Evidence indicates that the introduction of the National Curriculum has resulted in more rigorous planning. Most primary schools, including nursery and Key Stage 1 classes, are using two-year cycles of topics or themes with attention paid to the curriculum focus or foci of each topic. Recognizing that primary teachers are not going to give up on topic planning, the Department for Education documentation began to identify features of 'successful' topic work. For example in *Primary Matters* (Ofsted 1994b) these were listed as: an agreed whole-school system of planning and monitoring, sharing the expertise of curriculum coordinators; a fit with National Curriculum programmes of study using single, or subject, or grouping of subjects emphasis; and clear reference to objectives and learning outcomes with assessment opportunities identified as curriculum activities are planned.

However carefully infant teachers tried to plan, the sheer overload of content in the unpiloted Orders nevertheless made the legislated curriculum 'unmanageable'. They had put in up to fifty-hour weeks to try to make the model work. High levels of teacher stress were reported in all the research studies cited above. The demands of the job ate into their personal lives. Their dedication was extraordinary. As a teacher in the Pollard study said: 'I don't believe a nun has any more dedication to her duties than I do' (Pollard *et al.* 1994: 90).

The debate about the efficacy of a subject-based curriculum for young children (see Aubrey 1994; Edwards and Knight 1994) rather than a developmentally appropriate curriculum (Blenkin and Kelly 1994) rages on. The author's belief is that a model curriculum for 3–5-year-olds is best based on the original broader 'areas of learning and experience' set out by HMI in 1985 (see p. 95). These seem to put appropriate emphasis on aspects of young children's learning that early years educators, carers and parents know to be the most important: linguistic and literary, mathematical, aesthetic and creative, physical, scientific, technological, moral and spiritual. The HMI areas

dovetail neatly enough into the subject framework of the Key Stage 1 curriculum, designed for the needs of 5–7-year-olds and which in turn provides
the foundation for cross-phase continuity and progression for the education
of 7 to 16-year-olds. Key Stage 1 teachers should not cut themselves off from
this continuum. The areas of experience provide a framework within which
adults can structure learning experiences/opportunities for the needs of the
'whole child'. How those are translated into content will depend on the shared
interests of each small (home) or large (school) community of learners.

Teachers have long practised the art of transforming paper models into
workable systems in their classrooms. Despite their claim to espouse a
process-dominated curriculum, the evidence is that early years teachers have
tended to use content – the 'what' rather than the 'how' to learn – as their
starting point for planning. However, the National Curriculum has the potential to provide a framework for planning for progression in both the
practical and procedural skills children need, the 'how' of the curriculum, and
a clearly defined content, the 'what' of the curriculum. It is the practical and
procedural that have always proved so hard, despite the rhetoric, for teachers
to plan for and assess. The content is comparatively easy to deal with.

We are required by law, however, to deliver a curriculum based on a
subject framework. This can be reconciled to teachers' preferred ways of
working at Key Stage 1. If we return to the process model of curriculum
planning set out in Figure 4 (p. 100), we can see how some examples of
statements of attainment from the programmes of study can be mapped
on to the diagram. Supposing 'Rocks' is taken as the starting-point for a 4–
6-week unit of work for a Year 2 class. The 'what' and the 'how' of the
curriculum can be mapped on to the model as shown in Figure 5. The specific statements of attainment used to illustrate the point are drawn from
the subjects, but the overall planning is cross-curricular. They are at level 2,
the level at which most 7-year-olds are expected to function after two years'
experience of the National Curriculum.

Rocks and stones might be collected by or made available to the children
for initial discussions. Visits might be made to sites including natural rocks
and manufactured building/construction materials (e.g. beach, countryside,
waste land, building site, shopping centre). From group discussion (English),
children may begin to consider ways of describing similarities and differences
in the materials they observe – colour, shape, surface texture, weight, size
(science). This could lead to children representing their findings in a variety
of ways – for example, observational drawings of stones and rocks in varying conditions and situations, descriptive writing, photographs, all of which
help develop the skills of observation and classification. From these sensory
explorations, children may move on to devising experiments involving fair
tests on rocks. What would happen if we tried to build with various materials,
weighed them, made marks on and with them, used them in conjunction
with other materials in a variety of conditions? Children might, for example,

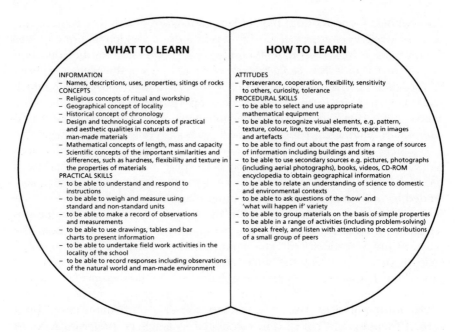

Figure 5 A content and process model for the National Curriculum
Source: Anning and Gates 1989: 27

see how many or what weight of bricks, pebbles, pumice stones, concrete, etc. would tear supermarket paper or plastic carrier bags. What happens to different kinds of rocks when they are put into water? How do they change in appearance and weight, and how much water do they displace? Results involving weight, length and displacement properties might be tabulated in mathematical form, initially in non-standard units, but, through collaboration and comparison of results, the need for standard units would soon emerge (mathematics).

Geographical and historical perspectives would emerge from a discussion of the sites. Reference books would be a valuable source of additional information. Story books and poetry chosen to complement the theme of rocks would stimulate the children's imaginations and perhaps lead to dance, drama, music and visual art. The study of carvings and shrines could also encourage children to talk about sacred rituals and forms of worship. The possibilities are endless, and using this cross-curricular approach it is possible to identify a wide range of aspects of learning from the National Curriculum programmes of study and incorporate them into the model (Anning and Gates 1989: 27).

The Revised National Curriculum Orders of 1995

In 1993, Sir Ron Dearing, a man who had been seen to be 'a safe pair of hands' when presiding over conflict at the Post Office, was appointed to oversee a review of the curriculum. A decision had already been made to collapse the two separate bodies responsible for the curriculum (the National Curriculum Council) and the assessment (School Examination and Assessment Council), into the School Curriculum and Assessment Authority (SCAA) to be based in London. Dearing began a process of extensive consultation with teachers. He was horrified to discover that primary teachers had to deal with 966 statements of attainment to deliver the statutory curriculum. A series of subject- and phase-specific working parties were set up and by May 1994 a draft, slimmed-down set of Orders – Sir Ron boasted that the primary curriculum was now 'one centimetre thin' – had been drawn up by SCAA. A day a week was freed up from the requirements of the Order to give more flexibility to teachers. The focus was to be on programmes of study as the basis of planning. Two hundred level descriptions replaced the 966 statements of attainment. Teachers were urged not to keep records of children based on fragmented 'checklist' systems but to ascribe children to whichever level description 'best fits' their pupils at a point of assessment. We have been promised a five-year moratorium on change.

In the Final Report (DFE 1993a: 31.4.12) the distinctive purpose of Key Stage 1 was defined as

> to lay the future foundations of learning by:
>   i. developing the basic skills in reading, writing, speaking, listening, number and information technology;
> ii. introducing young children to a broad range of interesting content spanning the subjects of the curriculum;
> iii. promoting positive attitudes to learning and helping young children to work and play together harmoniously.

Alternative models of the early childhood curriculum

It is also worth considering more radical models of curriculum design for young children. In the United States, Howard Gardner's seminal work on multiple intelligences (Gardner 1993a, b) has been promoted in Birmingham primary schools by the charismatic Chief Education Officer, Tim Brighouse. Gardner believes that the education system does not capitalize on the impressive cognitive and affective powers of a 5-year-old's mind, but instead alienates them by narrowing the curriculum to a narrow range of their intelligences, notably the linguistic and logical/mathematical, and ignoring six other important forms of intelligence – musical/auditory, visual/spatial, kinesthetic, interpersonal, intrapersonal and intuitive/spiritual.

Gardner's 'intelligences' map well on to the 'areas of learning and experience' identified by HMI in 1985.

In the United States, Keiran Egan (1991) has argued that we introduce children to 'the technologies' of writing and reading too early and in doing so depress their intellectual lives by forcing them to slow down to the rate at which they can function, using writing and reading, rather than an oral culture, for learning. Steiner would have approved strongly of Egan's argument. Egan argues that bipolar opposites and grand universal concepts – such as good/evil, big/small, hot/cold, right/wrong – should form the basis of curriculum design for young children. He criticizes current models as 'baby safe' and based on 'Disneyesque sentimentality'.

In Italy the work of Louis Malaguzzi (Edwards *et al.* 1993) in the city of Reggio Emilia has aroused international interest. Malaguzzi's approach to the education of 3–6-year-olds fosters their intellectual development through a systematic focus on symbolic representation. Children are encouraged to explore and make meaning of the world about them through all the natural 'languages' at their disposal, for example, words, movement, drawing, painting, building, sculpture, shadow play, dramatic play and music. Each school has a working artist's studio attached where children are encouraged to represent their thinking through a range of media.

In the UK, whilst Key Stage 1 teachers struggled to come to terms with the mechanics of implementing the National Curriculum, they have also been preoccupied with assessment at Key Stage 1, planning for children with special educational needs, and with the knock-on effects of the National Curriculum on the quality of education offered to children in nursery and reception classes. It is to these and other related issues that we turn in the final chapter.

6

Beyond the new ERA

Throughout the five years of the Education Reform Act there has been grow-ing hostility between educationists and policymakers. In 1993, the Secretary of State for Education, John Patten, launched a proposal to set up a one-year training scheme for non-graduates 'with a couple of A-levels' to teach children up to the age of 7. It was labelled 'The Mums' Army Scheme'. Early years educators reacted angrily. Doug McAvoy, General Secretary of the National Union of Teachers, summed up their outrage when he said that the proposed scheme was 'underpinned by a false and offensive assumption that teaching young children is easy, requiring fewer professional skills and less personal education' (reported in *The Independent*, 10 June 1993). Early childhood educators quickly and successfully lobbied parents and politicians for support to quash the initiative.

In the same year, English teachers – always formidable and articulate adversaries – rejected the Key Stage 3 SATs. In line with general trends in industrial legislation against unions in the UK in the 1980s, the strength of the teacher unions had been curtailed. Their power had also been lessened by public discontent about the industrial action taken by teachers in the 1970s. Nevertheless, in 1993 the unions rallied enough support to back both second-ary and primary teachers' refusals to carry out the SATs. Whilst 'in the wilder-ness' the unions had learned how to be more politically astute, and they won a court case on the grounds that the statutory requirements of assess-ment had resulted in 'unreasonable' workloads for teachers. Infant teachers had at last learned to say no.

Evidence from research projects on the effects of the educational reforms indicated that primary schools had parental support despite the media bash-ing to which they had been subjected. Hughes *et al.* (1994) reported that

85–95 per cent of parents were satisfied with their children's primary schools. *The Parent's Charter* (DES 1991c) emphasized their procedural rights as 'consumers' – choice of school, an annual written report on their child's progress, access to league table results in SATs of local schools and the annual governors' report, plus reports from the proposed four-year cycle of Ofsted inspections. The league tables were supposed to alert parents to the best schools to choose for their children. In fact, for many parents, a 'choice' of primary schools has always been illusory. There may be only one school within reasonable distance of their home and parents are increasingly fearful of letting children walk further than necessary on our unsafe streets. In any case, though keen that their children should do well, especially in the basics, they valued the 'human' features of a school – whether there was a welcoming atmosphere, good relationships between pupils, teachers and parents, whether their children were happy – rather more than its academic results. However Hughes' research indicated that they did want schools to provide clearer information about what their children were actually doing there and help in how they could best support them at home.

There is evidence that traditional school reports with vague statements – 'quite good' or 'shows interest in number' – and the feedback given by teachers at parents' evenings ('He's doing fine') were not helpful to parents. Since the introduction of the National Curriculum, the proliferation of jargon – attainment targets, levels, profile components – has made information given to parents even more opaque. As acronyms multiply, the restricted code amongst educators becomes increasingly inaccessible: we must not forget that for many people 'SATs', 'ATs', 'SCAA' and 'Ofsted' are meaningless strings of letters. Meaningless phrases generated by computer programmes such as SIMS as the basis for writing school reports are equally unhelpful to parents. Communicating with parents is an area for which there is a real staff development need – both at in-service and initial training levels.

Assessment

The innovative report on assessment in schools, the Task Group on Assessment and Testing Report (DES 1988a) presented a complex model for the assessment of pupils' progression through the National Curriculum. It was proposed that Teacher Assessments (TAs) should operate on a regular basis in classrooms alongside the formal assessment requirements, the Standard Assessment Tasks (SATs), controlled by the School Examination and Assessment Council (SEAC) and to be administered at the end of each key stage. The purposes of assessment were identified as:

- formative and diagnostic (both of which have a feed-forward function in planning appropriate learning experiences and activities for pupils)

- summative (which gives information about the overall achievements of pupils at the end of a defined period of learning)
- evaluative (which gives information about specific aspects of the work of a school or LEA).

The authors of the report made the following recommendations (DES 1988a: para 27):

> We recommend that the basis of the national assessment system be essentially formative, but designed also to indicate where there is a need for more detailed diagnostic assessment. At age 16, however, it should incorporate assessment with summative functions.

However, SATs began to dominate the political agenda and the status of TAs was systematically downgraded. Politicians believed that test results would identify poor schools and weak teachers in the state system. League tables of LEA results, compiled by finding the mean scores of each cohort of 7-year-olds in a school, were released and published in local and national newspapers even for the first supposedly unreported run of SATs in 1991.

Research and development groups were commissioned to design the SATs. They struggled to devise criterion-referenced tests for a teaching population conditioned into a norm-referenced mind set through years of administering standardized reading and mathematics tests and IQ tests for 11-year-olds (for the 11-plus selection system for secondary schooling). In the SATs models that emerged, assigning children to levels (most 7-year-olds were expected to achieve level 2 in subjects) was based on a complex system of assessing whether a child had 'achieved' on some precise indicators (for example, 'know and use addition and subtraction facts up to ten') and some excessively imprecise (for example, 'participate in a presentation'). Several attainment target level scores were aggregated within profile components in each subject (for example, writing, spelling and handwriting in the writing profile component of the English Order) and then profile component scores were further aggregated (for example, Speaking and Listening, Reading and Writing in English) to produce an overall subject level score. Inevitably, harking back to their traditional norm-referenced testing systems, teachers began to speak about a 'level 2 sort of child'.

Despite clear guidelines given by SEAC, the way in which SATs were administered by class teachers varied. Most Year 2 teachers had additional teacher support for the half-term in which the tests were carried out. Some teachers gave more 'help' to children than others (see Shorrocks *et al.* 1993). It became clear that social background, birth date, first language and, most hearteningly for pre-school interests, the effects of nursery education, all had effects on the SAT results of 7-year-olds. Summer-born children achieved lower levels (unless, as in Wales, tests were administered in their first language), social background variables depressed results and children who had attended nurseries (especially in inner cities) scored higher in English and mathematics, but not in science.

Teachers were also required to maintain a system of TAs and report children's levels of attainment to parents annually. There was an explosion of detailed, time-consuming, often ticklist-based record keeping systems (Evans *et al.* 1994) described by HMI as 'fervent but unfocused' (DES 1990b). It proved difficult for teachers to find a way to feedback the information they gathered directly and productively into planning the next set of curriculum activities. There was simply too much fragmentary detail recorded as attainment target levels for too many children.

In 1992, despite politicians' assurances that the first rounds of trialling the Key Stage 1 SATs would be unreported, the Government reneged on this commitment and published the results. The Tories were quick to criticize high-spending inner-city local authorities where results were low. Teachers felt betrayed.

Year by year, mastery statements in English and mathematics were tinkered with by test designers directed by politicians and their policymakers. Children could be assigned to different levels in a subject on the basis of apparently trivial criterion changes. For example, in the 1991 pilot SATs, mastery level for level 2 in writing required using 'at least two capital letters and at least two full stops' and 'more than half and at least five sentences correctly punctuated' for level 3. Only 38 per cent of the sample 7-year-olds met the level 2 criteria and 18 per cent level 3. A slight shift in the wording of the statements of attainment could radically alter these percentages. Such shifts were made year by year by the test designers. Thus comparisons of annual results were spurious. Yet the media conducted a relentless campaign about 'falling standards' in schools. Their criticisms were aimed directly at so-called 'poor teaching'. Anxious to defend themselves, infant teachers began to demand baseline testing for children at school entry (see Cline and Blatchford 1994) so that parents would be clear about their children's starting points as they entered Key Stage 1. An early and influential model was Sheila Wolfendale's (1989) booklet, *All About Me*, for completion by parents and care or education workers with the child.

After the Dearing Review, arrangements for testing 7-year-olds were 'simplified'. Only English and mathematics SATs were retained using a mixture of classroom tasks and paper and pencil tests covering reading, writing, spelling and number work. At level 2, three subgrades (A–C) were assigned to give greater definition to the assessments. Able children were able to take Key Stage 2 level 4 tests. Only these papers were marked externally. Year 2 class teachers, unlike their Year 6 Key Stage 2 colleagues, marked all other tests themselves. Four days per class of supply cover teaching was costed into LEA Grants for Education Support and Training (GEST) bids for the implementation of post-Dearing SATs, but these 'days' also had to provide time for teachers to be trained in the new testing procedures. From the GEST grant

LEAs also had to find the costs of auditing SATs in their areas by visits to schools and scrutiny of marked papers. In any case they had to pay 40 per cent of the total costs of implementing and monitoring the revised SATs to attract a 60 per cent government grant.

Special educational needs

The Education Act 1981 redefined the role that LEAs and schools were to play in the education of children with special educational needs. The Act reflected recommendations within the influential Warnock Report (DES 1978b) that as far as possible children with special educational needs should be integrated with rather than separated from pupils in mainstream schools in the United Kingdom. The Warnock Report indicated that there was likely to be a notional 2 per cent of the school population whose needs were sufficiently specialized to warrant a process defined as 'statementing'. The framework within which children should be 'statemented' was set out within Circular 1/83 (DES 1983). The process involved full parental consultation and was usually coordinated within LEAs by educational psychologists. The LEA was required to provide resources to meet the particular defined needs of statemented children.

A larger group of children, a further 18 per cent of the school population according to the Warnock Report, were expected to qualify as having 'a learning difficulty which called for special educational provision to be made' (para 1 (1) of the Education Act 1981). The Act (Section 1 (2)) defined a child over 5 years old who has learning difficulties as one who has

> a significantly greater difficulty in learning than the majority of children his age; or he has a disability which either prevents or hinders him from making use of educational facilities of a kind generally provided in schools, within the area of the local authority concerned, for children of his age.

The implementation of these policies was patchy. It was dependent upon both LEA commitment and school expertise (Hegarty et al. 1981). Some LEAs invested money and time in screening procedures across the whole population to identify children who qualified for additional resourcing (see for example ILEA's Classroom Observation Profile for infant teachers, Goldstein et al. 1984). Once children had been identified as having special needs, LEAs adopted a range of strategies to accommodate those needs. For some children whose needs could not be met in mainstream schooling, special school placements were attached to units within schools so that they could have specialized teaching for some of the school day, but were 'partially integrated' into the mainstream school for some aspects of school timetabling. In other situations additional teaching staff were attached to schools to work

alongside mainstream teachers, either within the classroom or by withdraw-
ing groups or individual children for specialized support. For particular children with defined physical needs (such as hearing or visual impairment or
spina bifida) or behaviour difficulties (such as hyperactivity, aggression or
severe withdrawal symptoms) or with acute learning difficulties, full-time
non-teaching assistants were employed to work with the children in a mainstream classroom.

Though most infant teachers were sympathetic towards the ideology of
integration enshrined in the Warnock Report, in practice, at school and classroom operational level, there were problems in implementing the ideology.
The first difficulty arose right at the identification point of children's special
educational needs from teachers' reluctance (already referred to in Chapter
3) to label children as 'different'. This reluctance is particularly acute when
the label implies 'of lower ability' – hence the range of euphemisms teachers
adopt in describing children, 'takes a long time to catch on', 'a slow learner'.
However, to go as far as to 'statement' children is perceived as assigning
an extreme label to them. Therefore there has been a tendency for the staff
to delay putting into motion the statementing procedures until the final year
of infant schooling. The result of the delay, though well intentioned, meant
that children were deprived of specialist help and additional resources during the first three formative years of schooling. On the whole, teachers have
proved to be more ready to request statementing procedures for those children whose behaviour is so disruptive that they make life extremely difficult
for both the teacher and the rest of the class. Physical disabilities are also
quickly identified and attended to. It is the children with learning difficulties
whom the teachers feel squeamish about identifying.

It is also fair to say that in some LEAs there has been so little specialist
support and resources made available to children with special educational
needs, that headteachers have simply given up the unequal battle to have
their rightful allocation of additional staffing or capitation as specified within
the legal framework of the Act. Consequently, they have delayed putting
into motion complicated and time-consuming statementing procedures.

If schools are assigned additional staff to support children with special
educational needs, there are particular management issues to be addressed
so that maximum benefits can be gained from their presence. The management issues arise at both school and classroom level. A headteacher must
decide if it is really legitimate to assign non-teaching assistants who have
been employed to support children with special educational needs to make
the coffee and tea for the teachers or to spend hours triple-mounting children's art work. A class teacher must learn the skills, rarely acknowledged
within initial or in-service training, of working collaboratively with other
professionals. They must also recognize that it is not good enough to simply
allow the pace of teaching/learning interactions to slow down as extra adult
help is fed into a classroom. In other words, the extra help needs a complete

rethink rather than replication of a style of classroom management. The strategies for effective team teaching need careful and intelligent consideration both at personal and operational levels.

The question of specialized expertise in the education of children with special needs is another problem within infant schools. Many LEAs have encouraged a policy whereby every school has a coordinator for special needs. Their role, as with curriculum specialists, is to offer up-to-date expertise and advice to all classroom teachers and to work alongside teachers to model effective teaching, classroom management and record-keeping strategies. The problem is that there have been few in-service courses on offer to keep such coordinators informed of the vast range of specialist knowledge that used to be centred on the now rapidly diminishing special schools.

The National Curriculum Council stressed that from September 1990 all children were entitled to participate in the National Curriculum (NCC 1989d). They urged minimal use of the arrangements, through Sections 17–19 of the Educational Reform Act, for exempting children: a process called 'disapplication'. If it was necessary to exempt children from the statutory requirements of curriculum coverage and assessment procedures, disapplication was to be seen as a temporary arrangement, not as a fixed category for children, and where disapplication was agreed, an alternative curriculum for the children must be specified. It was recognized that some children might take more time to progress through the curriculum. On the other hand, gifted children might move very quickly through the levels of attainment for certain subjects or at certain times of their school careers. It was suggested that children might work with a class of older or younger children for some subjects if this seemed appropriate, although it was stressed that there was no intention of keeping children 'down' or moving children 'up' on the basis of results in formal assessment only.

In 1994, a new Code of Practice on the Identification and Assessment of Special Educational Needs was established (DFE 1994a). Every school was required to publish policies and procedures for their children defined as having special educational needs. They must identify a SEN coordinator, a SENCO, whose responsibility was to oversee these arrangements. Five stages, with time scales specified, were defined for the processes of identifying and possibly statementing children with special educational needs. Parents must be involved at every stage. A *Citizen's Charter* guide for parents was published (DFE 1994b) setting out the school and LEA requirements under the code and listing voluntary sector agencies from which parents might seek support. For dissatisfied parents, regional special needs tribunals were set up at which SENCOs were likely to be asked to give evidence. Bowers (1994) predicted that tribunals were likely to deal with 700–1000 cases in the first year, though there was evidence that claims for additional support for dyslexic children dominated the first rounds of tribunals in 1995.

In 1995 the Government provided £7.3 million for the training of SENCOs, but hard-pressed LEAs had to find 40 per cent of these costs. In an article published in the *Times Educational Supplement*, Peter Mittler (1994), then Professor with Special Educational Needs Responsibilities at Manchester University, argued that the full costs of staff development for coordinators and teachers working with 'priority groups', children with sensory impairments, severe learning difficulties, or emotional and behavioural difficulties, should be met by central government. He also argued that all those with 'significant' SEN responsibilities should be required to have additional qualifications, as is currently the case with teachers working with children with visual and hearing impairments.

The most pressing problem for primary teachers in responding to the code is lack of time. Lewis (1992) reported that before the new code was introduced, primary teachers claimed that the demands of the National Curriculum and related assessment had reduced the time they could spend with children with special educational needs. Without additional staffing and related funding, it is difficult to see how they can conform to the additional requirements of the Code of Practice.

The education of under-fives

In the document, *A Framework for the Primary Curriculum*, sent by NCC to all primary schools, there was a clear statement that 'To establish artificial boundaries between the education of children under five and that received by five year olds would be both counterproductive and an opportunity lost' (NCC 1989a: para 4.5). We know that 25 per cent of under-fives are in mostly part-time nursery schools or nursery classes, but access for pre-fives to nursery education is dependent on huge variations in LEA provision. Over 50 per cent of 4-year-olds in maintained schools are admitted early into reception classes (sometimes taken out of nursery classes while they are still 4, sometimes admitted straight from home or playgroup provision) (source National Commission on Education 1993). Thus the UK school starting age is rapidly being established at a startling 4 years of age! HMI have stated that evidence they have collected from schools indicates that 'Taking all factors into account, children under five in nursery schools and classes generally receive a broader, better balanced education than those in primary classes' (HMI 1989a). In a survey of the quality of education for 4-year-olds in primary classes, they reported that 'For the majority of four year olds . . . there is an overemphasis on some aspects of the basic skills of literacy and numeracy' and 'The educational purposes of play and investigative work are not sufficiently understood and provided for' (HMI 1989b). HMI also indicated that very few of the teachers they observed had been trained to work with the under-fives.

By 1993, HMI reported that 80 per cent of what they had observed in reception classes was 'satisfactory or better' and that there was 'a better match of work to pupils' ability than is generally the case in primary classes' (DFE 1993c: 7). On the whole, reception-class teachers felt that the National Curriculum had 'broadened or enhanced their approach to the curriculum' (ibid.: 14). Still disappointing, however, was the quality of learning through play. 'Fewer than half of the teachers fully exploited the educational potential of play' (ibid.: 10).

Whether the under-fives are in nursery or reception classes, it makes sense for staff to be familiar with the requirements of the Key Stage 1 National Curriculum. Many of the statements of attainment for level 1 are well within the achievement of some 4-year-olds, and indeed some 3-year-olds. For example, the level 1 descriptor of the science Attainment Target, Experimental and Investigative Science, in the 1994 Science Order states that children should be able to 'describe simple features of objects, living things and events they observe, communicating their findings in simple ways, such as talking about their work or through drawings or simple charts'. Neither Maria Montessori nor Susan Isaacs would have had misgivings about this descriptor as the basis for objectives for their nursery curricula. The 1994 English Order descriptor for Attainment Target 1, Speaking and Listening, states that pupils should be able to

> talk about matters of immediate interest. They listen to others and usually respond appropriately. They convey simple meanings to a range of listeners, speaking audibly, and begin to extend their ideas or accounts by providing some detail.

In the 1994 Mathematics Order, the level 1 descriptor for Attainment Target 3, Space, Shape and Measures, states that

> When working with 3-D and 2-D shapes, pupils use everyday language to describe properties and positions. They measure and order objects using direct comparison, and order events.

Both these descriptors reflect the kind of objectives most nursery and reception-class teachers would encourage their pupils to be working towards.

The vital proviso, however, is that the *methods* by which children should be encouraged towards achievements should be based on 'children's interests and appetite for play, building upon these to achieve educational objectives which complement, and have much in common with, the curriculum which they will receive in later years' (HMI 1989a: para 65). We have explored elsewhere in the book the dangers of 'too formal, too soon' approaches to early education. Nor do we want 3–4-year-olds studying what are strangely defined as pre-reading, pre-maths or pre-science in a subject-specific way. The NCC document (NCC 1989a), however, makes the important distinction between the inappropriateness of pre-fives being offered 'the curriculum – from the point of view of the learner – as separate subjects', and stresses at the same time that the *teacher* be aware of what strands underlie the various collaborative, exploratory, manipulative and imaginative play situations in which the pupils engage. In this way, a teacher can 'use the spontaneity and enthusiasm of young children to provide starting points for further work' while at the same time establishing a sense of continuity and progression within the framework prescribed by the National Curriculum.

The evaluations of the beginnings of the National Curriculum have heightened awareness of the difficulty of defining 'good practice' in the education of 3–5-year-olds. The different forms of educational provision offered to our pre-fives reflect the confused results of the uneven, unequal and unfair funding arrangements and resources provided by the local authorities across the country or dictated by the *laissez-faire* approach towards nursery education of central government policies. Moreover, different beliefs and practices emanating from past policies and ideologies in early years educational and childcare provision are reflected in the confusion amongst teachers of under-fives as to appropriate curriculum models they should be offering. In many reception classes, 4-year-olds are being offered a pale reflection of the British nursery school tradition of structured play provision and practical or individual activities in baking, sand-and-water play, craftwork, table-top toys, etc. – a tradition which sits uncomfortably in infant classrooms, as we have indicated, alongside the elementary school tradition of teaching the basics of literacy and numeracy. The US tradition of 'cognitively orientated' curricula such as High/Scope coexists uneasily with the Developmental Curriculum with its emphasis on children moving freely around self-chosen practical learning activities. Some nursery classes attached to primary schools have moved to a thematic approach to planning to fit in with the demands of whole-school planning. In the daycare centres, the staff place heavy emphasis on the physical and social well-being of the child, with perhaps the most structured teaching time being devoted to language development. Children are likely to meet any one or a combination of these curriculum models before they filter into the National Curriculum at five. Or their parents may decide to exercise their right to keep the child at home until their fifth birthday.

If we have legislated for an entitlement to a National Curriculum at five, however, should there not also be an entitlement to a recognized quality of education for pre-fives? SCAA (DFEE 1996a) have produced a set of 'desirable outcomes' for children attending any form of pre-school provision under the headings: personal and social development; language and literacy; mathematics; knowledge and understanding of the world; and physical and creative development. For a critique of the pre-school curriculum set out in the document, see Anning (1995b). The education of under-fives has become an all-party focus of political interest and potential vote-catcher. In *Learning to Succeed* (National Commission on Education 1993: 132), a visionary report sponsored by the Paul Hamlyn Foundation on the future of education in the

UK, the authors argued for 'a statutory requirement on local authorities to ensure high-quality, publicly funded nursery education for all 3- and 4-year-olds whose parents wish it'. The Tory policy is to encourage 'diversity' in provision and a voucher system offering parents of all 4-year-olds £1100 towards payment for 'a nursery place' was piloted in four LEAs in 1996. Complications arising from this market-led approach to nursery provision are predictable. Refunds accruing to LEAs currently offering reception class places for 4-year-olds are simply recycled as a costly paper exercise into their current school funding arrangements. The likelihood is that private nursery day care and education will raise their fees, since most better-off parents are clearly able to pay the current going rate for pre-school provision without a subsidy. If the independent sector were to put the additional income gained from the voucher scheme into training for their staff, that would be beneficial to the children, because at present many staff employed in independent nursery provision are not formally qualified.

In 1989, the Children Act defined the duties placed on social services to monitor the quality of care for the under-fives. There is evidence that children most at risk of a 'poor start' to school (and consequently the rigours of the National Curriculum) are those from 'disadvantaged' homes (Mortimore and Blackstone 1982) and/or those who attend day nursery provision (Osborn and Milbank 1987). How then can we ensure that there is, as far as possible, equal access to the kinds of pre-school education which will give all our children equal entitlement to a good start to schooling?

In the first instance, within the UK there must be more research into the long-term effects of different types of pre-school provision on the educational achievements of children. With hard data, rather than vague aspirations, at their disposal, the various vested interests dealing with under-fives – playgroup associations, social services, local education authorities, private daycare and nursery education providers – might be able to work within a framework where good quality pre-school education and care are clearly defined and exemplified. A start has already been made in promoting a multidimensional approach to quality indicators by the National Children's Bureau. The Bureau has published a range of influential material for some time, but recent publications from the Under-Fives Unit have been particularly helpful: *Working With Children: Developing a Curriculum for the Early Years* (Drummond et al. 1989) and *Young Children in Group Day Care. Guidelines for Good Practice* (National Children's Bureau 1991). The DFEE have produced a set of guidelines entitled *Next Steps* outlining how vouchers, quality assurance, and inspection arrangements for ensuring that the 'desirable outcomes' set out by the SCAA are to be achieved (DFEE 1996b). The inspection of all providers expected to register for voucher status is likely to be a costly and cumbersome exercise.

Ofsted inspection instruments for primary schools include a comprehensive and well-principled schedule for the inspection of nursery classes. The recommendations of the Rumbold Committee, *Starting with Quality* (DES

1990c) for resourcing good-quality educational provision for 3- and 4-year-olds were a staff:pupil ratio of 1:13, preferably half-day attendance and a curriculum 'which emphasises first-hand experiences and which views play and talk as powerful mediums for learning' (ibid.: 35: 13e). It is to be hoped that these quality indicators are also included in pre-school providers' criteria for delivering and resourcing effective pre-school education.

Initial training is undergoing a radical restructuring to comply with the new Government regulations for school-based training, set out for primary courses in Circular 14/93 (DFE 1993b). The policy requires 'transfer of resources from the institutions to their partnership schools' (ibid.: 6.37). However, there is a tension between increased demands for training Key Stage 1 teachers in National Curriculum subject knowledge and the capacity or range of curriculum expertise a small primary school might have to offer for such training. It is also important that initial training courses for the education of 3–7-year-olds acknowledge the particularities of working with a multiprofessional approach. Teachers of young children must know how to collaborate with, supervise and train support workers, and be taught the skills of professional collaboration with social workers, health visitors, day care staff and educational welfare officers. In many Higher Education-based initial training courses for teachers of young children, these issues are scarcely addressed. A bonus for students in the proposed school-based training model is that many school staff are able to model and teach this expertise for intending teachers.

Towards the twenty-first century

The issues of assessment, special educational needs, a curriculum for the under-fives and training teachers to teach 3–8-year-olds are just some of the many concerns preoccupying infant teachers as they struggle to adapt to the new demands put upon them by a decade of reforms. The levels of stress in infant schools are high. There simply is too much coming at the teachers too fast. Nevertheless, because of their commitment to the children, Key Stage 1 teachers are struggling to keep abreast of the changes demanded of them. There is a great resilience there. Early years teachers are however particularly alarmed by the politicizing of education. They feel threatened by the military and business-world jargon – audits, cost-effectiveness, consumers, performance indicators, loss leaders, commando-style units for failing schools – which is increasingly and, they feel, inappropriately applied to the education of children. It is designed to intimidate.

We should not be afraid of changes. We have already seen that classroom practice is immensely resistant to changes initiated from outside rather than inside the classroom. There is the story of a group of Cherokee Indians who were baffled when some well-meaning American administrators were anxiously planning to protect from the ravages of the weather the totem pole they had newly carved for an American Indian Cultural Centre. The Cherokees simply said that it did not matter if the totem pole weathered. First of all, that was the way totem poles were. Second, when the pole began to crumble away they would always know how to carve another one, a variation perhaps on their newly finished design.

The theme of the changes and continuities in infant schooling explored in this book could be represented by the metaphor of the totem pole, open to the effects of forces from outside, but at the heart belonging to the craft knowledge and quiet confidence of the generations of Indians who had gone before. In the end, it is the teachers who form the heart of any educational system. What matters is that they are not afraid to address in an analytical way the kinds of dilemmas identified in this book, and to create new ways of working which maintain a respect for their own culture, traditions, and craft knowledge. Infant teachers should be given the personal and professional space they deserve to do exactly that.

References

Adams, M. J. (1990) *Beginning to Read,* Cambridge, Mass.: MIT Press.

Alexander, R. J. (1984) *Primary Teaching,* Eastbourne: Holt, Rinehart & Winston.

Alexander, R. J. (1992) *Policy and Practice in Primary Education,* London: Routledge.

Alexander, R. J., Wilcocks, J. and Kinder, K. (1989) *Changing Primary Practice,* Lewes: Falmer Press.

Anning, A. (1987) 'An analysis of primary teachers' understanding of how children learn and its relationship to their teaching strategies', unpublished MEd thesis, University of Leicester.

Anning, A. (1988) 'Teachers' theories about children's learning', in J. Calderhead (ed.) *Teachers' Professional Development,* Lewes: Falmer Press.

Anning, A. (1994) 'Dilemmas and opportunities of a new curriculum: design and technology with young children', *International Journal of Technology and Design Education* 4: 155–77.

Anning, A. (ed.) (1995a) *A National Curriculum for the Early Years,* Buckingham: Open University Press.

Anning, A. (1995b) *The Key Stage Zero Curriculum: A Response to the SCAA Draft Proposals on Pre-School Education,* London: ATL publications.

Anning, A. and Billett, S. (1995) 'Four year olds in infant classes in small and large classes', in P. Broadhead (ed.) *BERA Dialogues,* Clevedon: Multilingual Matters.

Anning, A. and Gates, J. (1989) 'The National Curriculum and good infant practice', *Education 3–13* 17, 3: 25–8.

Anning, A., Brown, D., Galton, M. and Kinch, T. (1986) 'Attitudes and the infant teacher: conflicts in society', *Child Education* June: 15–22.

Argyris, C. and Schön, D. A. (1976) *Theory in Practice: Increasing Professional Effectiveness,* San Francisco, Calif.: Jossey-Bass.

Armstrong, N. and McManus, A. (1994) 'Children's fitness and physical activity: a challenge for PE', *British Journal of Physical Education* 21, 1: 6–10.

Ashton, P., Kneen, P., Davies, F. and Holley, B. (1975) *The Aims of Primary Education:*

A Study of Teachers' Opinions, London and Basingstoke: Macmillan Education for Schools Council.

Asoko, H. (1995) 'Science', in A. Anning (ed.) *A National Curriculum for the Early Years*, Buckingham: Open University Press.

APU (Assessment of Performance Unit) (1984) *Science in Schools Age 11: Report No 4*, London: HMSO.

Athey, C. (1980) 'Parental involvement in nursery education', *Early Childhood* 1, 3, December: 2–8.

Aubrey, C. (1994) *The Role of Subject Knowledge in the Early Years of Schooling*, London: Falmer Press.

Auld, R. (1976) *William Tyndale Junior and Infants Schools Public Inquiry*, London: ILEA.

Bamberger, J. (1991) *The Mind Behind the Musical Ear*, Cambridge, Mass.: Harvard University Press.

Barrett, G. (1986) *Starting School; An Evaluation of the Experience*, School of Education, University of East Anglia.

Barrie, J. M. (1915) *Peter Pan and Wendy; The Story of Peter Pan extracted from Peter and Wendy*, illustrated by P. D. Bedford, authorized school edn., London: Henry Frowde/Hodder & Stoughton.

Barrow, R. (1984) *Giving Teaching Back to Teachers*, Brighton: Wheatsheaf.

Bassey, M. (1978) *Nine Hundred Primary School Teachers*, Windsor: NFER.

Beard, R. (ed.) (1995) *Rhyme, Reading and Writing*, London: Hodder & Stoughton.

Bellett, E. (1995) 'Religious Education', in A. Anning (ed.) *A National Curriculum for the Early Years*, Buckingham: Open University Press.

Bennett, D. (1987) 'The aims of teachers and parents for children in their first year at school', in *Four Year Olds in School: Policy and Practice*, NFER/SCDC Report, Windsor: NFER.

Bennett, J. (1979) *Learning to Read with Picture Books*, Gloucester: Thimble Press.

Bennett, N. (1976) *Teaching Styles and Pupil Progress*, London: Open Books.

Bennett, N. and Kell, J. (1989) *A Good Start: Four Year Olds in Infant Schools*, Oxford: Basil Blackwell.

Bennett, N., Desforges, C., Cockburn, A. and Wilkinson, B. (1984) *The Quality of Pupil Learning Experiences*, London: Lawrence Erlbaum.

Bennett, S. N., Wragg, E. C., Carre, C. G. and Carter, D. G. (1992) 'A longitudinal study of primary teachers' perceived competence and concerns about National Curriculum implementation', *Research Papers in Education* 7: 53–78.

Bereiter, C. and Engelmann, S. (1966) *Teaching Disadvantaged Children in Pre-School*, Englewood Cliffs, NJ: Prentice-Hall.

Berlak, A. and Berlak, H. (1981) *Dilemmas of Schooling: Teaching and Social Change*, London: Methuen.

Bernstein, B. B. (1971, 1975) *Class, codes and controls*, Vols. 1 and 3, London: Routledge & Kegan Paul.

Blenkin, G. V. and Kelly, A. V. (eds) (1987) *Early Childhood Education: A Developmental Curriculum*, London: Paul Chapman.

Blenkin, G. V. and Kelly, A. V. (1994) *The National Curriculum and Early Learning: An Evaluation*, London: Paul Chapman.

Blyth, J. E. (1984) *Place and Time with Children Five to Nine*, Beckenham: Croom Helm.

Blyth, W. A. L. (1976) *Place, Time and Society 8–13: Curriculum Planning in History, Geography and Social Science*, Glasgow and Bristol: Collins/ESL.

Blyth, W. A. L. (1984) *Development, Experience and Curriculum in Primary Education*, Beckenham: Croom Helm.

Board of Education (1931) *Report of the Consultative Committee on the Primary School*, Hadow Report, London: HMSO.

Board of Education (1933) *Report of the Consultative Committee on Infant and Nursery Schools*, Hadow Report, London: HMSO.

Bowers, T. (1994) 'A trying time?', *Special Children* 75: 9–10.

Brearley, M., Bott, R., Davies, M. P., Glynne-Jones, M. L., Hitchfield, E. M., Johnson, J. E. L. and Tamburrini, J. R. (1969) *Fundamentals in the First School*, Oxford: Basil Blackwell.

Brittan, E. M. (1976) 'Multicultural education 2. Teacher opinion and aspects of school life. Part One: changes in curriculum and school organisation', *Educational Research* 18, 2: 96–116.

Brook, A. and Driver, R. (1984) 'The development of pupils' understanding of the physical characteristics of air across the age range 5–16 years, Leeds', *Children's Learning in Science Project*, CSSME, University of Leeds.

Brown, G. and Desforges, C. (1979) *Piaget's Theory: A Psychological Critique*, London: Routledge & Kegan Paul.

Browne, N. and France, P. (1986) 'Only cissies wear dresses: a look at sexist talk in the nursery', in G. Weiner (ed.) *Just a Bunch of Girls*, Milton Keynes: Open University Press.

Bruner, J. S. (1960) *The Process of Education*, Cambridge, Mass.: Harvard University Press.

Bruner, J. S. (1966) *Towards a Theory of Instruction*, Cambridge, Mass.: Harvard University Press.

Bruner, J. S. (1972) 'Functions of plays', in Bruner (ed.) *Play*, Harmondsworth: Penguin.

Bruner, J. S. (1980) *Under Five in Britain*, Oxford Pre-School Research Project, London: Grant McIntyre.

Bruner, J. S. and Haste, H. (eds) (1987) *Making Sense: The Child's Construction of the World*, London: Methuen.

Bryant, P. and Bradley, L. (1985) *Children's Reading Problems*, Oxford: Blackwell.

Buxton, L. G. (1982) 'Emotional responses to symbolism', *Visible Language* XVI, 3: 215–20.

Campbell, R. J. (1985) *Developing the Primary School Curriculum*, London: Holt, Rinehart & Winston.

Campbell, R. J. and Neill, S. R. StJ. (1994) *Curriculum Reform at Key Stage One: Teacher Commitment and Policy Failure*, Harlow: Longman for the Association of Teachers and Lecturers.

CACE (Central Advisory Council for Education, England) (1967) *Children and their Primary Schools*, Plowden Report, London: HMSO.

Chazan, M., Laing, A. and Harper, G. (1987) *Teaching Five to Eight Year Olds*, Oxford: Basil Blackwell.

Chomsky, N. (1976) *Reflections on Language*, London: Fontana.

Clark, M. M. (1994) *Young Literacy Learners*, Leamington Spa: Scholastic Publications.

Clarricoates, K. (1980) 'The importance of being Ernest, Emma, Tom, John . . .', in R. Deem (ed.) *Schooling for Women's Work*, London: Routledge & Kegan Paul.

Clay, M. (1975) *What Did I Write?*, London: Heinemann Educational.

Clay, M. (1979) *Reading: The Patterning of Complex Behaviour,* London: Heinemann Educational.

Cleave, S. and Brown, S. (1989) *Meeting their Needs,* Windsor: NFER/Nelson.

Cleave, S. and Brown, S. (1991a) *Quality Matters,* Windsor: NFER/Nelson.

Cleave, S. and Brown, S. (1991b) *Early to School: Four Year Olds in Infant Classes,* Windsor: NFER/Nelson.

Cleave, S. and Sharp, C. (1986) *The Arts: A Preparation to Teach,* Slough: NFER.

Clement, R. (1993) *The Readiness of Primary Schools to Teach the National Curriculum Art,* Plymouth: Rolle Faculty of Arts and Education, University of Plymouth.

Clift, P., Cleave, S. and Griffin, M. (1980) *The Aims, Role and Deployment of Staff in the Nursery,* Report of the National Foundation of Educational Research in England and Wales, Windsor: NFER.

Cline, T. and Blatchford, P. (1994) 'Baseline assessment. Selecting a method of assessing children at school entry', *Education 3–13* 22, 3, October: 10–15.

Coe, J. (1966) 'The junior school: approaches to non-streaming', *Forum* 8: 76–9.

Constable, H. (1995) 'Design and technology and information technology', in A. Anning (ed.) *A National Curriculum for the Early Years,* Buckingham: Open University Press.

Copple, C., Sigal, I. E. and Saunders, R. (1979) *Educating the Young Thinker: Classroom Strategies for Cognitive Growth,* New York: D. Van Nostrand.

Corsaro, W. A. (1979) ' "We're friendly, right?" Children's use of access rituals in a nursery school', *Language in Society* 8: 315–36.

Cowie, H. (ed.) (1984) *The Development of Children's Imaginative Writing,* London: Croom Helm.

Cox, C. B. and Dyson, A. C. (eds) (1971) *The Black Papers in Education,* London: Davis-Poynter.

Cox, C. B. and Boyson, R. (eds) (1977) *Black Paper 1977,* London: Temple-Smith.

Csiksentmihalyi, M. T. (1979) 'The concept of flow in play', in B. Sutton Smith (ed.) *Play and Learning,* New York: Gardner Press.

Curtis, S. J. and Boultwood, M. E. A. (1962) *An Introductory History of English Education since 1800,* 2nd edn, London: University Tutorial Press.

Davies, B. (1989) *Frogs and Snails and Feminist Tails: Pre-School Children and Gender,* Sydney: Allen and Unwin.

Davies, C. (1994) 'I can't teach music – so we just sing', in C. Aubrey (ed.) *The Role of Subject Knowledge in the Early Years of Schooling,* London: Falmer Press.

Dawson, D. (1995) 'Music', in A. Anning (ed.) *A National Curriculum for the Early Years,* Buckingham: Open University Press.

Dearden, R. F. (1968) *The Philosophy of Primary Education,* London, Routledge & Kegan Paul.

De Lyon, H. and Migniuolo, F. (eds) (1989) *Women Teachers,* Milton Keynes: Open University Press.

Department for Education (1992) *Education Observed. The Implementation of the Curricular Requirements of ERA: An Overview by HM Inspectorate of the Second Year,* London: HMSO.

Department for Education (1993a) *The National Curriculum and its Assessment: Final Report,* London: School Curriculum and Assessment Authority.

Department for Education (1993b) *The Initial Training of Primary School Teachers: New Criteria for Course Approval,* London: HMSO.

Department for Education (1993c) *First Class. The Standards and Quality of Education in Reception Classes,* London: HMSO.

Department for Education (1994a) *Code of Practice on the Identification and Assessment of Special Educational Needs,* London: Central Office of Information.

Department for Education (1994b) *Special Educational Needs. A Guide for Parents,* London: Central Office of Information.

DFEE (1995) *Physical Education in the National Curriculum,* London: HMSO.

Department for Education and Employment (1996a) *Desirable Outcomes for Children's Learning on Entering Compulsory Schooling,* London: HMSO.

DFEE (1996b) *Next Steps,* London: HMSO.

DES (1977a) *A New Partnership for Our Schools,* Taylor Report, London: HMSO.

DES (1977b) Circular 14/77, London: HMSO.

DES (1978a) *Primary Education in England: A Survey by HM Inspectors of Schools,* London: HMSO.

DES (1978b) *Special Educational Needs,* Warnock Report, London: HMSO.

DES (1979) *A Framework for the School Curriculum,* London: HMSO.

DES (1981a) *The School Curriculum,* London: HMSO.

DES (1981b) *West Indian Children in Our Schools,* Interim Report of the Committee of Enquiry into the education of children from ethnic minority groups, the Rampton Report, London: HMSO.

DES (1982a) *Education 5 to 9: An Illustrative Survey of 80 First Schools in England,* London: HMSO.

DES (1982b) *Mathematics Counts,* Cockcroft Report, London: HMSO.

DES (1983) *Assessment and Statements of Special Educational Needs,* Circular 1/83, London: HMSO.

DES (1984) *Educational Support Grants,* Circular 6/84, London: HMSO.

DES (1985a) *Better Schools,* White Paper Cmnd 9469, London: HMSO.

DES (1985b) *The Curriculum from 5 to 16,* Curriculum Matters 2, HMI series, London: HMSO.

DES (1985c) *Science 5–16: A Statement of Policy,* London: HMSO.

DES (1987) *Educational Reform: Government Proposals for Schools,* London: HMSO.

DES (1988a) *National Curriculum Task Group on Assessment and Testing: A Report,* London: HMSO.

DES (1989a) *National Curriculum: From Policy to Practice,* London: HMSO.

DES (1989b) *Aspects of Primary Education: The Teaching and Learning of Science,* London: HMSO.

DES (1989d) Circular No 5/89, *Education Reform Act 1988, The School Curriculum and Assessment,* 22 Feb 1989, DES Publications.

DES (1989e) Statistical Bulletin 7/89, London: HMSO.

DES (1990a) *Mathematics at Key Stages 1 and 3,* London: HMSO.

DES (1990b) *Standards in Education 1988–89. The Annual Report of Her Majesty's Chief Inspector of Schools,* London: HMSO.

DES (1990c) *Starting with Quality,* Rumbold Report, London: HMSO.

DES (1991a) *Mathematics in the National Curriculum,* London: HMSO.

DES (1991b) *National Curriculum Art Working Group Interim Report,* London: HMSO.

DES (1991c) *The Parent's Charter,* London: HMSO.

DES (1992) *The Implementation of the Curricular Requirements of the Education*

Reform Act. Science Key Stages 1, 2 and 3. A Report by Her Majesty's Inspectorate 1990–91, London: HMSO.

DES/WO (1987) *The National Curriculum 5–16: A Consultative Document,* London: HMSO.

Desforges, C. and Cockburn, A. (1987) *Understanding the Mathematics Teacher: A Study of Practice in First Schools,* Lewes: Falmer Press.

Donaldson, M. (1978) *Children's Minds,* Glasgow: Fontana/Collins.

Dowling, K. (1984) 'Development of musical schemata in children's spontaneous singing', in W. R. Crozier and A. J. Chapman (eds) *Cognitive Processes in the Perception of Art,* Amsterdam: Elsevier.

Driver, R. (1983) *The Pupil as Scientist,* Milton Keynes: Open University Press.

Driver, R., Squires, A., Rushworth, P. and Wood-Robinson, C. (1994) *Making Sense of Secondary Science. Research into Children's Ideas,* London: HMSO.

Drummond, M. J., Lally, M. and Pugh, G. (eds) (1989) *Working with Children, Developing a Curriculum for the Early Years,* Under Fives Unit, National Children's Bureau, Nottingham: Nottingham Group/NCB.

Early Years Curriculum Group (1989) *Early Childhood Education, The Early Years and the National Curriculum,* Stoke-on-Trent: Trentham Books Ltd.

Edwards, A. and Knight, P. (1994) *Effective Early Years Education,* Buckingham: Open University Press.

Edwards, A. D. and Westgate, D. P. G. (1987) *Investigating Classroom Talk,* Lewes: Falmer Press.

Edwards, C., Gandini, L. and Forman, G. (eds) (1993) *The Hundred Languages of Children. The Reggio Emilia Approach to Early Childhood Education,* Norwood, NJ: Ablex.

Edwards, D. and Mercer, N. C. (1989) *Common Knowledge: The Development of Understanding in the Classroom,* London: Routledge.

Egan, K. (1988) 'The origins of the imagination and the curriculum', in K. Egan and D. Nadamer (eds) *Imagination and Education,* Milton Keynes: Open University Press.

Egan, K. (1991) *Primary Understanding,* London: Routledge.

Engelmann, S., Osborn, J. and Engelmann, T. (1972) *DISTAR Learning Program,* Chicago, Ill.: Science Research Associates.

Evans, L., Packwood, A., Neill, S. R. StJ. and Campbell, R. J. (1994) *The Meaning of Infant Teachers' Work,* London: Routledge.

Forman, A. E. and Cazden, C. B. (1985) 'Exploring Vygotskian perspectives in education: the cognitive value of peer interaction', in J. V. Wertsch (ed.) *Culture, Communication and Cognition: Vygotskian Perspectives,* Cambridge: Cambridge University Press.

Fountain, S. (1990) *Learning Together: Global Education 4–7,* Cheltenham: Stanley Thorne.

Froebel, F. W. (1826) *The Education of Man,* New York: Appleton.

Fromberg, D. P. (1990) 'An agenda for research on play in early childhood education', in E. Klugman and S. Smilansky (eds) *Children's Play and Learning: Policy Implications,* New York: Columbia University Teachers' College Press.

Gage, N. (1985) *Hard Gains in the Soft Sciences: The Case of Pedagogy,* CEOR Monograph, Bloomington, Ind.: Phi Delta Kappa.

Galton, M. (1987) 'An ORACLE chronicle: a decade of classroom research', *Teaching and Teacher Education* 3, 4: 299–314.

Galton, M. (1989) *Teaching in the Primary School,* London: David Fulton.

Galton, M. and Simon, B. (1980) *Progress and Performance in the Primary Classroom,* London: Routledge & Kegan Paul.

Galton, M. and Williamson, J. (1992) *Group Work in the Primary Classroom,* London: Routledge.

Galton, M., Simon, B. and Croll, P. (1980) *Inside the Primary Classroom,* London: Routledge & Kegan Paul.

Gardner, H. (1993a) *Multiple Intelligences: The Theory in Practice,* New York: Basic Books.

Gardner, H. (1993b) *The Unschooled Mind: How Children Think and How Schools Should Teach,* London: Fontana Press.

Garvey, C. (1977) *Play,* London: Fontana/Open Books.

Gilligan, C. (1982) *In a Different Voice,* Cambridge, Mass.: Harvard University Press.

Gipps, C. V. (1994) *Beyond Testing: Towards a Theory of Educational Assessment,* London: Falmer Press.

Golby, M. (1988) 'Traditions in primary education', in M. Clarkson (ed.) *Emerging Issues in Primary Education,* Lewes: Falmer Press.

Goldstein, W., Underwood, M., Bysouth, J. and Rabinowitz, A. I. (1984) *Classroom Observation Procedure,* ILEA: Schools Psychological Service.

Good, T. and Brophy, J. (1986) 'Teacher behaviour and student achievement', in M. Wittrock (ed.) *Handbook of Research on Teaching,* 3rd edn, New York: Macmillan.

Graham, D. (1993) *A Lesson For Us All: The Making of the National Curriculum,* London: Routledge.

Hall, N. (1987) *The Emergence of Literacy,* UKRA Teaching of Reading Monography, London: Edward Arnold.

Harland, J. and Kinder, K. (1992) *Mathematics and Science Courses for Primary Teachers,* Windsor: NFER.

Harlen, W., Darwin, A. and Murphy, M. (1977a) *Asking Questions: A Leader's Guide,* Edinburgh: Oliver & Boyd.

Harlen, W., Darwin, A. and Murphy, M. (1977b) *Finding Answers: Match and Mismatch,* Edinburgh: Oliver & Boyd.

Haste, H. (1987) 'Growing into rules', in J. S. Bruner and H. Haste (eds) *Making Sense: The Child's Construction of the World,* London: Methuen.

Hegarty, S., Pocklington, K. and Lucas, D. (1981) *Educating Pupils with Special Needs in the Ordinary School,* Windsor: NFER/Nelson.

HMI (1989a) *The Education of Children Under Five,* London: HMSO.

HMI (1989b) *Report by HM Inspectors on a Survey of the Quality of Education for Four Year Olds in Primary Classes – Reference 339/89/NS,* London: DES.

HMI (1989c) *The Teaching and Learning of History,* London: HMSO.

HMI (1989d) *The Teaching and Learning of Geography,* London: HMSO.

HMI (1991) *Aspects of Primary Education. The Teaching and Learning of Information Technology,* London: HMSO.

Hillgate Group (1986) *Whose Schools? A Radical Manifesto,* London: Claridge Press.

Hillgate Group (1987) *Reform of British Education,* London: Claridge Press.

Hirst, P. H. (1974) *Knowledge and the Curriculum,* London: Routledge & Kegan Paul.

Hohmann, M., Banet, B. and Weikart, D. P. (1979) *Young Children in Action,* Ypsilanti, Mich.: High/Scope Press.

Holt, J. (1968) *How Children Learn,* London: Pitman.

Holt, J. (1984) *How Children Fail,* revised edn, Harmondsworth: Penguin.

Hughes, J. and Marsden, W. (1994) (eds) *Primary School Geography,* London: David Fulton.

Hughes, M. (1986) *Children and Number,* Oxford: Basil Blackwell.

Hughes, M., Wikeley, F. and Nash, T. (1994) *Parents and their Children's Schools.* Oxford: Blackwell.

ILEA (1978) *People Around Us: Unit 1: Families;* (1979) *People Around Us: Unit 2: Friends;* (1980) *People Around Us: Unit 3: Work,* London: ILEA and A. & C. Black.

ILEA (1987) *The Early Years: A Curriculum for Young Children,* London: ILEA Centre for Learning Resources.

Isaacs, S. (1929) *The Nursery Years,* London: Routledge & Kegan Paul.

Isaacs, S. (1948) *Childhood and After,* London: Routledge & Kegan Paul.

Kerr, J. F. (ed.) (1968) *Changing the Curriculum,* London: University of London Press.

Kinder, K. and Harland, J. (1991) *The Impact of Inset: The Case of Primary Science,* Slough: NFER.

King, R. (1978) *All Things Bright and Beautiful? A Sociological Study of Infants' Classrooms,* Bath: John Wiley.

Klein, M. (1949) *The Psycho Analysis of Children,* trans. A. Stracey, 3rd edn, London: International Psycho-analytical Library 22.

Kohlberg, L. (1976) 'Moral stages and moralization: the cognitive-developmental approach', in T. Lickona (ed.) *Moral Development and Behaviour,* New York: Holt, Rinehart & Winston.

Lawton, D. (1980) *The Politics of the School Curriculum,* London: Routledge & Kegan Paul.

Lewis, A. (1992) *Primary Special Needs and the National Curriculum,* London: Routledge.

Little, A. and Willey, R. (1983) *Studies in the Multi-Ethnic Curriculum,* London: Schools Council.

Little, V. (1990) 'A National Curriculum in History: a very contentious issue', *British Journal of Educational Studies* 38, 4.

Lowenfeld, M. (1935) *Play in Childhood,* London: Gollancz.

McCutcheon, G. (1980) 'How do elementary teachers plan? The nature of planning and the influences on it', *Elementary School Journal* 81, 1: 5–9.

Mackay, D., Thompson, B. and Schaub, P. (1970) *Breakthrough to Literacy,* Teachers' Manual, Harlow: Longman.

McMillan, M. (1923) *Education Through Imagination,* London: Deit.

MacNamara, A. (1995) 'Mathematics', in A. Anning (ed.) *A National Curriculum for the Early Years,* Buckingham: Open University Press.

Manzer, R. A. (1970) *Teachers and Politics,* Manchester: Manchester University Press.

Marshall, S. (1963) *An Experiment in Education,* Cambridge: Cambridge University Press.

Meadows, S. and Cashdan, A. (1983) *Teaching Styles in Nursery Education,* London, final report to SSRC, unpublished.

Meadows, S. and Cashdan, A. (1988) *Helping Children Learn, Contributions to a Cognitive Curriculum,* London: David Fulton.

Millar, S. (1968) *The Psychology of Play*, Harmondsworth: Penguin.

Mills, J. (1991) *Music in the Primary School*, Cambridge: Cambridge University Press.

Mittler, P. (1994) A Post-Code Address, *Times Educational Supplement*, May 13, p. 21.

Montessori, M. (1972) *Dr. Montessori's Own Handbook*, first published in English 1914, New York: Schocken Books.

Moog, H. (1976) *The Musical Experience of the Pre-School Child* (English translation by C. Clarke), London: Schott.

Mortimore, P. and Blackstone, T. (1982) *Education and Disadvantage*, London: Heinemann.

Mullin, B., Morgan, V. and Dunn, S. (1986) *Gender Differentiation in Infant Classes*, University of Ulster at Coleraine, Northern Ireland: Equal Opportunities Commission.

Nash, R. C. (1973) *Classrooms Observed*, London: Routledge & Kegan Paul.

National Children's Bureau (1989) *Working with Children: Developing a Curriculum for the Early Years*, London: National Children's Bureau.

National Children's Bureau (1991) *Young Children in Group Day Care. Guidelines for Good Practice*, London: National Children's Bureau.

National Commission on Education (1993) *Learning to Succeed. A Radical Look at Education Today and a Strategy for the Future. Report of the Paul Hamlyn Foundation National Commission on Education*, London: William Heinemann.

NCC (National Curriculum Council) (1989a) *A Framework for the Primary Curriculum*, York: NCC.

NCC (1989b) *National Curriculum: From Policy to Practice*, National Curriculum Information Pack 1, York: NCC.

NCC (1989c) Circular 5/89 *Education Reform Act: The School Curriculum and Assessment*, 22 February 1989, York: NCC.

NCC (1989d) Circular no 5. *Implementing the National Curriculum: Participation by Pupils with Special Educational Needs*, May 1989, York: NCC.

NCC (1991) *Report on the Monitoring of the Implementation of the National Curriculum Core Subjects 1989–90*, York: National Curriculum Council.

NCC/WO (National Curriculum Council/Welsh Office) (1989a) *English in the National Curriculum*, London: HMSO.

NCC/WO (1989b) *Mathematics in the National Curriculum*, London: HMSO.

NCC/WO (1989c) *Science in the National Curriculum*, London: HMSO.

NCC/WO (1989d) *Design and Technology for Ages 5–16*, York: NCC.

NCC/WO (1989e) *Technology 5–16 in the National Curriculum*, November 1989, York: NCC.

NEU (National Education Union) (1870) *A Verbatim Report of the Debate in Parliament during the Progress of the Elementary School Bill*, reported in N. Whitbread (1972) *The Evolution of the Nursery Infant School*, London: Routledge & Kegan Paul.

NFER/SCDC (National Foundation for Educational Research/Schools Curriculum Development Council) (1987) *Four Year Olds in School: Policy and Practice*, Windsor: NFER.

Nelson, K. (1977) 'Cognitive development and the acquisition of concepts', in R. C. Anderson, R. J. Spiro and W. E. Montegue (eds) *Schooling and the Acquisition of Knowledge*, Hillsdale, NJ: Lawrence Erlbaum.

Newcastle Commission (1861) *Royal Commission Report*, Newcastle Commission (Elementary Education).

Newson, E. and Newson, J. (1977) *Perspectives on School at Seven Years Old*, London: Allen & Unwin.

Nias, J. (1988) 'Informal primary education in action: teacher accounts', in W. A. L. Blyth (ed.) *Informal Primary Education Today*, Lewes: Falmer Press.

Nias, J. (1989) *Teachers Talking: A Study of Teaching as Work*, London: Routledge & Kegan Paul.

Nicholls, R. (1986) (ed.) *Rumpus Schema Extra*, January, Saltburn Cleveland LEA.

Nuffield Primary Science (1993) London: Collins Educational.

Nutbrown, C. (1994) *Threads of Thinking. Young Children Learning and the Role of Early Education*, London: Paul Chapman.

Ofsted (1993a) *Science at Key Stages 1, 2 and 3. Third Year 1991–92*, London: HMSO.

Ofsted (1993b) *Science Key Stages 1, 2 and 3. Fourth Year*, London: HMSO.

Ofsted (1993c) *Technology at Key Stages 1, 2 and 3. A Report by HM Inspectorate on the Second Year*, London: HMSO.

Ofsted (1993d) *Physical Education at Key Stages 1, 2 and 3. First Year*, London: HMSO.

Ofsted (1994a) *Science and Mathematics in Schools*, London: HMSO.

Ofsted (1994b) *Primary Matters. A Discussion on Teaching and Learning in Primary Schools*, London: Ofsted Publications Centre.

Osborn, A. F. and Milbank, J. E. (1987) *The Effects of Early Education*, Report from the Child Health and Education Study, Oxford: Clarendon Press.

Peters, R. S. (1966) *Ethics and Education*, London: Allen & Unwin.

Piaget, J. (1932) *The Moral Judgement of the Child*, London: Routledge & Kegan Paul.

Piaget, J. (1962) *Play, Dreams and Imitation in Childhood*, New York: Norton.

Piaget, J. (1971) *Science of Education and the Psychology of the Child*, London: Longman.

Piaget, J. (1977) *The Moral Judgement of the Child*, Harmondsworth; Penguin.

Piaget, J. and Inhelder, B. (1956) *The Child's Conception of Space*, London: Routledge & Kegan Paul.

Pilling, D. and Kellmer Pringle, M. (1978) *Controversial Issues in Child Development*, London: Paul Elek for National Children's Bureau.

Pollard, A. (1985) *The Social World of the Primary School*, Eastbourne: Holt, Rinehart & Winston.

Pollard, A. (1988) 'Coping strategies and the multiplication of differentiation in infant classes', in A. Cohen and L. Cohen (eds) *Early Education: The School Years*, London: Paul Chapman.

Pollard, A., Broadfoot, P., Croll, P., Osborn, M. and Abbott, D. (1994) *Changing English Primary Schools? The Impact of the Education Reform Act at Key Stage One*, London: Cassell.

Prindep (1989) *Changing Classroom Practice: Decisions and Dilemmas*, Prindep, 110 Merrion House, Leeds, LS2 8DT.

Raban, B., Clark, U. and MacIntyre, J. (1994) *Evaluation of the Implementation of English in the National Curriculum at Key Stages 1, 2 and 3 (1991–1993): Final Report*, London: School Curriculum and Assessment Authority.

Reid, J. and Donaldson, M. (1979) *The Written Word: Teachers' Manual to Link Up Reading Scheme*, Edinburgh: Holmes McDougall.

Richards, C. (1982) *Primary Education 1974–80*, in Richards, C. (ed.) *New Directions in Primary Education*, Lewes: Falmer Press.

Robinson, K. (ed.) (1982) *The Arts in School*, Gulbenkian Report, London: Calouste Gulbenkian Foundation.

Rosen, H. (1984) *The Nurture of Narratives: Stories and Meanings*, London: National Association for the Teaching of English.

Rosenshine, B. (1987) 'Direct instruction', in M. Dunkin (ed.) *Teaching and Teacher Education*, Oxford: Pergamon Press.

Rousseau, J. J. (1762) *Emile, Book 2*, quoted in P. Abbs (ed.) (1987) *The Living Powers*, Lewes: Falmer Press.

Rubin, Z. (1980) *Children's Friendships*, London: Fontana.

Rudduck, J. (1986) 'Curriculum change: management and meaning?', *School Organization* 6, 1: 107–15.

School Curriculum and Assessment Authority (1995a) *Physical Education in the National Curriculum*, London: SCAA Publications.

SCAA (1995b) *Key Stages 1 and 2, Design and Technology: The New Requirements*, London: SCAA Publications.

Sharp, C. (1990) *Developing the Arts in Primary Education: Good Practice in Teacher Education*, Slough: NFER.

Sharp, R. and Green, A. (1975) *Education and Social Control: A Study in Progressive Primary Education*, London: Routledge & Kegan Paul.

Shorrocks, D., Frobisher, L., Nelson, N., Turner, L. and Waterson, A. (1993) *Implementing National Curriculum Assessment in the Primary School*, London: Hodder & Stoughton.

Sinclair, J. McH. and Coulthard, R. M. (1975) *Towards an Analysis of Discourse: The English Used by Teachers and Pupils*, London: Oxford University Press.

Skinner, B. F. (1974) *About Behaviourism*, London: Cape.

Sleap, M. and Warburton, P. (1994) 'Physical activity levels in pre-adolescent children in England', *British Journal of Physical Education, Research Supplement* 14: 2–6.

Smith, E. A. and Holden, C. (1994) 'I thought it was for picking bones out of soup. Using artefacts in the primary school', *Teaching History* 76, June.

Smith, F. (1971) *Understanding Reading*, New York: Holt, Rinehart & Winston.

Smith, F. (1978) *Reading*, Cambridge: Cambridge University Press.

Smith, F. (1982) *Writing and the Writer*, London: Heinemann Educational.

Smith, P. K. (ed.) (1984) *Play in Animals and Humans*. Oxford: Basil Blackwell.

Smith, P. K. and Cowie, H. (1988) *Understanding Children's Development*, Oxford: Basil Blackwell.

Southgate, V., Arnold, H. and Johnson, S. (1981) *Extending Beginning Reading*, London: Heinemann for the Schools Council.

SPACE (Science Process and Concept Exploration) Research Reports (1990–94), Liverpool: Liverpool University Press.

Spencer, C., Blade, M. and Morsley, K. (1990) *The Child and the Physical Environment*, Chichester: John Wiley.

Spender, D. (1982) *Invisible Women: The Schooling Scandal*, London: Writers & Readers.

Spock, B. (1946) *Baby and Child Care*, New York: Pocket Books.

Stannard, J. (1988) 'Focus on the Curriculum 3–7', *Child Education* September: 8–9.

Steiner, R. (1926) *The Essentials of Education*, London: Anthroposophical Publishing.

Stones, E. (1984) *Supervision in Teacher Education*, London: Methuen.

Sugden, D. (1990) 'Development of physical education for all', *British Journal of Physical Education* 21, 1: 247–57.

Summers, M. (1992) Improving primary school teachers' understanding of science concepts – Theory into practice, *International Journal of Science Education* 14, 1: 25–40.

Swann Committee (1985) *Education for All*, Swann Report, Cmnd 9453, London: HMSO.

Swanwick, K. (1992) *Music Education and the National Curriculum*, London: Tufnell Press.

Sylva, K., Roy, C. and Painter, M. (1980) *Childwatching at Playgroup and Nursery School*, London: Grant McIntyre.

Tann, C. S. (1981) 'Grouping and group work', in B. Simon and J. Willcocks (eds) *Research and Practice in the Primary Classroom*, London: Routledge & Kegan Paul.

Taylor, P. H., Exon, G. and Holley, B. (1972) *A Study of Nursery Education*, Schools Council Working Paper 41, London: Evans/Methuen Educational.

Taylor, R. (1986) *Educating for Art: Critical Response and Development*, Harlow: Longman.

Taylor, R. and Andrews, G. (1993) *The Arts in the Primary School*, London: Falmer Press.

TES (1990) *Tests Fail to Jolt Real-Book Faithful*, 27 July 1990: 4.

Tizard, B. and Hughes, M. (1984) *Young Children Learning: Talking and Listening at Home and at School*, London: Fontana.

Tizard, B., Blatchford, P., Burke, J., Farquar, C. and Plewis, I. (1988) *Young Children at School in the Inner City*, Hove: Lawrence Erlbaum.

Tizard, J., Schofield, W. N. and Hewison J. (1982) 'Collaboration between teachers and parents in assisting children's reading', *British Journal of Educational Psychology* 52: 1–15.

Topping, K. (1984) 'Paired reading', *Child Education*, December: 10–11.

Topping, K. (1985) 'Paired reading', *Child Education*, January: 10–11.

Tough, J. (1976) *Listening to Children Talking*, London: Ward Lock Educational.

Troyna, B. and Hatcher, R. (1992) *Racism in Children's Lives*, London: Routledge and National Children's Bureau.

Turiel, E. (1978) 'Distinct conceptual and development Domains: social convention and morality', in S. Meadows (1986) *Understanding Child Development*, London: Hutchinson Education, p. 235.

Turiel, E. (1983) *The Development of Social Knowledge. Morality and Convention*, Cambridge: Cambridge University Press.

Tutchell, E. (ed.) (1990) *Dolls and Dungarees: Gender Issues in the Primary School Curriculum*, Buckingham: Open University Press.

Tyler, R. W. (1949) *Basic Principles of Curriculum and Instruction*, Chicago, Ill.: University of Chicago Press.

Van der Eycken, W. and Turner, B. (1969) *Adventures in Education*, London: Allen Lane.

Vygotsky, L. S. (1962) *Thought and Language*, New York: John Wiley.

Vygotsky, L. S. (1978) *Mind in Society* (edited by M. Cole), Cambridge, Mass.: Harvard University Press.

Walkerdine, V. (1985) *Psychological Knowledge and Educational Practice: Producing the Truth about Schools*, Bedford Way Papers 25, University of London, Institute of Education.

Waterland, L. C. (1985) *Read with Me: An Apprenticeship Approach to Reading*, Gloucester: Thimble Press.

Watson, B. G. (1987) *Education and Belief*, Oxford: Blackwell.

Webb, L. (1974) *Purpose and Practice in Nursery Education*, Oxford: Basil Blackwell.

Weiner, G. (1985) *Just a Bunch of Girls*, Milton Keynes: Open University Press.

Wells, G. (1987) *The Meaning Makers: Children Learning Language to Learn*. New Hampshire: Heinemann Educational.

Wetton, P. (1990) *Physical Education in the Nursery and Infant School*, London: Routledge.

Whitbread, N. (1972) *The Evolution of the Nursery Infant School: A History of Infant and Nursery Education in Britain 1800–1970*, London: Routledge & Kegan Paul.

Whyte, J. (1983) *Beyond the Wendy House: Sex Role Stereotyping in Primary Schools*, York: Longman for Schools Council.

Wiegand, P. (1991a) 'The known world of the primary school', *Geography*, 76: 143–9.

Wiegand, P. (1991b) 'Does travel broaden the mind?', *Education 3–13* 19: 54–8.

Wiegand, P. (1995) 'Geography', in A. Anning (ed.) *A National Curriculum for the Early Years*, Buckingham: Open University Press.

Wilkinson, A. (1986) *The Quality of Writing*, Milton Keynes: Open University Press.

Willes, M. J. (1983) *Children into Pupils*, London: Routledge & Kegan Paul.

Wolfendale, S. (1989) *All About Me*, London: National Children's Bureau.

Wood, D. (1990) *How Children Think and Learn*, Oxford: Basil Blackwell.

Woods, P. (1993) *Critical Events in Teaching and Learning*, London: Falmer Press.

Wragg, E. C., Bennett, S. N. and Carre, C. G. (1989) 'Primary teachers and the National Curriculum', *Research Papers in Education* 4, 3: 17–37.

Wright, C. (1992) 'Early education: multiracial primary school classrooms', in D. Gill (ed.) *Racism and Education*, London: Sage.

Young, M. F. D. (ed.) (1971) *Knowledge and Control*, London: Collier Macmillan.

Name index

Abbott, D., 118, 125, 132
Adams, M. J., 109
Alexander, R., 9, 18, 51, 78, 80–1, 123, 124
Andrews, G., 125
Anning, A., 9, 32, 45, 46, 52, 62, 72, 100, 114, 119, 134, 146
Argyris, C., 49
Armstrong, N., 128
Arnold, H., 77, 83, 84
Ashton, P., 13, 43
Asoko, H., 116
Athey, C., 27–9
Aubrey, C., 132
Auld, R., 6

Bamberger, J., 127
Banet, B., 27
Barrett, G., 59, 61
Barrie, J. M., 12
Barrow, R., 22
Bassey, M., 101
Bate, M., 40, 60
Bellett, E., 131
Bennett, D., 50, 51
Bennett, J., 108
Bennett, N., 6, 9, 18, 37, 52, 77, 82, 84, 85–6, 87, 88, 90, 101, 106, 111, 114, 116, 124

Bereiter, C., 93
Berlak, A., 49
Berlak, H., 49
Bernstein, B. B., 37
Billett, S., 9
Blackstone, T., 147
Blade, M., 123
Blatchford, P., 18, 37, 70–1, 74, 79, 88, 101–2, 111, 124, 140
Blenkin, G. V., 44, 97, 105, 132
Blyth, J. E., 121
Blyth, W. A. L., 97
Bott, R., 15
Boultwood, M. E. A., 2
Bowers, T., 143
Boyson, R., 104
Bradley, L., 40
Brearley, M., 16
Brittan, E. M., 68
Broadfoot, P., 118, 125, 132
Brook, A., 116
Brophy, J., 93
Brown, G., 23
Brown, S., 9
Browne, N., 42
Bruner, J. S., 22, 23, 34, 56, 57
Bryant, P., 40
Burke, J., 18, 37, 70–1, 74, 79, 88, 101–2, 111, 124

Subject index

A NATIONAL CURRICULUM FOR THE EARLY YEARS

Angela Anning (ed.)

- What does the National Curriculum mean to pupils and teachers at Key Stage One?
- How have teachers and children coped with the ongoing changes?
- How has subject teaching altered in infant classrooms?

In *A National Curriculum for the Early Years*, Angela Anning and her team of contributors set out to examine these issues. Infant teachers and their pupils were the guinea pigs for the introduction of the National Curriculum over a five-year period. Despite many reservations about a subject-based curriculum for young children, teachers struggled to interpret the National Curriculum Orders into a workable, if not manageable, curriculum in their classrooms.

The contributors to this book, each expert in a subject discipline, have kept in close touch with practising and intending infant teachers as the National Curriculum was operationalized in primary schools. They have used their teacher networks, as well as research evidence, to tap into the strategies used by infant teachers to cope with the planning, delivery and assessment of the National Curriculum subjects and the effects of government policy changes on young children's learning.

Together the contributors provide a timely analysis of subject-discipline-based education for young children and look ahead to the prospects for those subjects at Key Stage One in the second half of the 1990s.

This book will be essential reading for anyone involved in the education of young children.

Contents

A national curriculum for Key Stage One – English – Mathematics – Science – Design and technology and information technology – Geography – History – Art – Music – Physical education – Religious education – The way ahead: Another national curriculum for Key Stage One? – Author index – Subject index.

Contributors

Angela Anning, Hilary Asoko, Roger Beard, Eileen Bellett, Helen Constable, David Dawson, Carolyn Jones, Ann MacNamara, Patrick Wiegand, Elizabeth Wood.

176pp   0 335 19431 1 (Paperback)   0 335 19432 X (Hardback)

EFFECTIVE EARLY YEARS EDUCATION
TEACHING YOUNG CHILDREN

Anne Edwards and Peter Knight

In this concise and accessible guide, the authors are sympathetic to the particular
demands of teaching three to eight year olds and offer practical solutions to the
complex issues that are currently faced by early years educators. In recognizing
the demands on practitioners, they provide new and challenging frameworks for an
understanding of the practice of teaching young children and draw upon international
research to offer a sound model of early years subject-structured teaching which has
the quality of children's learning at its centre. Their aim is to support teaching
expertise through stimulating teachers' thinking about children's development,
motivation, ways of learning and the subjects they teach. These topics are clearly set
in the complex institutional settings in which practitioners work and ways of taking
and evaluating action are offered.

Contents
*Introduction: education from three to eight – Becoming a pupil – Children's learning
– A curriculum for the early years – Subjects and the early years curriculum – The
organization of the learning environment – Parents and professionals – Developing
the curriculum – Developing the organization – Endpiece – References – Index.*

176pp   0 335 19188 6 (Paperback)   0 335 19189 4 (Hardback)

QUALITY EDUCATION IN THE EARLY YEARS

Lesley Abbott and Rosemary Rodger (eds)

Lesley Abbott and her team of contributors identify and explore high quality work (and what shapes it) in early years education. They show us children and adults variously working and playing, talking and communicating, learning and laughing, caring and sharing in a rich tapestry of case studies which highlight quality experiences and interactions. Every chapter is based around a particular case study, each one tackling a different issue: the curriculum, play, assessment, roles and relationships, special needs, partnerships with parents, and equal opportunities.

All the writers work together in early years education on a day-to-day basis enabling them to pool their different expertise to create a balanced but challenging approach. They give inspiring examples of, and outline underlying principles for, quality work and ask important questions of all those involved in the education and care of young children.

Contents

Introduction: The search for quality in the early years – A quality curriculum in the early years: Raising some questions – 'Play is fun, but it's hard work too': The search for quality play in the early years – 'Why involve me?': Encouraging children and their parents to participate in the assessment process – 'It's nice here now': Managing young children's behaviour – 'She'll have a go at anything': Towards an equal opportunities policy – 'We only speak English here, don't we?': Supporting language development in a multilingual context – 'People matter': The role of adults in providing a quality learning environment for the early years – 'You feel like you belong': Establishing partnerships between parents and educators – 'Look at me – I'm only two': Educare for the under threes: The importance of early experience – Looking to the future: Concluding comments – Bibliography – Index.

Contributors

Lesley Abbott, Janet Ackers, Janice Adams, Caroline Barratt-Pugh, Brenda Griffin, Chris Marsh, Sylvia Phillips, Rosemary Rodger, Helen Strahan.

224pp   0 335 19230 0 (Paperback)   0 335 19231 9 (Hardback)